REEL WOMEN

The World of
Women Who Fish

by

Lyla Foggia

THREE RIVERS PRESS
New York

The author wishes to thank Keppie Keplinger for the use of the cover photo (circa 1935) featuring her mother, Mary Lee Barnes (foreground); her aunt, Ruby McIntyre (left); and her grandmother, Ella Barnes (right) — all truly Reel Women.

The author also wishes to clarify any confusion that may result from the similarity between the title of this book and the business Reel Women Fly Fishing Adventures owned by Lori-Ann Murphy, which offers angling destination adventures, among other services, and can be contacted at P.O. Box 289, Victor, ID 83455; phone (208) 787-2657.

Published by Three Rivers Press, 201 East 50th Street, New York, New York 10022. Member of the Crown Publishing Group.

Random House, Inc. New York, Toronto, London, Sydney, Auckland

http://www.randomhouse.com/

THREE RIVERS PRESS and colophon are trademarks of Crown Publishers, Inc.

Printed in the United States of America.

Design by Principia Graphics.

Library of Congress Cataloging-in-Publication Data is available upon request.

First published in hardcover by Beyond Words Publishing Inc. in 1995.

ISBN 0-609-80028-0

10 9 8 7 6 5 4 3 2 1

First Paperback Edition

This book is dedicated to my beloved husband and favorite fishing partner, Kelly Neal, and to the practice of catch-and-release for the future preservation of our fisheries

Table of Contents

Introduction vi
Prologue – Angling's First Great Legend:
      Dame Juliana Berners 1

Part I: Women's Legacy in Fly Fishing 8
  1 Trailblazers in Fly-Fishing History 13
  2 Patterns of Excellence: Fly Tiers in History 33
  3 The Woman Flyfishers Club 45
  4 A Living Legend: Joan Salvato Wulff 51
  5 Fly Fishing's Trailblazers Today 71
  6 More Patterns of Excellence: Fly Tiers Today 107

Part II: Women's Legacy in Big-Game Saltwater Angling . . . 128
  7 "The Anglerettes" of the 1930s and 1940s 133
  8 The Grande Dames of the Sea from the 1950s
     through the 1970s 147
  9 A Living Legend: Marsha Bierman 165
 10 Women Making Big-Game History Today 179

Part III: Women's Legacy in Bass Fishing 194
 11 A Living Legend: Sugar Ferris 203
 12 Top Pro Bass Anglers 213

Part IV: Women's Legacy in Science and Industry 240
 13 Four Pioneering Spirits 243

Part V: The First-Ever Women's Angling
       Resource Directory 260
National and Regional Organizations 261
State and International Clubs, Businesses, and
   Services Offered by or for Women 264
Schools, Travel Services, Clothing, and Miscellaneous . . . 280
Angling Books Written by or for Women:
   A Selected Bibliography 283

Appendices
Bass'n Gal All-Time Earners 286
Notes 287
Acknowledgments 291
Photography Credits 292

Index 293

Introduction

Until now, the history of women and fishing has only existed as scattered fragments of information, waiting to be assembled into a coherent whole, waiting to tell us what we have always suspected but could never confirm: women have distinguished themselves in fishing by establishing historic precedents, setting unfathomable world records, and otherwise changing the face of the sport through their ingenuity and daring.

Indeed, the history of modern sportfishing begins with a woman, an early 15th-century nun and noblewoman named Dame Juliana Berners, who is credited with writing the first tracts on both hunting and fishing. So remarkable was her "Treatyse of Fysshynge wyth an Angle," which appeared in 1496, that it has been hailed as "one of the best and most durable pieces of prose writing of its time."[1] It has also had a profound influence on the five centuries of angling literature that have followed.

Reel Women is filled with historic milestones attributed to the women who have followed Dame Juliana. For instance, Sara Jane McBride, a self-educated entomologist and prize-winning fly tier, wrote the first American papers on the life cycles of insects from an angler's point of view, which appeared in leading American journals in 1876. Mary Orvis Marbury compiled and authored the first definitive book on American fly patterns, published in 1892, which served as an instrumental force in dispelling the mass confusion surrounding the names that flies were called at the time. Cornelia "Fly Rod" Crosby was one of the country's first outdoors columnists and national sports celebrities, and by 1895 her fame had reached mythical proportions.

WOMEN TROUT FISHING AT WAGON
WHEEL GAP, COLORADO, CIRCA 1890.

Examples of women and their landmark accomplishments in the 20th century include Carrie Stevens, who revolutionized the way streamer fly patterns are tied when she whipped up the famous Gray Ghost in 1924. Francesca LaMonte of the American Museum of Natural History in New York helped pioneer marine research and produced seven groundbreaking books on fresh- and saltwater fish, beginning in the mid-1930s. Helen Robinson was one of a trio of people responsible for devising a technique for teasing a billfish to an artificial fly in the 1960s—a technique that is practiced around the world today. About the same time, Kay Brodney became the first woman to courageously explore the remote jungles of South America in search of freshwater fish so rare that few are aware of their existence even today. International fly-fishing luminary Joan Wulff indelibly altered the way flycasting is taught, through the school she established with her late husband, Lee Wulff, and her long-running magazine column and books. Marsha Bierman's short-rod standup technique for catching billfish is regarded as the most innovative influence on big-game angling since the sport's official inception in 1898. Most recently, Sugar Ferris introduced the first all-women's bass-fishing circuit in 1976, opening the doors to the world of professional tournaments for women.

They are but a few of the extraordinary women—past and present—whose lives and achievements are chronicled in this book, each one significant in her own way.

Why do we need to know about them? These compelling figures symbolize the innate spirit that too often lies dormant within our souls. They embody those qualities that are within the grasp of each one of us, but which our inner consciousness, like a strict governess, rarely acknowledges as a legitimate exhibition of behavior for women. Through their lives, we are reminded of what we can and might be doing with our own lives—whether or not we ever pick up a fishing rod. Through their actions, they show us a way out of the limited menu of roles we've come to accept for ourselves, though we have the physical capabilities and mental capacities to face almost every challenge presented to men. More than anything, they are the role models who can help guide and center us as we cope with these increasingly complex and often troubling times.

They also represent an invisible dynasty of collective female experience. By amassing their achievements and contributions in a single volume, we discover that women not only have a history in fishing but have also *made* history in the sport. As we follow the daisy chain of their lives through the ages, we also discover that there are many threads and parallels that bind them together into a culture all their own.

Without exception, they are tenacious, persevering, and keenly in touch with their native instincts. To them, fishing is a reflective act, a state of mind, and a metaphor for life in how each one views herself in alignment with the universe. What it has never been, even before conscientious anglers embraced the modern concept of catch-and-release, was a personal contest of egos measured by the number of fish dumped on a dock or fillets packed home at the end of a day on the water. In fact, every contemporary woman you will encounter in this book is a conservation advocate, using her prominence in the sport as a forum for alerting the public to the paramount need for preservation and restoration of our fisheries, both as anglers and concerned world citizens.

It will always be a puzzle how the myth got started that women do not fish, or at least do not fish in significant numbers comparable to men. Certainly there are ample references within this book to indicate that women have been participating in the sport for hundreds of years. There are also statistics to indicate that women have comprised approximately one-third of all anglers for at least the last 10 years, the only period of time in which quantifiable surveys have been taken.[2] If we have underestimated their participation, it is perhaps a result of two key factors: as late as the 1960s, many states did not require women to buy a fishing license,[3] and even today, few states ask for an angler's gender on the form that is filled out at the point of purchase for either an annual or temporary license.

Also perplexing is the prevailing myth that men want to keep the sport of fishing all to themselves. Of course, there will always be those for whom the sport is as much an escape from "the little woman" as a chance to spend time exclusively in the company of men. But it can be assumed that most of the millions of women who fish do so with their husbands or other male loved ones, since women are rarely observed on the water in groups of two or more without a man present, unless in a tournament or learning situation. But the president of a large angling organization says that the male members who have wives or girlfriends as fishing companions are treated with special envy and respect by the rest of the membership. Perhaps this book will aid their efforts to entice their female loved ones into a sport that has served as the primary bond in many of the relationships represented in this book.

The year 1996 is a watershed for women in angling. First and foremost, it is the 500th anniversary of the publication of Dame Juliana's phenomenally astute treatise on fishing of 1496. Equally worthy of recognition is the 20th anniversary of the inception of Bass'n Gal in 1976 as well as the 40th anniversary of the founding of the International Women's Fishing Association in 1955. Indeed, these three events, along with every other imprint left by women over the last five centuries, is a testament to the fact that women have a legacy in angling.

May this book help change how we perceive women — and the sport — forever.

Angling's First Great Legend: Dame Juliana Berners

She was, as the legend goes, noble in birth and spirit, sociable, solitary, dashing, beautiful, learned, and intellectual. In some accounts she fled to field sports to avoid love; in another she might have retired to a convent "from disappointment." The seeming conflict between nun and sportswoman together with the scarcity of evidence for assertions made about her, have been the cause of spirited argument among generations of antiquaries.

—JOHN MCDONALD, *The Origins of Angling*[1]

Christopher Columbus wasn't even born when an English nun and noblewoman, Dame Juliana Berners, reputedly penned the first tracts on fishing and hunting.

The year 1996 marks the 500th anniversary of the publication of Dame Juliana's "Treatyse of Fysshynge wyth an Angle."[2] For the angling world, it is the granddaddy of historic milestones: the treatise is universally recognized as both "the first writing on modern sportfishing"[3] and the wellspring from which five centuries of angling literature has flowed.

For women, it is a birthstone of even greater significance, symbolizing the first tangible thread of our unfolding legacy behind a rod. "The Treatise appears to put women squarely into the fishing picture almost from the start," Silvio Calabi notes in his book, *The Illustrated Encyclopedia of Fly-Fishing*.[4]

Who is this extraordinary woman whose looming presence has reigned over the sport through the ages? Little about her is known, except for several early but obscure accounts. The first is from a book published around 1559 called *Lives of the Most Eminent Writers of Great Britain*: "She was an illustrious female, eminently endowed with superior qualities both mental and personal. Amongst the many solaces of human life she held the sports of the field in the highest estimation."[5]

Another invaluable reference is provided by author Ernest Schwiebert, drawn from critical evidence in the *Biographia Britannica* (date unknown), which, he writes, "describes the Treatyse at considerable length, and vouches for the character and authorship of the noblewoman who compiled its richly illuminated pages. It clearly identifies the author of the "Treatyse of Fysshynge wyth an Angle" as the prioress of Sopwell Nunnery near St. Albans. It describes her as a gentlewoman of noble lineage, much celebrated in her time for her wisdom, scholarship, and charm; and she was apparently well versed in the field sports."[6]

How Dame Juliana acquired her astute knowledge of how, when, and where to fish is a missing puzzle piece probably lost forever. Her document, nevertheless, is one of the richest how-to manuals ever produced. In a time when one didn't have a tackle store to turn to, Dame Juliana provides indispensable, step-by-step instructions on everything a novice angler would need to know, including how to build a rod, construct a hook, dye horsehairs and braid lines, select and preserve natural baits, and dress flies and choose patterns based on the months of the year. Amazingly, her treatise also has expert advice on where and

THE HISTORY OF MODERN SPORTFISHING BEGINS WITH 15TH-CENTURY NUN AND
NOBLEWOMAN DAME JULIANA BERNERS OF ENGLAND, WHO IS CREDITED WITH
WRITING THE FIRST TRACTS ON HUNTING AND FISHING, PUBLISHED IN 1486 AND
1496 RESPECTIVELY. THE SOURCE OF THIS FANCIFUL DEPICTION IS UNKNOWN.

how to catch fish, stern cautions against trespassing and poaching, and a visionary sermonette on the need for conservation.

Dame Juliana's treatise was so remarkable that historian John McDonald has hailed it as "the origin of modern angling" and "one of the best and most durable pieces of prose writing of its time," adding that "for most of two centuries, the fifteenth and sixteenth, it was alone the standard work on the sport and put its stamp on all subsequent history. In the ages before the treatise almost nothing is known about the sport."

Ernest Schwiebert in his book, *Trout*, also sings its praises: "It was a remarkable monograph on the sport, totally without precedent in English or any other language.... It clearly represented the birth of fly-fishing literature as such, and it was written by an angler with considerable experience on the rivers of England—it is richly unique in both character and scope."

Even so, the legend of Dame Juliana is comprised more of myth than fact. While various authorities believe she wrote both treatises between 1420 and 1450, it is probable that neither was published within her lifetime. Her tract on hunting appeared first, in 1486, in the initial edition of *The Boke of St. Albans*, reportedly the first sporting book in England. In 1496, the fishing treatise was added when the second edition of *The Boke* was issued.

Although no one has quibbled over Dame Juliana's byline on the hunting treatise—which had little influence on that sport, then or later—ironically she would ultimately reap her greatest fame from an enduring debate over her authorship of the fishing treatise.

According to Schwiebert, "The controversy over the authenticity and existence of Berners was largely fuelled in 1881, when William Blades attempted to demolish Dame Juliana and her claims to authorship of the 'Treatyse' in the facsimile reprint of the work published in that year by Elliot Stock. Our chronological proximity to this edition, and our tragicomic predilection toward muckraking in this century have perhaps recruited an army of doubters."

Adding to the problem has been the varying spellings of Dame Juliana's last name and the fact that she was given the only byline in either edition. But, we must not forget, there has never been another candidate, or even the hint of one. Nor has anyone been able to produce tangible evidence that it could *not* have been Dame Juliana. Furthermore, Schwiebert produces convincing proof—which he credits to John McDonald's thorough investigation into the matter—in the form of handwritten margin notes from a 16th-century copy of the treatise, which name her father and brother and critical other dates and places.

Clearly, Schwiebert, one of the most highly regarded writers in the history of fly fishing, feels that the controversy is without merit. Another is Joan Wulff, the world's most celebrated woman in fly fishing today. In her book, *Joan Wulff's Fly Fishing*, she writes with persuasive feminine logic: "It is easy to believe that [the treatise] was written by a woman.... What man would suggest, for instance, that to take care of hornets, bumblebees, and wasps for bait, one should bake them in bread? [Dame Juliana] also suggests feeding maggots with mutton fat and with cake made of flour and honey and to keep them in a 'bag of blanket, kept hot under your gown or other warm thing.' No man would say this, would he?"[7]

Canadian author and accomplished fly fisher Mallory Burton also remains unfazed in her enthusiasm for this first great female angling role model: "In this extraordinary tract ... she explains everything so accurately and so thoroughly that nary a woman in the past five hundred years has bothered to rehash her basic advice, though countless men, of course, have made a career of it. I daresay Dame Juliana was a formidable female angler in her day."

Clearly it is time to dispense with the debate on whether Dame Juliana Berners wrote the treatise on fishing. But in the event there are those still harboring doubts about her existence or authorship, I propose the following perplexing question: *Are we to believe that 500 years ago a woman would be credited with authoring a document she did not write — when it's extraordinary enough that a woman would be credited at all?*

Dame Juliana was undoubtedly the greatest first act that any legacy could hope for!

PART I

Women's Legacy in Fly Fishing

My mother found a piece of artwork about fishing that she gave me some years ago. It's a simple picture of someone in a boat and describes fishing as "a perpetual series of occasions for hope." In a tumultuous world, this may be the best reason of all to flyfish.

—LESLIE FOSTER, DENVER, COLORADO

Fly fishing is really the perfect sport for women. For so many hundreds, no thousands, of years, we have been told how to act, who we are and should be, and just plain molded into what we are not.

In our acceptance of this, we have often lost our ability to use our instincts, make decisions, and feel a part of the natural world. Fly fishing is the perfect activity to reconnect with all the natural, wonderful, wildish instinctive qualities that make up a true woman.

—DOROTHY SCHRAMM, PENTWATER, MICHIGAN

The origin of women and fly fishing remains an unsolved mystery. Acceptance of Dame Juliana Berner's authorship of the first treatise on angling provides at least one benchmark for women's participation in the sport: the early to mid 15th century, the time in which she lived and wrote. But was she the first? Probably not. It's hard to believe that Dame Juliana was the only woman fishing in her day or that women had not fished with artificial flies at some point in the prior 13 centuries—according to some authorities, the method of fishing with a hook disguised by feathers and/or fur began with the Macedonians in the first century A.D.

Moving forward in time, illuminating evidence has surfaced to suggest that women indeed indulged themselves in this delightful pastime prior to the 20th century. For example, Paul Schullery in his book, *American Fly Fishing: A History*, tells us that in 1737 William Penn's daughter wrote to her brother in England, asking him to send her more fishing equipment. Schullery quotes from her letter as follows:

> *"My chief amusement this summer has been fishing. I therefore request the favour of you when Laisure Hour will admit, you will buy for me a four joynted strong fishing Rod and Real with strong good Lines and asortment of hooks the best sort."*[1]

Susie Isaksen in *The American Fly Fisher*[2] notes that Paul Fisher's *The Angler's Souvenir*, published in London in 1835, and John J. Brown's *American Angler's Guide*, published in New York in 1845, both mention sightings of numerous women seen fly fishing.

Holly Morris's anthology, *Uncommon Waters: Women Write About Fishing*,[3] includes a late 1800s essay anonymously written by a woman, titled "Woman's Hour has Struck," which was originally published in *Fishing in North America 1876–1910* as "A New Hand at the Rod." It is a rib-tickling account of this woman's ingenious plot to requisition a man's rod without his knowledge, and her joy at catching her first trout despite the risk of having to endure his wrath.

In 1895, the first woman was observed fly fishing in the Catskills in upstate New York in the companionship of Theodore Gordon, who is credited as the founder of the American school of dry-fly fishing. According to Austin M. Francis in *Catskill Rivers: Birthplace of American Fly Fishing*, "She wore a tam-o'-shanter, sweater, short jacket, and skirts, with stout shoes and leggings.... As she fished, her long skirts caressed the ripples, creating the illusion that she moved along on the surface of the stream." Francis also relates that even though this mysterious woman broke Gordon's heart, he later said of her: "The best chum I ever had in fishing was a girl, and she tramped just as hard and fished quite as patiently as any man I ever knew."[4]

Francis also provides us with Fred White's enlightening reminiscences, recorded in 1923, of observing women fly fishers in the Catskills since the turn of the century:

> *"I remember distinctly the first woman at Beaverkill to put on boots and, even with a knee length skirt, dare to brave the disapproval of the porch sitters at Davidson's. It simply wasn't done and she came pretty near being regarded as fast as the water that rippled about her knees. Now the river is full of 'em and they don't bother with skirts either. And they catch fish — some of them — and big ones, too. Whether you like it or not the women are here to stay in trout fishing as on the golf course and at the ballot box, and when all is said and done, I believe it to be an excellent thing — for the women. They can wear my second best waders any time."*[5]

And then there is the galaxy of extraordinary lights whose lives are portrayed in this section, representing the dynasty of women who have excelled in the sport from 1876 to the present.

"In the five hundred years since Dame Juliana's time, the women who have gained notoriety in this field can be counted on two hands: McBride, Crosby, Marbury, Frost, Stevens, Grieg, Darbee,

Shaw and Dette," writes contemporary fly-fishing legend Joan Wulff in her second book, *Joan Wulff's Fly Fishing: Expert Advice from a Woman's Perspective.* "The good news is we can be proud of every one of them. We are not starting from scratch; we have a heritage!"[6]

Indeed we do.

CHAPTER 1

Trailblazers in Fly-Fishing History

CORNELIA "FLY ROD" CROSBY

"BONEFISH" BONNIE SMITH, FRANKEE ALBRIGHT, AND BEULAH CASS

KAY BRODNEY

HELEN ROBINSON

AND OTHER SIGNIFICANT FIGURES

Five of the women who etched a permanent place in fly-fishing history were indisputably among the best the sport has ever produced; another never picked up a fly rod but co-pioneered a revolutionary technique that is practiced throughout the world today by fly fishers angling for billfish.

Thanks to their contributions, we will never again think of women's participation in this branch of the sport as only a recent phenomenon.

Cornelia "Fly Rod" Crosby LATE 1800s • MAINE

If the First Lady of American fly fishing in the 19th century had properly confined herself to the delicate tasks expected of Victorian women (namely, parlor chat and afternoon teas), she'd be known today only as *Miss* Cornelia Thurza Crosby. But Cornelia, dear soul, was uncontrollably consumed by the undainty pastime of catching trophy-size fish (as well as bringing in the last legally hunted caribou in the state of Maine), which led to her enduring moniker of "Fly Rod" Crosby instead.

Fondly referred to as "the firecracker of our ancestors" by contemporary fly-fishing legend Joan Wulff,[1] Cornelia remains one of the few women in American history to have reached that rare stratosphere of public recognition where gender ceases to become an issue.

How did she do it? By racking up a succession of firsts that rivaled even the best efforts of men at the time. She was not only Maine's first registered guide, but she also pioneered use of the lightweight fly rod and artificial lure for women, authored possibly the first-ever nationally syndicated outdoors column, and reigned for three decades as one of the first prominent sports celebrities capable of filling an arena on name value alone. Not to be overlooked, she was also the "wearer of the first liberated woman's hunting suit (including bustle) seen in the woods," according to Victor Block in *Outdoors Unlimited*.[2]

Born in 1854 to Lemuel and Thurza Crosby of Phillips, Maine, Cornelia worked odd jobs in summer camps in Rangeley, Maine, as a young girl, where, according to legend, she learned the fundamentals of fishing from friendly Indians and local guides, and she was adept with both a rod and a rifle by her teens.

Following graduation from an Episcopal school, she worked briefly as a bank clerk until contracting tuberculosis and being told by her physician to "take to the woods" to recover her health—a prescription that undoubtedly thrilled her! Just before her departure, a friend presented her with the prototype of a lightweight fly rod to field test and, notes Kenneth Smith in *Discover Maine*, "in Cornelia's hands the fly rod became a magic wand that launched her amazing career."[3]

Smith also reports that "she caught so many huge salmon and trout that the local sports nicknamed her 'Fly Rod.' Her fishing talents, combined with her innovative fly-tying skills, provided her with a state-wide reputation as one of the premier anglers in Maine. Cornelia hooked these creations [her artificial

BY 1895, CORNELIA "FLY ROD" CROSBY WAS A NATIONAL SPORTS CELEBRITY AS A RESULT OF HER EXTRAORDINARY ANGLING AND HUNTING SKILLS AND POPULAR SYNDICATED OUTDOORS COLUMN.

flies] around the band of her felt hat, instituting a sports fashion which has lasted until today."

What led Cornelia to write for publication is not known, but there's no disputing that it was an extraordinary ambition for a woman at the time. J. W. Bracket, the editor of *The Maine Woods*, is said to have given her the byline, "Fly Rod's Notebook," and launched her career nationally by distributing her column to other papers. "While major newspapers in Boston, Philadelphia, New York and Chicago routinely detailed her exploits," explains Smith, her articles at the same time appeared in such prestigious publications as *Field and Stream* and *Shooting and Fishing*, according to historian Austin S. Hogan in *The American Fly Fisher*. In fact, Hogan notes, her piece was often "the only one on angling to appear in the latter, a New York publication."[4]

"The image that reflects from her writing is that of a school girl having the most delightful time travelling from lake to lake, meeting people from Oregon, Iowa, California, shop talking with guides and interviewing hotel keepers about the new accommodations.... In reality, behind the daintiness was the sharp intelligence that spelled money for the lodge owner, the boat builder, the guide and the State of Maine. Not only was she a master of the fly rod, Cornelia Crosby was a one lady advertising agency," Hogan adds.

Cornelia could have just as easily been nicknamed "Rifle" as "Fly Rod." Her marksmanship was so widely admired that Buffalo Bill invited her to tour with his Wild West Show (an offer which she apparently declined), and a 1905 friendly exhibition shooting match with Annie Oakley was the talk of the region for years.

By 1895, Cornelia "had become a star employed by the Maine Central Railroad to advertise the advantage of travelling by rail to the fishing resorts," writes Hogan. Each year, her tour would include arenas throughout the eastern United States, climaxed by appearances at the Sportsman's Shows in New York and Boston. "Taking advantage of her talent for showmanship, they put her in charge of their exhibits and with a coterie of guides and two beautiful Indian girls, Fly Rod pulled them in by the thousands."

But it was more than her skills with a rod and rifle that sent shivers through the crowds. Fly Rod had *star quality!* Sporting an outfit that featured a skirt "nearly a foot shorter than accepted fashion," Smith writes, she literally dazzled them. "Tall, attractive, and modest, with a resonant speaking voice and attired as she was, the effect was electric. Crowds flocked, lingering for her lectures and demonstrations. Cornelia's garb served to create a new fashion trend for American woman."

Even so, she was once again the frontierswoman when out of sight of her admiring public. "Along with her notebook, Cornelia carried a special rod custom-made by Charles Wheeler of Farmington . . . and a Winchester with which she hunted bear and caribou. At the peak of her popularity, the stage that brought her to a wilderness hotel [also] carried her birch bark canoe lashed to the top," recounts Hogan.

Who knows how long Cornelia could have kept up such a demanding career, if it hadn't been sidelined by a misstep off a slow-moving train at the age of 50. And while the resulting injuries kept her off the road and out of the woods for the rest of her life, this robust woman nonetheless survived another 40 years, until 1946, when she died two days after turning 92.

Cornelia was indeed a trailblazer in the true sense of the word!

"Bonefish" Bonnie Smith, Frankee Albright, and Beulah Cass 1940s–1950s • FLORIDA

During World War II, when young women across the country were discarding their aprons and heading for aircraft

SISTERS BEULAH CASS, "BONEFISH" BONNIE SMITH, AND FRANKEE ALBRIGHT (LEFT TO RIGHT) FISHED THEIR WAY INTO SALTWATER FLY-FISHING HISTORY AS FAMOUS GUIDES IN THE FLORIDA KEYS DURING AND AFTER WORLD WAR II.

factories and shipyards, sisters "Bonefish" Bonnie Smith, Frankee Albright, and Beulah Cass did something even more remarkable for the times. When Bonnie's husband joined the Armed Forces, the three sisters picked up the slack and literally guided themselves into saltwater fly-fishing history in the Florida Keys. And though their husbands would ultimately receive the largess of acclaim as famous guides in the area, time has not snuffed out the legend of the three sisters and their notable achievements.

Bonnie was the first to venture to the Keys, where she met and married flats guide Bill Smith in the late 1930s. "Bonnie was more than just the wife of a fishing guide," remarks author David Foster in *Gray's Sporting Journal*. "She loved to fish and most people in Islamorada considered her uncanny in her talent."[5]

It's possible that Bonnie's husband, Bill, had not yet picked up a fly rod when she was given one by George LaBranche from his personal collection. LaBranche, one of the most influential figures in dry-fly fishing after the turn of the century, also hired the dean of Keys guides, Preston Pinder, to teach her how to use it. "Pinder did such a good job that in the late 1930s his eager student was able, in turn, to teach her two sisters, Beulah and Frankee, how to flycast when they moved from Georgia to join her," relates George X. Sand in *Saltwater Fly Fishing*.[6]

The fact that Bill would be the first, in 1939, to catch a bonefish on an artificial fly foreshadows an event that would put Bonnie on the map during his wartime absence. It seems that in 1942, one of Bill's childhood friends, Charles "Barrel" Bowen, was about to be shipped overseas and approached her with a special request. "'There is one thing I'd like to do—in case I don't come back,' Bowen told Bonnie earnestly. 'I'd like to catch a bonefish on a fly, like Bill did,'" recounts Sand. Bowen not only got his bonefish, but he and Bonnie were back at the dock within two hours! It was a remarkable feat, considering that "what makes [a bonefish] the ultimate quarry in the sport is that you must see it—sometimes from eighty feet away—before you can cast to it," declares Dick Brown in *Fly Fishing for Bonefish*. "You stalk it like a predator. You track it down, you take aim, and cast with precision. You must make no mistakes. The ruthless, primitive instincts of this skittish creature leave no room for error."[7] No wonder everyone else was going after them with spinning gear. How many would have the casting skill, even today, to drop a fly right in front of a fish's nose over such a distance? But Bonnie certainly did.

Also during the war, Bonnie guided another young soldier, Jimmie Albright, to his first bonefish. Stationed aboard a deep-sea fishing vessel out of Fort Lauderdale, Florida, Jimmie was introduced to Bonnie's sister, Frankee, and they eventually married.

Immediately after the war, many of the servicemen who had been trained or stationed in Florida found their way back to the Keys. Among them was Joe Brooks, later a renowned angling author, whom Bonnie guided to his first permit on a fly.

During those postwar years, according to Sand, Bonnie and Bill "built one of the best known and most successful guide businesses in the Keys," with a celebrity clientele that included baseball great Ted Williams and movie actress Madeline Carol. In honor of her Midas touch with the game fish that everyone admired but few could catch, Bonnie became "Bonefish" Bonnie within the saltwater fly-fishing fraternity.

By 1950, catching a permit on a fly rod was the challenge of the day. Bonnie and Bill, along with Joe and Mary Brooks and a few others, tried their luck in 1950, to no avail. In 1952, a year after Joe had brought in the first one, Bonnie caught hers, becoming the first woman to take a permit, a women's record that had not been broken by the time Sand published his landmark book in 1970.

Meanwhile, Frankee was racking up her own list of achievements. Among them was a 48.5-pound tarpon on an Orvis rod and 12-pound test tippet, in just 50 minutes. She also guided an elderly George LaBranche to his first bonefish on a fly. That he chose her to guide him instead of one of the sisters' husbands says much about Frankee's stature as a professional guide at the time.

The youngest of the three sisters, Beulah Cass, gave up guiding early to become a successful real-estate developer in Islamorada. By the mid-1960s, "Bonefish" Bonnie had retired from guiding and spent much of her time teaching the fundamentals of flats fishing to others. (She and Frankee also became passionate orchid growers.) Bonnie died in the 1970s; Beulah, in the early 1990s; and Frankee, at the age of 84, in January 1995.

We can be proud of the fact that the Laidlaw sisters did what few women have been able to accomplish. They left their footprints in the shifting sands of saltwater fly-fishing history.

Kay Brodney 1950s–1980s • WASHINGTON, D.C.

"You'd be surprised how few people know about Kay Brodney," Lefty Kreh, one of the fly-fishing world's legendary writers, told me.

It was a refrain that I would find repeated in Jim Chapralis's tribute to her angling *par excellence* upon her death in 1994: "Even the world's most knowledgeable anglers probably haven't heard of her. It's not because her angling experience and accomplishments were limited—they were indeed very rich and extensive—but because Kay was a private person. Her life was an endless ribbon of angler vs. fish confrontations that took place not at posh fishing resorts, but mostly in wilderness settings, where a hammock would be her bed and a dug-out her cruiser."[8]

As impersonal as labels are, it's hard to resist calling Kay Brodney the Indiana Jones of women's angling heritage. Kay, however, would never have been bothered with collecting valuable antiquities like Indiana, even if she had to step over them in the jungle on the way to what she cherished more: a great fishing hole.

And just as the fictional Indiana led a double life, so did Kay. Hers was as a librarian who spent every vacation period in her later years stalking the uncharted wildernesses of South America.

"She did it all," recounts Chapralis in *The PanAngler* newsletter. "Kay fished in Argentina and was one of the first anglers to take a dorado on a fly. She fished the jungles of Brazil camping out in areas where the Indians were considered unfriendly. 'We didn't carry any weapons—and I think they knew this and therefore we weren't considered threats,' she said. But what if they attacked? 'If we die, we die,' she replied. Gulp.

"She fished Rupununi ranch in Guyana with Stu Apte and longtime friend Peter Gorinsky," Chapralis continues. "When it was impossible to get into Venezuela to fish for peacock bass (in the days when oil-rich Venezuela didn't need tourists) she spent a month in Colombia trying to cut through the gobs of red tape. She smuggled across the border. She fished for steelhead in British Columbia and giant salmon in Quebec. A few years ago, she went on a world wide trip and was gone for about a year."

Born in 1920, Kay grew up in Wisconsin and did some fishing as a child, but did not get the fly-fishing bug until 1948, when she happened upon a casting tournament in San Francisco's Golden Gate Park. "I saw those lines swishing

LIBRARY OF CONGRESS LIBRARIAN KAY
BRODNEY, SHOWN HERE IN A PRIMITIVE
DUGOUT CANOE, PIONEERED FISHING
EXPEDITIONS INTO THE REMOTE JUNGLES
OF SOUTH AMERICA, BEGINNING IN
THE 1960S.

about and it changed my whole life," she later related to *Sports Illustrated*'s Clive Gammon. "Women weren't recognized for doing much distance casting then, just accuracy events. Once [in 1950] I took third place in the Western Championship down at Long Beach. I went to get my prize but I found I hadn't qualified because I wasn't a man."[9]

By her mid-30s, Kay had become a self-described "card-carrying fishing bum," according to Gammon. "She never had much money and she went through about 50 jobs, the steadiest one clerking at a railroad office. But she did manage to acquire a Volkswagen Camper. It took her all over northern California fishing for steelhead and shad."

She relocated to Seattle, which put her within driving distance of her favorite steelhead rivers, the Dean and Kispoix in British Columbia. But even then, trying to finance her angling forays was difficult without the wages that came with a college education.

While working two jobs, as a clerk-typist and cataloguer, she eventually returned to school and earned a bachelor's degree in zoology. When sexual discrimination reared its ugly head on one of Kay's jobs, however, she realized that a master's in library science was the only way she could make enough money to support her unique lifestyle. So she headed to Rutgers University in Camden, New Jersey. After graduation, she began a long career at the Library of Congress in Washington, D.C.

Meanwhile, in 1962, Kay took her meager savings and headed for the Florida Keys, where Stu Apte, one of the sport's prominent figures, was with her the day she landed a 137.6-pound tarpon on 12-pound tippet. "Right in front of Ted Williams [the baseball great] and a multitude of other people, Kay caught this humongous tarpon. At the time, there had only been one, maybe two, caught bigger than that by anybody on a fly," Apte says, noting that fly-fishing legend Joe Brooks's world record was only 11 pounds heavier at 148.5 pounds and that Kay had made her own fly rod, line, and fly. (No store-bought tackle for her, then or later!)

From there, she apparently turned her attention to the jungles of South America, "[and] we're talking fishing the real outback country, not five miles from a comfortable air-conditioned oasis," notes Chapralis. Accompanied by an outfitter, "they often probed uncharted waters, slept outside and fought the elements, and 'trespassed' areas where unfriendly natives observed them constantly with a baleful eye. These trips were for weeks at a time, and I don't know of any visiting angler—including the late A. J. McClane—who has spent more time fishing South American jungles than Kay Brodney."

Apte recalls that "she would go off and do things—actually go and do them—that men would only contemplate the possibility of doing, but never do. If she was a man, [there's] no telling *where* she would have gone."

In the early 1980s, when Kay was 61 and the head of the Library of Congress's Life Sciences Subject Catalog Section, *Sports Illustrated*'s Gammon was given the unenviable assignment of shadowing her while she stalked two elusive freshwater fish, the tucunare and the arapaima, deep within the Amazon rain forest of Brazil. For Gammon, it would turn out to be almost as dangerous as covering a war from behind the enemy lines.

From the moment he set down in a patch of cleared jungle in the middle of nowhere to the day of his anxious departure, Gammon found himself dodging venomous and bone-crushing snakes, electric eels, vampire fish, piranhas, wild pigs, deadly spiders, vampire bats, jaguars, "endlessly attacking" cabouri flies, and stingrays—not to mention surviving daily rations of mysterious origins.

Meanwhile, the indomitable Kay was completely oblivious to it all. "People think that I'm a mad, brave old woman to come out fishing in a place like this, living like an Amerindian," Kay told him. "But, hell, I've been robbed twice on the streets of D.C., and each time it was more frightening than anything I've met in a rain forest."

Unfortunately, Kay paid a hefty price for her far-ranging freedom. "She picked up this terrible disease," says Joan Wulff, her friend since the early 1950s. Sitting on a stump in the middle of a jungle clearing, "after a while, she realized she was being bitten by some kind of tiny, tiny thing. She said she was bitten from her feet up to her waist. And so she thought that's where the disease came from which attacked the inside of her arteries and scarred them.

"She ended up with restricted circulation. They put her on terrible drugs. She gained weight. The sun affected her and made her break out, and yet in 1992, she met me in Great Falls, Montana—I flew out there—and we drove up to Calgary for a Federation of Fly Fishermen's conclave. And we came back down and went to the Missouri River, where we spent five days fishing; except that she didn't fish. She sat in the boat and I fished. I mean, it was unbelievable what she was going through, and yet she did not act as if she was putting up with anything. She just put up with it."

It was apparently true of every obstacle Kay faced in life. "She never complained about her infirmities or inconveniences. She was a very courageous lady," says Apte.

We lost this intrepid spirit on July 21, 1994, at the age of 74. It's obvious that Kay's life force was sustained by a personal challenge entirely outside the realm of the average angler: fishing where no one had dared venture before. "Her life was so remarkable: the things that she did, the places that she went, and the way she went about it," says Apte. "I mean, she was fearless!"

Helen Robinson never fished anything but conventional tackle. And yet, in collaboration with her husband, Webster Robinson, and Captain Lefty Reagan, she pioneered a technique for teasing billfish to an artificial fly that is practiced around the world today.

In the late 1930s, Web (as he was known to his friends) severely injured his back in an automobile accident. Helen suggested they take up fishing so that Web could build up the muscles that supported his spine and possibly relieve the constant pain. They ventured down to the Florida Keys from their New York home base and "began to wade the flats, particularly at Marvin Key, which is outside of Key West. And they waded these flats almost everyday for years," angling writer Lefty Kreh recalls from his long friendship with them.

In 1959, Web developed an overwhelming urge to go after big-game fish, though he was already 63 and Helen was 59. They bought a boat and hired Captain Lefty Reagan—who, Kreh shares, was "regarded by me and many others as one of the *great* pioneers in offshore fishing, particularly in the Keys"—and set off on a four-year fishing trip to Panama, Peru, Chile, and other points. When they finally returned to Florida, Web sat down and tallied up their catches: he had 115 black marlin to his credit (double that of anyone else in the history of the sport) and Helen had 37. Among Helen's catches, however, were two world records, a 796-pounder on 80-pound test and a 584-pounder on 50-pound line, which brought her tremendous prestige within the saltwater world.

Somewhere in the early 1960s, Web, who approached angling the way a scientist goes after a cure for a life-threatening disease, got another inspiration. Since no one had

HELEN ROBINSON'S REVOLUTIONARY
TECHNIQUE FOR TEASING BILLFISH
TO AN ARTIFICIAL FLY, WHICH SHE
INVENTED IN THE 1960S WITH HER
HUSBAND AND THEIR CAPTAIN,
IS PRACTICED AROUND THE
WORLD, TODAY.

ever caught a billfish on an artificial fly, he suggested the three of them team up to see if it was possible.

So while Lefty ran the boat and Web stood by ready to cast, Helen became the master teaser. "Most of the billfish that Web Robinson ever caught anywhere were caught with Helen actually teasing the fish up to the boat so he could make the cast," says Kreh, one of her ardent admirers. If done correctly, Kreh adds, a sailfish will be "so excited [by the teaser bait] that when you throw a fly in, it's like rolling a wine bottle in a jail cell. I mean, they're going to jump all over this damn thing.

"Helen became a consummate teaser of billfish. She was absolutely superb at figuring out when a fish was really hot and would take the fly. Once the fish was [ready], of course, then it was Web's problem. But up until the point that she directed him to throw the fly, she was in control."

So while Web received all the acclaim "as the most innovative ocean angler since Zane Grey"[10] and the one who would go down in the record books as the first angler to capture a sailfish by "pure" flycasting, it was Helen who actually provided the talent that produced the results.

More than anything else, however, what made all of their achievements possible was a bond that superceded even their remarkable passion for angling. "Helen and Web were totally devoted to each other," says Kreh. "Web was a great big handsome imposing man, probably six foot two. And Helen was a little tiny gal, I don't think over five foot two. But [she] had a mind like a steel trap. Brilliant woman."

Web died in the 1970s, almost 30 years before Helen. So deep was their love that Helen committed herself to completing the rest of his dreams after his death. By now in her early 70s, she took the footage he had shot and produced a public-television documentary called "Marlin to the Fly." She also appeared in and produced a BBC special called "The Old Lady and the Sea," shot off Australia. When it was all done, legend has it that Helen put down her rod for the last time.

Other Significant Figures

Although little has been written about Mary Brooks, she is universally admired throughout the fly-fishing world. Soon after World War II, she met her famous writer-husband Joe Brooks when he visited Canada and she took him fishing. According to their friend Lefty Kreh, Joe had suffered with alcoholism for years, but Mary had a profound effect on his life. "They fell in love, got married, and from that day until Joe died, he never had another drink," Kreh says with glowing admiration for both.

From the 1950s to the 1970s, Kreh says, Joe was "probably the best-known fishing writer in the world," and Mary accompanied him everywhere. Together they pioneered fly fishing in Africa, Central and South America, Iceland, Norway, and New Zealand, among other remote places. Equally expert in saltwater and freshwater, she was one of the first women to take bonefish on a fly and set a world record for a 39.75-pound Atlantic salmon on 20-pound test leader tippet on a 9.5-foot bamboo rod.

Although many people are under the impression that Mary never fished again after Joe died in 1972, she wrote in a letter to me that she in fact settled in Montana "and enjoyed the spring creek fishing until I developed arthritis in my fingers to the point that I could not handle the tiny flies and 6X and 7X tippets. Fortunately, I discovered golf at that time and can still grip a golf club, and at 84 years of age am playing 3 or 4 days per week."

But as Kreh notes, she is so highly regarded as both a person and angler that "I hated to see *us* lose her."

Louise Brewster Miller was another legend in her own right who was married to one of the deans of fly fishing, Sparse Grey Hackle, author of the classic *Fishless Days, Angling Nights*. Born in 1900, Louise was nicknamed "Lady Beaverkill" by her husband, after the famous Catskills river which they often fished.

According to her granddaughter, Margot Page, those who saw Louise fish "say that she was a better fly fisher than my grandfather." But tradition being what it was in the 1920s and 1930s, Louise was typically left at home to care for their four children while Sparse headed to the Catskills on weekends. There were other frustrations as well, particularly her exclusion from Sparse's men-only angling club which did not allow women in their building. "She would sit on the [club's] porch knitting, getting closer and closer to the door as the years went by, until finally she earned her way in there occasionally because she was so skilled and they liked her a lot," Margot says.

"There can be a perception of this sport as elitist and snobby. My grandmother strung together equipment she could find," Margot adds. "She had beautiful Garrison rods because they were good friends with Everett Garrison [the rod builder]. But her waders were patched. She was a true Yankee and there was nothing elitist about her. She loved the fact that you met such wonderful people on the stream."

Margot herself did not take up fly fishing until she met her husband, Tom Rosenbauer, one of the prominent young men in the sport. So it was not until her grandmother was 86 that they finally ventured out with their rods together. "When I saw her cast, it was the most beautiful thing I'd ever seen," Margot recalls of that memorable day. "Even at 86, after not picking up a rod for ten years, it was crisp and calm and a thing of beauty. So natural to those old hands."

Although Louise had to give up fishing several years before her death at the age of 92, because of a bad knee and wrist, "she never stopped talking about it," Margot says. "If you had a room full of people and put a fly fisher in the room, she would go right over to that person. That was all she wanted to talk about!"

Fishing became a special bond between Louise and Margot, especially since the angling bug never took hold with Louise's daughters (including Margot's mother). Louise gave Margot one of her beloved Garrison rods as a wedding present and lived to see Margot spread her wings as a writer and the editor of the American Museum of Fly Fishing's prestigious journal, *The American Fly Fisher*. And one can only imagine the pride she would have felt when Margot's first book, a highly praised collection of personal essays titled *Little Rivers: Tales of a Woman Angler*, appeared in 1995.

In her eloquent introduction to Holly Morris's anthology of essays, *Uncommon Waters: Women Write About Fishing*, Margot writes: "'Think of me when you fish,' she once told me wistfully."

CHAPTER 2

Patterns of Excellence: Fly Tiers in History

ELIZABETH BENJAMIN

SARA JANE MCBRIDE

MARY ORVIS MARBURY

CARRIE STEVENS

AND OTHER SIGNIFICANT FIGURES

No matter when they worked, the women who distinguished themselves in the art of fly tying have been, by nature, a breed of their own: ingenious, artistic, and industrious. In terms of the latter, they had to be; fly tying has never been a road to great fortune. Yet many of them managed to insert themselves into the history of the sport by twisting fur or feathers around a hook in such a way that neither fish or fisher*men* could resist.

Those to be celebrated from another era are...

Elizabeth Benjamin 1858–60 • PENNSYLVANIA

"The first was also the least known, and as far as can be told was *not* of much influence on other fly tiers. But she is extremely interesting, one of the most intriguing characters in nineteenth-century fly tying," writes Paul Schullery in his definitive tome, *American Fly Fishing: A History*.[1]

Elizabeth Benjamin is indeed one of the more obscure fly-tying personages out of the past, and we know of her now only because, according to Schullery, historian Austin Hogan uncovered a letter written in the 1930s by her only child, Joseph, at the age of 81.

The wife of a railroad conductor, Elizabeth's moment in history occurred during one of the Benjamins' summer sojourns to Ralston, Pennsylvania, just prior to the Civil War. As her son Joseph related in his letter, Ralston was famous for its speckled brook trout, for which city anglers flocked to the area "loaded down with all kinds of fancy fishing tackle" between the years 1858 and 1860. What they encountered, however, were fish so fickle that most returned home with empty creels.

But Elizabeth happened to notice that the local tavern owner, Mr. Conley, seemed to have all the luck. Every afternoon he'd head out fishing and each evening return home with a mess of trout to fry up. Intrigued, she followed him down to the creek, making sure to stay out of sight, and watched the largest trout gobble up his flies the moment they touched the water. Upon returning home, she told her husband of her fortuitous discovery, "and they worked nights making nets," Joseph recalled, to snare the insects that hovered around the creek, which were placed under "glasses on a table until they would 'shed their coats.'" Elizabeth then sent her son out gathering feathers from the "roosters, chickens, ducks, pigeons and bird nests" in the area, which she "fastened by hand to fishhooks with different colored silk thread." Elizabeth's flies were so successful, Joseph related, that word quickly spread among the visiting anglers who "paid her fabulous prices for all she could make."

It was not to be the only time that a woman suddenly found herself in the fly-tying business as a result of stumping nature and saving her fellow fishermen from many fishless days on the water. Three-quarters of a century later, Carrie Stevens, another non-tier, would revolutionize the way certain patterns were tied thereafter as a result of a chance inspiration.

Almost two decades later, a self-taught entomologist by the name of Sara Jane McBride wrote what Kenneth M. Cameron in *The Fly Fisher* has called "the first American papers of any consequence on the subject of aquatic insects from the angler's point of interest."[2]

Her extraordinary theses first appeared in 1876 in *Forest and Stream* as a three-part series called "Metaphysics of Fly Fishing" and in *Rod and Gun* a year later under the title of "Entomology for Fly Fishers." Adding to the prestige of having her work published by such prominent journals was *Forest and Stream*'s editorial blessing, which read: "The subject matter of these articles we believe to be altogether new in the Angling Literature of America, and certainly reflects much credit upon the author, who shows herself to be a patient and close observor."

Sara would also distinguish herself as a fly tier, for which she won a bronze medal at the 1876 Centennial Exposition, and find a permanent place in the annals of the applied art when Mary Orvis Marbury referred to her findings in *Favorite Flies and their Histories* in 1892.

Sara "was way ahead of her time," current fly-fishing legend Joan Wulff declares in *Joan Wulff's Fly Fishing*. "The fly-fishing fraternity, as a whole, didn't have a clue about insect life and most fly patterns were what we now call 'attractors.'"[3]

One can only wonder what local gossip must have accompanied sightings of Sara grubbing around in the mud while studying the various stages of insect life as well as the effects of water temperature and climatic conditions on the "food-rich" Spring Creek, which ran through Caledonia, New York, near Rochester on Lake Ontario. Considering that "fancy flies" were still the fashion of the day, it's unlikely she had the approval of many!

There's no doubt, however, that she was a woman who understood her mission fully. One of five children of well-known Irish-born fly tier John McBride, Sara apparently learned the craft before her inquiring mind took her off in search of new methods.

Not surprising for the times, she went uncredited within the scientific community, whose job it was to document stream insect life in its natural habitat. Whether it was her lack of academic credentials, the possibility that her research had treaded on too many fragile egos, or the simple fact of her gender, Sara's work was not even acknowledged in an important report of the time, the New York State Fishery Commission's 1877–78 study of Spring Creek. "Too bad," notes Cameron, "for although [J. A.] Litner [the report's author] worked from water and moss samples sent to him by [Seth] Green, Sara probably could have provided him with all stages of the most important insects."

Though Sara's achievements are now a well-documented part of fly-fishing folklore, facts about her personal life remain largely a mystery. By consulting original census records, Cameron was able to establish her birth at about 1845, and it can be assumed that she never married, based on her continuing use of her family name. In June of 1879, *Forest and Stream* reported that she was "about to close up her business" and six months later ran "a cheerful and chatty letter" from her about a particular tackle company, Cameron notes. After that, she completely vanished without a trace!

"It is fitting, at least, that she is remembered through the work of Mary Orvis Marbury," adds Cameron. "The two women were opposites in many ways, and their approaches to fishing and flydressing were quite different. One was an original, the other a collator, but they were alike in their ability to achieve in a field where women were otherwise treated as the handmaidens of a masculine pastime."

One of the prominent figures in the history of fly fishing, Mary Orvis Marbury achieved her fame inadvertently. She simply saw a problem and proceeded to solve it by compiling and writing the first definitive reference book on American fly patterns, *Favorite Flies and Their Histories*,[4] published in 1892.

It was an astounding accomplishment. Over 500 pages in length, with 32 color plates featuring 290 different regional patterns, Mary's book was the long-awaited answer to a dilemma that threatened to paralyze both the sport and the fly-tying industry that served it.

It seems that by the 1870s, fly fishing had become so popular in this country that anglers were fervently developing new artificial fly patterns, as well as producing variations on old standbys, to fish the specific waters in their own region. And like pollen spread by a summer breeze, the most successful of those patterns ventured across state lines, carried by visiting fly fishers who hoped their magic would have the same profound effect on their home streams and lakes. The patterns often underwent further modifications and even name changes as they were passed from hand to hand in new locales.

It wouldn't have mattered what anyone called their flies or how they made them if every angler tied his own. But even then, in the late 1800s, many anglers turned to professional fly-tying companies to replenish their supplies, and many of them were sorely disappointed when the patterns that came back in the mail were not the ones they had intended to order.

As the head of the Orvis Company's fly-tying department, Mary was one of those fly-tying professionals forced to cope with the growing mass confusion. As she explained in the pages of *Favorite Flies and Their Histories*:

MARY ORVIS MARBURY, THE DAUGHTER OF
THE FOUNDER OF THE FAMOUS ORVIS
COMPANY, WROTE HER WAY INTO FLY-FISHING
HISTORY WITH AN 1892 BEST-SELLING BOOK
ON AMERICAN FLY PATTERNS THAT DIVERTED
AN ESCALATING CRISIS.

You would hear him [a customer] describe his favorites, and such descriptions! He would declare, "for an all-round fly, give me a Professor with a green body!" meaning a Grizzly King. The next might say, "Now I tell you, the best fly for black bass, every time, is a large-sized Ferguson with a green body and a speckled wing;" again a Grizzly King was intended. One who wrote the above to us pitifully added, "But I can no more get the right Ferguson; I have ordered of many dealers, and they always send the wrong fly." A specimen of the Grizzly King was sent to help him out of his dilemma, and he wrote back gratefully, saying, "You are the first I have met in a long time who knew the real Ferguson."

The first child and only daughter of Charles and Laura Orvis, Mary was born in 1856, the same year her father started the long-famous company that introduced affordable rods, reels, and finely tied flies to the mass public. And though her two brothers went on to become prominent Manchester, Vermont, citizens, it was Mary whose outstanding achievements would bring prestige and respect to the family business.

At the age of 20, in 1876, she took over the company's commercial fly-production department, after apprenticing under the auspices of an expert dresser hired by her father to teach her the craft. "Mary's half-dozen tiers, all young women, worked upstairs in a white clapboard building on Union Street that still belongs to Orvis," notes Silvio Calabi in *The Illustrated Encyclopedia of Fly-Fishing*.[5]

By 1890, Mary's tiny but industrious operation was not only turning out untold quantities each year of the 434 different patterns listed in the Orvis mail-order catalog but struggling to keep up with special orders as well. It was undoubtedly the latter that produced the crisis which led her father, Charles, to do a mass mailing to leading anglers in the nation's fishing hotspots, soliciting detailed information on their favorite flies and how to fish them.

The project was an immense success. Over 200 fly fishermen in 38 states responded, whose letters Mary edited for inclusion in her text. *Favorite Flies and Their Histories* was not only an instant best-seller—with over six printings in America and England in just four years—but a highly celebrated one as well.

"It has been given credit, more than any other event, for helping standardize the tangle of fly-pattern names and dressings that had by then become the curse of American fishermen and fishing tackle dealers," writes Paul Schullery in *American Fly Fishing: A History*. "It was a magnificent book.... Not the least, it gave Mary a lasting place in the pantheon of famous angling writers."

Adds historian Kenneth Cameron in *The Fly Fisher*: "The book was infused with a talented intelligence—not talented merely as a writer, although the prose is clear enough, but talented also in her grasp of fishing and in her knowledge of how to appeal to literate flyfishermen.... It is, above all, a visual feast, the most sumptuous of readily available American angling books of the period."[6]

Despite her enduring achievement, Mary's life was filled with mysteries that even historians Austin Hogan and Paul Schullery, who had access to the family's archives for their official chronicle, *The Orvis Story*, were not able to unravel. "We know only enough of Mary's personal life to suspect it was not a happy one," they write, pointing to an unsuccessful marriage to John Marbury in 1877 and the death at an early age of her only child, a son.[7]

Perhaps the most telling insight into her obviously complex personality was her unfulfilled ambition to be the artist rather than the chronicler, as she expresses in *Favorite Flies and Their Histories*.

To create history one should be a great general, an inventor, or an explorer, but to those of us who are not so fortunate as to be creators is permitted the more humble mission of recording what is accomplished by others.

We confess, though, that we are not quite content in this latter capacity, but are ambitious to submit some day to the angling fraternity a series of imitations of natural insects peculiarly our own.

For whatever reasons, Mary never did. And yet her mark on angling history is undisputed, as evidenced by the headline attached to her obituary in London's *Fishing Gazette* in 1914: "Death of the Most Famous but one Female Angling Author."

The first? Dame Juliana Berners, of course.

Carrie Stevens 1924 · MAINE

On July 1, 1924, Carrie Stevens, a milliner by trade and a world-class fly fisher and expert shot by reputation, on an impulse, whipped up an artificial fly out of gray feathers to resemble a smelt.

She attached her crude creation to her line, and on its maiden voyage across the placid water of the Upper Dam pool of Lake Mooselookmeguntic in western Maine, it landed her a six-pound, 13-ounce brook trout—the largest recorded in those parts in 13 years!

Too excited to unhook it, Carrie grabbed her netted fish with one hand and her rod with the other, and raced down to the center of town to weigh it. "There, at the hotel to witness Mrs. Stevens' catch, were some of the country's most affluent anglers, men whose private rail cars were parked beside the railhead at Middle Dam. As Mrs. Stevens showed off her fish, the assemblage of anglers became curious as to what fly she had used," recounts Susie Isaksen in *The American Fly Fisher*.[8]

"The talk around the potbellied stoves that night was about one subject only, and you know what it was! The tycoons in the cabins and the others in the hotel ordered Gray Ghosts as fast as Carrie could dress them and took them home to proudly pass around. The new fly was launched—probably the most famous streamer pattern ever originated," writes Joseph D. Bates in *Streamers and Bucktails: The Big Fish Flies*.[9]

Not only did Carrie's Gray Ghost revolutionize the way streamer flies would be tied thereafter, but her fish took second prize in *Field and Stream*'s annual competition that year. And this was a woman who had never tied a fly before!

From the publicity generated by the *Field and Stream* article as well as the verbal wildfire that flashed through the Rangeley Lakes region, this 42-year-old housewife was suddenly inundated with orders and virtually thrust into the fly-tying business.

Operating under the name of Rangeley's Favorite Trout and Salmon Flies, she single-handedly produced some 2,000 specimens a year at a $1.50 each, providing her with an annual income of about $3,000! It should be noted that her growing client base included such angling notables as President Herbert Hoover and author Zane Grey.

The Gray Ghost may have been the most famous, but Carrie's handiwork over the years also resulted in more than two dozen successful streamer patterns that endure today. And yet she guarded her particular tying methods like a corporation protects a trade secret, divulging the particulars to only one person, author Joseph D. Bates, who was allowed to publish them in his book, *Streamer Fly Tying and Fishing*, long after her retirement.

Twelve days after Carrie died in 1970, friends and admirers, as well as the governor of Maine, gathered to erect a permanent plaque at the site of her greatest angling achievement, on the edge of the Upper Dam pool. It reads in part: "This table is placed here to honor a perfectionist and her original creations which have brought recognition to her native Maine and fame to the Rangeley Lakes region."

It should also be noted that Carrie Gertrude Stevens and Cornelia "Fly Rod" Crosby were two of the three individuals whose names would eventually become fixtures in the folklore of the Rangeley Lakes region.

Other Significant Figures

A contemporary of Mary Orvis Marbury, Carrie Frost established a commercial fly-tying company with a small staff of women in Stevens Point, Wisconsin, in 1890. It's likely that her pioneering operation had much to do with the area's prominence at the end of World War II as the fly-tying capital of the world. Much like the factories of women who labored in the garment industry in New York, Stevens Point had its factories of women who spent long hours behind their vises dressing flies, turning out some ten million a year.

Elizabeth Greig was known as "The First Lady of U.S. Fly Tying," notes Eric Leiser in his book, *The Dettes: A Catskill Legend*.[10] After apprenticing for six years in Scotland, Elizabeth settled in New York about 1930 and worked for Jim Deren's Angler's Roost for many years. Although it hardly seems possible, this extraordinary fly dresser "tied without a vise, using only her fingers and a pair of scissors for all procedures," Leiser points out.

Earline Powell, wife of Walton Powell of the Powell Rod Company in Chico, California, took up winding flies, much like other women pick up crocheting and knitting, upon the birth of one of her five children. Although it's hard to imagine how she kept up with all the work, Earline, who was born in 1917, also assisted in her husband's growing business while running her own fly shop and serving as a founding member of the Chico Fly Fishing Club. Through the years, her flies gained such a wide following that orders poured in by mail from such faraway places as Rome and Germany, where they were particularly popular with American GIs.

In the state of Oregon, the name Audrey Joy will always be fondly remembered. Audrey maintained a queenly presence on the sixth floor of the family-owned department store Meier & Frank in downtown Portland, where she produced her prized flies on a converted Singer treadle sewing machine while customers waited for their orders. If a loyal customer called up in desperation from some faraway location, Audrey would whip up the specified order, then rush it down to the bus terminal with specific directions to the driver to "look sharp for her friend at a certain village or bend of the river."[11] When the idea was first floated to start the Flyfisher's Club of Oregon, who did they turn to? Audrey, of course, who pulled out her file of prestigious clients and gave the club all the names and addresses necessary to round up their charter membership.

CHAPTER 3

The Woman Flyfishers Club

FOUNDED 1932 • NEW YORK

Like so many good things cooked up by women, it started on an impulse. Julia (Mrs. Tappen) Freeman Fairchild and Frank (Mrs. Karl) Hovey-Roof Connell were whiling away a lazy afternoon in 1931, porch-sitting and listening to Tappen Fairchild's absorbing reminiscences of how his membership in the all-male Angler's Club of New York had enriched his life with far-flung adventures and irreplaceable friendships. And then it hit them: *Why not a club just for women?*

In no time at all, Julia and Frank had established the first women's fishing organization in the world, simply by recruiting 35 founding members—another 22 would join within a year—and filing incorporation papers as The Woman Flyfishers Club on January 28, 1932. The initiation fee was set at a modest $2; annual dues were $5.

If there's one element in particular that has bound the Flyfishers together over the decades, it was Julia Fairchild's inspired leadership as its presiding president for 39 years. "Mention her name to any Flyfisher and she will undoubtedly exclaim, 'Julia is the most extraordinary person!' and then proceed to tell you why," Austin M. Francis noted in his highly respected tome, *Catskill Rivers*, in 1983.[1] We are indebted to Francis (unless otherwise noted) for the following rare glimpses into the Club's long and glorious history.

THE FIRST WOMEN'S FISHING ORGANI-
ZATION IN THE WORLD, THE WOMAN
FLYFISHERS CLUB ENJOYS A 1933 OUT-
ING. GUIDING LIGHT JULIA FAIRCHILD
IS THE ONE HOLDING THE FLY ROD.

"The secret of Julia Fairchild's success is her love for people. She was always looking after the needs of her fellow Flyfishers. Jane Smith recalls a recent outing when the two of them were passing out fishing beats to the various members. 'After she had suggested easier stretches for several women in their seventies, Julia suddenly turned to me and said, "Jane, you know, I think we'd better go way up to the top two beats. It's pretty rough fishing up there. I think you and I should go up there." Now this was when she was already past ninety!'"

Because of Julia's unassailable standards regarding how women should conduct themselves in the outdoors, the Club was welcome everywhere it went. "Joe Knapp, whose wife Margaret was a Flyfisher, was very fond of hosting her fellow members at annual outings on his Beaverkill water. 'They are the most remarkable women,' he said. 'They come; they bring everything they own; they never borrow anything; they keep very few fish; and when they go away they take everything they own. I wish my men friends were like that; the men come in here with those hobnail boots and ruin Margaret's floors and then take all the damn fish home with them.'"

Julia also taught her brood the virtue of self-reliance, as Jane Smith, who succeeded her as president, enthusiastically conveyed to Francis: "One of the things Julia was very firm on was that we were women who were not dependent on anybody but ourselves. We were expected to take care of our own equipment, to know what flies we had, to clean our own fish in places where they didn't have somebody to do it for us. This made quite an impression on me; we didn't come up and forget our wading sneakers."

Outings were always a joyous occasion. Before they acquired their own waters and clubhouse, their annual rendezvous on the Beaverkill River was often punctuated with playful antics at the end of the day at a nearby 19th-century fishing hotel. "At bedtime we felt like girls at boarding school as we flitted about the halls in pajamas, gossiped in each other's rooms, and on a few occasions, had an athletic contest. Mary King and Jane Smith outdid us all in pushups and standing on the head!" one member happily related to Francis.

And over the years, special memories would cement them together, such as the time the members "visited Gioia Gould Larkin, and fished Dry Brook. We finally persuaded her that her baby should not be born in a trout stream. So we all climbed into the car in fishing attire and at five o'clock headed for the Margaretville Hospital. Gioia's son was born at six; we suggested Brown or Brook as an appropriate name."

Although it was their aim from the beginning, it took five years for the Flyfishers to secure their own Catskills head-quarters and waters. Since such streamfront properties rarely hit the market, when Julia and her husband, Tappen, happened to hear about a spread on the Willowemoc that was destined for the auction block, they rushed over to the county seat and paid the back taxes, then secured a lease from the late owner's widow.

It could hardly be called paradise, but it was close enough for this hardy bunch. The 265-acre spread came with a mile of stream frontage, which they were able to add to by obtaining permission to fish the adjacent three miles. The only problem was that the cottage was rather primitive, to say the least. It came with no electricity, which also meant no refrigeration. But they were hardly discouraged, as Julia delightedly recounted in the club's 40th-anniversary bulletin: "[Members] had to stop in Livingston Manor and haul in hundred pound blocks of ice which continued to drip all the way in, but enough remained to be dumped into the ice box outside the kitchen door.

There was always enough left to make the martinis." After dismissing the caretaker who came with the property for lack of visible results from his alleged efforts, they rolled up their sleeves and got to work. "The river was small and overgrown, but many of us spent useful days chopping out suckers and clearing debris from the many winter storms to get a chance to cast in a pool or two," Julia added.

Their beloved retreat served them well until 1946, when the owner of record suddenly had a change of heart and took back her land. Undaunted, the Flyfishers set out again, looking for a place they could call their weekend home. Four years and one frustrated relocation later, they finally found what has become their permanent lair.

It's no wonder Julia was so admired by her clan that they affectionately dubbed her "Dame Julia," after our first great angling legend. Though the needs of the Flyfishers would always rank as one of her chief priorities, she never wavered in her commitment to conservation. Over the years, according to Susie Isaksen in *The American Fly Fisher*,[2] Julia wrote endless letters to presidents, senators, congressmen, secretaries of the interior, and anyone else in a pivotal position concerning the protection of our natural resources. She also guided the Flyfishers on a successful crusade to persuade the State of New York to establish the much-needed Cold Spring Harbor Fish Hatchery.

"She was definitely a woman way before her time," a current member related to me. "Her commitment to the environment and her tireless work to save watersheds, forests, gardens, open spaces, and even a fish hatchery on Long Island, all took place before most people were even aware of the need for such foresight."

Add to that the fact that the club's original doctrine—in 1932!—included a provision for "the protection and propagation of fish and game," which Julia was instrumental in drafting, and there's no doubt that this dedicated fly fisher was worthy of the many distinctions that came her way.

Before Julia retired as president in 1971, she would receive an invitation to raise the American flag with Secretary of the Interior Stewart L. Udall at the 50th commemoration of the National Park Service in 1966, the Garden Club of America's Conservation Committee Certificate in 1967, and a privileged seat on the national board of Trout Unlimited, to mention but a few of her honors.

Perhaps it's something about fishing that brings such contentment to the soul that fishers seem to live longer than those who spend little time in the outdoors. Julia Fairchild was still wading streams up until her death at 97; Frank Connell, who lived to be 102, fished right up to her 98th birthday.

Significant of the unique and enduring tradition Julia and Frank created in their lifetimes, The Woman Flyfishers Club will celebrate its 65th anniversary in 1997.

CHAPTER 4

A Living Legend: Joan Salvato Wulff

NEW YORK

"She has done for casting what Stephen Hawking did for physics.... She stands alone in her ability to communicate its mechanics as well its human aspects," *Fly Rod & Reel* magazine declared in 1994 upon designating Joan Salvato Wulff their Angler of the Year.[1]

"She has probably done more for women in fishing, especially on the international scene, than any one else," Jim Chapralis of *The PanAngler* has also written.[2]

From the moment she won her first casting title in 1938 at the age of 11, Joan Wulff's illustrious career has spanned almost six decades, at least double that of any other woman in the history of angling. And it's not over.

It's not just that her name is synonymous with fly fishing (particularly casting) throughout the world today. No other woman has more profoundly impacted the sport in general and more widely influenced succeeding generations of young women—not a few of whom have strived to emulate her.

At 69, Joan can look back on a lifetime of pioneering achievements. By the time she was 34, she had distinguished herself with an unprecedented 17 national and one international casting titles, established a women's record distance cast of 161 feet, and become the first woman ever to win the Fisherman's

Distance Event against all-male competition. During this same period, she also forged a path for women in the profession of angling by apparently becoming the first woman ever offered a salaried contract by a tackle manufacturer, an arrangement that lasted from 1959 to 1975. Besides long-distance casting, Joan was also the only woman competing in as many as 15 of the 16 national tournament categories during those years, which many will be startled to learn included baitcasting and spinning, since we think of her as a fly-fishing purist.

During the next 23 years, while married to Lee Wulff, she became the first and only casting columnist with a monthly feature in a national periodical. The author of two highly regarded books on fly fishing, her first, *Joan Wulff's Fly Casting Techniques*,[3] has been hailed as the best on the subject. Equally important, by founding the Joan and Lee Wulff Fishing School in the Catskills in upstate New York in 1979, she and Lee created an institution that has long been regarded as the standard in the field, even today with the proliferation of schools, classes, and workshops throughout the country.

Like so many of the women who have soared to the top of their respective branches, Joan was introduced to fishing at an early age. As she wrote in the introduction to her second book, *Joan Wulff's Fly Fishing: Expert Advice from a Woman's Perspective*, "As is true of many of the women of my generation who fly fish, my father was a fly fisherman. Mother was not. It became apparent the first time I accompanied them for an evening of fly fishing for bass that Dad had all the fun while Mom got yelled at for not keeping the rowboat at the right distance from bass cover. Unencumbered by the knowledge that women didn't fish, it was obvious to me then, at age five or six, that it was better to be the fisherman than the rower."[4]

Born in 1926 and raised in a suburb of Paterson, New Jersey, her chosen career path was undoubtedly influenced by her father's consuming involvement in the outdoors. Jimmy Salvato was not only the proprietor of the Paterson Rod and Gun Store but also the outdoors columnist for the *Paterson Morning Call* as well as an avid hunter, tournament caster, angler, and conservationist.

Each summer, Jimmy would spend his Sunday mornings at Paterson's local casting club. Meeting at the club, along with competing in tournaments, was such a popular pastime before and after the war that when sons stood tall enough to handle a fly rod, they were naturally initiated into this pleasant ritual. Not much thought was given to bringing daughters along, since few girls—or women—expressed an interest in this physical sport. But then Joan Wulff has always been the exception.

When Jimmy Salvato invited Joan's eight-year-old brother to accompany him one Sunday, ten-year-old Joan was crestfallen. "I *wanted* to fly cast," she recounts in *Fly Fishing*. "Gaining Mom's permission to try it with Dad's fly rod one afternoon, I went to the casting club dock, put the rod together and flailed away. Oops! The tip and butt sections separated, and with no fly on the leader to stop it, the tip went into the six-foot-deep pond water. Home I went, crying and afraid of my father's anger. Mom may have been, too, because when our next-door neighbor came home from work, an hour before Dad would come in for dinner, she asked for his help. We went back to the dock with a garden rake and, bless Mr. Kuehn, he snagged it in a few minutes.

"The dad I didn't know very well, the authoritarian figure in my life, the man of whom I was a little bit afraid, asked me to join him and Jimmy the next Sunday at the casting club."

The year was 1937. At the same time she took up casting, Joan also began studying tap, ballet, and acrobatics with

Eleanor Egg. "I am convinced that the dancing lessons improved my casting because they taught me to use my whole body to back up my limited ten-year-old strength," she later assessed.

At the age of 11, she was already on her way to stardom by winning her first casting title, the New Jersey Sub-Junior All-Around Championship. At 12, she caught her first trout on a fly. And at 13, her world suddenly opened up as she got to travel to regional tournaments, including one in Washington, D.C. She also began *teaching* tap dancing.

Winning casting events not only got her picture in the paper, giving her even more incentive to practice and compete, but it also provided a much-needed release for a budding young woman stranded in a rural setting. "I was a kid in a family where my father was Italian, so I was never encouraged to be active socially, and I was not pretty," she says. "I went to high school in another town where I had to go by bus, so that in order to go to basketball games or something like that, it was always out of the question because you had to take two buses to get there. So casting was an outlet, and it gave me some little notoriety or whatever you call it. It let me be somebody other than this homely girl who had no social life. And I got to travel. I loved to travel."

The year Joan graduated from high school, in 1943 at the age of 16, she entered her first national competition and won the dry-fly accuracy event against other women. In fact, one or more national titles would come her way each year between 1943 and 1960. Yet, she says disarmingly, "I'm not a terribly good competitor. I get nervous and all those sorts of things. But I loved fly casting because of the grace and beauty of it. That felt like what I was meant to do. And I think it is. I was born to fly cast."

Because it was post–World War II, few families had the resources to send their children to college, and besides, young women were expected to head into teaching, nursing, or secretarial jobs. Joan did the latter. As she relates in a humorous passage in *Fly Fishing*, "Although I took college preparatory courses in high school, when my guidance counselor asked what my plans were ('I don't know') and what I liked to do ('fly cast and dance'), she suggested secretarial school."

Life as a secretary would not, however, last long. Her brief position as a junior secretary at a large advertising firm in New York City paid only $25 a week. At the same time, her Saturday sessions as a dance instructor paid $20 a *day*. When Eleanor, her former dancing teacher, suggested they start a school together, Joan leaped at the chance. Theirs would be the "perfect partnership" for the next eight years, and it also allowed Joan the freedom to spend her summers competing in amateur casting tournaments.

While other young women headed into marriage and motherhood, Joan fell in love with the most mythical event of them all—distance casting—before the emergence of lightweight graphite rods and modern fly lines. And, like successful career women do today, she found a mentor, William Taylor, one of the best in the country. In fact, she drove him to and from practice sessions where she would serve as his gillie, just so she could absorb his sage advice and witness his brilliance in action. "Watch my cast. Tell me what my backcast is doing," he'd say to her.

"I didn't know anything, but I got to know what beautiful casting looked like, because he was exceptional," she remembers. Taylor also customized a slightly lighter rod for her, to accommodate her tiny five-foot, five-inch frame. Even so, she says, it took "every ounce of my strength. I had to use all of my body. I had to be absolutely disciplined in order to pick that line up off the water."

In 1945, she received her first national publicity, a feature article titled "No Flies on Joanie" in *American* magazine, for which she was photographed in shorts, hip boots, and creel. Then, in 1948, legendary hotelier and devoted angler Charles Ritz spotted her impeccable form at the New York Sportsmen's Show and invited her to participate in the first European competitions to take place after the war—the French National Tournament in Paris and the International Casting Tournament in London. And though she was competing against both men and women, professionals and amateurs, Joan walked away with the ⅝-ounce plugcasting championship in the latter. It was an incredible achievement for a 21-year-old, especially a woman, but it was just the beginning.

Meanwhile, Joan continued to devote nine months of each year to transforming several hundred students into little Fred Astaires and Ginger Rogers. So there was "very little" time for actual fishing, aside from competition casting, "because you can't do everything," she now reflects. "And the other thing is that in my family, girls did not go out on the streams alone." Add to that the ill-fitting gear available to women at the time, and you wonder if the women fishing the Catskills in their billowing skirts at the turn of the century weren't actually better off. "The waders were impossible. You had to buy a man's wader or a boy's hip boot, so you were held back," she explains.

By 1952, though her dancing school days had been blissful—she was, after all, clearing $150 a week, which "was a lot in those days"—Joan "decided that if I didn't leave that dancing school, I'd be there happily teaching at age 75, never having lived anything else." So she opted to make angling a career, though no other woman—and only a couple of men—had attempted it outside the traditional occupations like running a tackle shop or charter boat. Remember, those were the days before there were big bucks for endorsements. Even now, some 40 years later, few women are paid to represent a brand name. Back then, the two or three men managing to eke out a living solely in the angling profession survived only by combining sports-show appearances with in-store promotions, Joan says. But, undaunted, she decided to charge ahead.

While demonstrating fine casting at the myriad outdoors and sportsmen's shows that occurred like clockwork each winter, she got to know the people at Ashaway Line & Twine Company, then the producer of world-class fishing lines. They made her their "goodwill ambassador," which sounded grand even though it was a major drop in pay from the dancing school—"$4 for every report I sent in. I was paying my own expenses," Joan laughs. Though it was a modest start, it didn't matter, because it gave her the opportunity to travel to places she had never seen and to polish her self-confidence. "I would go into a town cold, look in the phone book, and then go into the stores," she recalls.

During the winter of 1954, at the age of 27, she toured the Midwest in a casting exhibition that featured silent-screen star Monte Blue as emcee. "When I showed up in my shorts, hip boots, and creel, which was everyone's idea of a girl fisherman's costume, Monte took me aside and told me he wanted to try something different," Joan recounts in *Fly Fishing*. "'Wear a dress,' he said, 'a long one, and we'll wow 'em.' Leaping at the chance to portray casting as feminine, I bought a strapless, ankle-length white dress with silver leaves on it, high-heeled sandals, and to complete the outfit, rhinestones for my hair.

"The combination was perfect, and Monte presented my act beautifully, speaking softly while I was casting of grace, timing, and beauty. I didn't cast at targets but, instead, used one rod and then two, creating as many interesting patterns with the fly lines as I could in time with the music. 'Up a Lazy River' was a natural, and the audiences responded. It couldn't last forever, though, and without either Monte or an orchestra the costume didn't play as well mixed in with lumberjacks, retrievers, and

Sparky the seal." In fact, Joan laughs now, when she walked out on the stage in her long dress at her very next appearance, minus Monte, "They just looked at me as if I had gone out naked."

Joan wasn't the only woman performing around the country in exhibitions at that time. There were several others, though none also represented a manufacturer during the off-months. What kept them going, despite the miserable wages, was the understanding that "a woman could do this and presume that someday she'd get married and somebody would take care of her. I mean, you didn't make a living at this," she reflects.

Meanwhile, she was still racking up national casting titles. In the summer of 1951, she not only garnered five more but cemented her place in the record books by becoming the first woman in history to win the Fisherman's Distance Event, on a 131-foot cast, *against all-male competition.* To put this into perspective, remember that this was the era of Ozzie and Harriet, and June Cleaver, when women—at least on television—were *vacuuming* in high heels!

Somewhere in the mid-1950s, Joan was offered a job that would take her to Miami to serve as the southern rep for another angling manufacturer. On her way down, she pondered the wisdom of this move after stopping off at tackle stores on behalf of Ashaway, where she was clearly left with the "impression that men had absolutely no respect for a woman traveling alone on the road." Joan did not take the job, but she did stay in Miami. While continuing to do shows and represent Ashaway, she got married and had a child.

By 1959, she had also secured a contract with the largest tackle company in the world, the Garcia Corporation, which paid her an unheard-of $4,000 a year for 100 days of appearances, along with such percs as first-class air travel and limousines wherever she went on company business. Considering the fact that the women's movement was still a decade away, it was a remarkable milestone for a woman working in a field dominated by men.

By 1961, Garcia had hired another woman, Ann Strobel, who would also find fame on the sports-show circuit. This allowed Joan to cut back her touring territory to Florida so she could concentrate on rearing her young son. "Ann was the one who really did spend her life on the road demonstrating," Joan says.

Garcia also paid Joan to compete in various events, such as the Key Colony Beach Sailfish Tournament, where she took home the winning trophy for a 60-pound Atlantic sailfish, the largest caught in that competition in years. (The fish, which Garcia originally had mounted for its own offices, now hangs at the Wulff School of Fly Fishing.)

In 1960, after 22 years of gearing herself up for the pressures of competition, Joan entered her last tournaments, one of which would also prove to be her most important. At a registered event in New Jersey, she laid her line down at an astounding 161 feet, establishing a new unofficial women's record. It was "unofficial" only because there weren't enough female distance casters to qualify the event. But she did it nonetheless, and it was a feat, indisputably, that would have brought home the gold if this had been the Olympics.

After scaling the Mount Everest of casting achievements, Joan, now 33, decided to leave competitive casting and *just* fish. "I couldn't compete in 15 events and maintain that and have a family and all those things — so something had to give," she explains. "And that's what gave. So then I started to fish in greater earnest. I had always fished with good fishermen, but I had never fished as much as I would have if I had been a man, just because of the difference in our lives and the fact [that women of my generation] didn't go off in the woods by themselves into wild places."

Two years later, she had her second child while continuing to make appearances for Garcia. Somewhere in the early 1960s, she began receiving wider media attention, including guest spots on "Captain Kangaroo" and Regis Philbin's very first late-night talk show in San Diego.

In 1967, a life-altering twist of fate brought her together with Lee Wulff, whom author and editor Silvio Calabi has called "the most outstanding angler and angling conservationist of the 20th Century."[5] An internationally renowned outdoors filmmaker, Lee was also a producer of "The American Sportsman" series for the ABC network, for which he was preparing to shoot a show about bluefin tuna fishing. (Like Joan, Lee was accomplished in all aspects of the sport, not just fly fishing.) Wanting to make the dramatic point that bringing in the giant tuna was a team effort, he had selected pop singer Kay Starr, who weighed a mere 100 pounds, to serve as his angler. But she got sick at the last moment, so an emergency call went in to Garcia, which in turn called Joan, who, at 122 pounds, not only saved the show by landing a 572-pounder but hooked the love of her life as well.

The day they were married, less than a year later, Lee jokingly called up Joan's boss at Garcia—for whom he had also been making films—and boasted, "I just married a girl who *used* to work for you!" Apparently, he wasn't kidding. "That was the end of my career for a year," Joan laughs. "And then we both went back to work for Garcia."

To the angling world, they were, and would remain, the Royal Couple of the sport. And there's little wonder why. It was the merger of two of the leading lights of the angling world.[6] During the next 23 years, their union would have a profound impact on the sport—fly fishing in particular. As a producer, director, editor, and writer, Lee continued to film shows all over the world for various companies and "The American Sportsman," which often featured

Joan as the guest angler. Between 1969 and 1972, the Wulffs also crisscrossed the country as Garcia's emissaries, both promoting the sport of fly fishing and the urgency of conservation.

Through endless clinics and dinner programs, they shared their angling wisdom and skills during what was the formative period of a new era for fly fishing in America. Finally, there were experts who could answer questions and share finely honed techniques. Equally important, a woman was standing on the platform as a guest speaker, which motivated men to bring their wives to these dinners. Each time, after Lee spoke, Joan would demonstrate the art of fine casting, using the Fly-O (an indoor practice rod with yarn instead of line, invented by Lee and used prominently today as a teaching tool at their Catskills school). Not only were those "the fun years," Joan says, "but I do think that it helped. I do think that those appearances really helped to make women feel that they could be part of this."

For three years beginning in 1972, they slowed down, traveling only to Colorado each summer as guest instructors for the American Sportsman's Club, which was where Joan discovered her ultimate calling in life. "I knew that I loved to teach. Lee was not a teacher in the obvious sense. He was more a college professor, somebody who makes you think, challenges everything, a leader. And I'm the teacher who takes you from where you are to the next step."

By 1975, they began to reassess an idea that had been brewing for some time: establishing a permanent fly-fishing school of their own. "Lee was 20 years older than I was, and I know that he saw the idea of a school as something that would be good for me if he weren't around," Joan says.

Next came the decision of where to locate it. Their 500-acre home base in New Hampshire was not convenient to New York or well-regarded for its trout fishing. So they turned their attention to the ten acres Lee had long owned on the Battenkill River, near Manchester, Vermont. But before they got to revisit the site, fate intervened in the form of an invitation from the Federation of Fly Fishers for Lee to speak at a conclave in the Catskills.

Amazingly, Lee had not been back to the Catskills for 35 years and Joan for 25. "There were fishermen *everywhere*," Joan recalls with relish, "and the rivers were full. And the catch-and-release area was brimful. And we looked at each other and said, 'This is the place for a fishing school!'" It was also ideally located just two hours from New York.

A year later, in 1979, the Joan and Lee Wulff Fishing School (now known as the Wulff School of Fly Fishing) permanently opened its doors on a 100-acre spread in Lew Beach, on the historic Beaverkill River in the heart of the Catskills. For the Wulffs, it marked a major change in their lives at a time when most people would be gearing up for retirement: Joan was now 52; Lee 73. Through their determination, they not only created one of the most important institutions in the fly-fishing world but made it possible for the average person to become accomplished in a sport that had long been regarded as the pastime of an upper class. In 1981, they would also become an instrumental force in the establishment of the Catskill Fly Fishing Center and Museum, just as Lee had done in 1965 as a founding member of the Federation of Fly Fishers.

Soon after establishing the school, Joan says, Lee "began pushing" her to write about casting. Though she had toyed with the idea of starting an outdoors magazine for women in the early 1970s and had written a few things for "Garcia's Annual" in the late 1950s, Joan was at first reluctant. But Lee persisted, finally convincing her that writing was the most powerful way of sharing knowledge and raising standards. Despite her prominence in the field, however, outdoors and angling magazines were not yet ready to publish an article authored strictly by a woman. They insisted that each byline include both Wulff names, even though Joan was the one doing about 99 percent of the writing. "It really bothered me that it couldn't be *me*," she says.

By 1980, she had her first monthly casting column—on all kinds of casting, not just fly—in *Outdoor Life* for fourteen issues. "I was the token woman on the masthead," she notes, adding that when her editor left the magazine, she was let go. Nonetheless, it was a significant breakthrough: Joan had become the first person ever—man or woman—with a monthly casting column in a national periodical.

In 1981, when editor John Merwin moved from *Fly Fisherman* to *Rod & Reel* (now known as *Fly Rod & Reel*), he brought Joan aboard as the latter's permanent casting columnist. Fourteen years later, "Joan Salvato Wulff's Fly-Casting" not only appears each month in this prominent fly-fishing periodical, but it ranks as the longest-running feature on that topic in any major publication.

"What writing did for me was to make me understand what I was doing. Here I'd been casting from 1937 on, and I now had to put it on paper. And that is a helluva job," she says, pointing out that in *teaching* casting, you simply say, "Watch me. Do it like this." But to describe it on paper meant dissecting her own performance, not unlike what a choreographer goes through laying out a new ballet.

By 1985, Lee and author/publisher Nick Lyons were urging her to write a book. "I looked at all of the books that were available on casting, and they didn't tell you enough. They didn't tell you *how* to do it," she recalls. The two-year project again required her to "figure out exactly what your hands and arms do and where the line goes and the physics of it. So what my book did was give you the mechanics of it—'This had to happen. This is the result of this happening.' That sort of thing. The point was to take the mystery out of it."

Joan Wulff's Fly Casting Techniques appeared in 1987 to rave reviews. "These days, books on any subject don't seem to be around for long, but this book is still the only one to explain casting factually," commented Pete Woolley in *Fly Rod & Reel*. It was also a shining moment for the woman who had always seen herself as a great supporter of creative people but never the artist herself. "That was my first contribution to the world in terms of anything," she says, proudly. "That was the first thing that *I* ever created."

By 1991, Joan's second book, *Joan Wulff's Fly Fishing: Expert Advice from a Woman's Perspective*, was published. Astoundingly, she wrote both books while turning out the monthly column, running the Wulff School, and fulfilling the myriad other commitments that were a constant in the Wulffs' demanding personal schedules.

Though it was never a major focus of Joan's life, her efforts to produce gear to accommodate women's specific needs must be mentioned, if only to fill in the gaps to the long struggle that has finally resulted in a major awakening by manufacturers to this growing segment of the fly-fishing population.

Beginning in the early 1970s, Joan became possibly the first advocate for gear and clothing designed just for women. In 1971, she developed a line of rods—spinning, plug, and fly—for Garcia and was told by their salesmen, "We can't sell them."

"And so that didn't work, and I still have those some-where in my house," she says, clearly disappointed. Somewhere around the mid-1970s, a manufacturer put out "Lee and Joan Wulff" vests, "but they didn't really work," she recalls. Finally, in

"SHE HAS DONE FOR CASTING WHAT
STEPHEN HAWKING DID FOR PHYSICS,"
"FLY ROD & REEL" DECLARED OF JOAN
WULFF IN 1994.

the mid-1980s, Amerex issued a "Stream-Designed" edition, and a new Joan Wulff–designed vest debuted in 1995.

In 1978, as a consultant to Red Ball, Joan tried to persuade them to issue a women's line of waders. "I remember arguing with them about the design of their waders," she recalls. The line they were passing off for women "had a yoke through the crotch, so that in the back it looked like the back end of an antelope. It was absolutely vulgar-looking. And I finally got them to go just for the natural V-thing, and then they came out with flyweights, and that changed everything, because flyweights were the waders we'd been looking for." Joan still has a photo of herself in the new flyweights, clicking her heels in the air as a message to consumers that they were light enough to dance in. Also, in 1978, graphite rods appeared, literally revolutionizing the sport. "So those two factors, the waders and the rods, were very, very big to getting women into the field," she explains.

In 1991, the angling world lost the incomparable Lee Wulff. But instead of retiring on her laurels, Joan has carried on like the indomitable spirit she always was. After a lifetime of living out of a suitcase, she is now staying home more; completing her third book, which is soon to be published by Lyons & Burford; tending to the Royal Wulff product line; serving as the steward of the land holdings she and Lee acquired; and, most recently, supervising the design of the Lee Wulff exhibits for the Catskill Fly Fishing Center and Museum's brand-new facility.

But nothing competes with her undivided devotion to teaching. "My mind, when it's doing nothing else, thinks about teaching," she says, bursting with enthusiasm. "*This morning*, for instance, I figured out that I need two more mirrors in my fishing school. If you're teaching—and if you have a passion, which this is for me—you're always trying to distill it and to make it easier for people to understand. So I'm refining constantly, because I only have people for a weekend."

Fly-fishing instruction today is readily available through most local fly shops as well as a number of specialized regional schools. So why do men and women—many of them senior statesmen and CEOs—make the weekend pilgrimage each April through June to the Wulff School of Fly Fishing? To learn at the elbow of a master, of course. "Her instruction is totally void of ego or attitude. Egos or attitudes can't possibly improve technique. Joan always had a kind of Joy-of-Sex attitude about casting: it's simple, fun and you never stop working on it—and, best of all, when your casting improves, so does your fishing," writes Pete Woolley in *Fly Rod & Reel*.

One is always taking the chance of stepping off a diving board and landing in an empty pool with statements like *If there had never been a Joan Wulff, there probably wouldn't be as many women in fly fishing today.* In this case, however, it's true. Sure, there have been many women who have fished for six decades. But there has been only one who devoted most of her life to this male-dominated profession, long before women flocked to such nontraditional careers as law, medicine, business, science, and politics. That she chose to treat a career in angling as an unfolding challenge has established an inspirational endowment of sorts for both women who fish and those who may never pick up a rod, simply because she *did it* and did it *as well or better* than most of her male counterparts.

I leave you with this eloquent final statement on the great Joan Wulff, again provided by Woolley in *Fly Rod & Reel*:

> *Joan not only embodies the strength and excellence we strive for, but in doing so she doesn't lose the grace and sensitivity of the woman she is. Her continued blossoming since Lee's passing is no*

surprise to those who truly know her. The blend of her strength and femininity parallels the marriage of casting and fishing that truly makes Joan our Angler of the Year. We will always look up to her.

And we will, too.

CHAPTER 5

Fly Fishing's Trailblazers Today

MAGGIE MERRIMAN

CATHY BECK

RHONDA SAPP AND DONNA TEENY

JENNIFER OLSSON

CHRISTY BALL AND LORI-ANN MURPHY

KELLY WATT

Only two decades ago, women did not choose careers as professional guides, tackle-shop owners, fishing instructors, or tackle manufacturers ... unless they were Joan Wulff.

But just as others have done in law, medicine, business, and other previously male-dominated professions, women have since penetrated the ranks of the fly-fishing sport with professionalism, ingenuity, style, and grace.

At the vanguard of this new era are a league of women who possess a rare combination of can-do spirit and cutting-edge skill which will undoubtedly inspire more women to get out of the office or home and into the outdoors.

Among those blazing a trail for others to follow are ...

Maggie Merriman MONTANA AND CALIFORNIA

"Today the path [Mary Orvis Marbury] blazed is being followed by luminaries like Joan Salvato Wulff and Maggie Merriman," Silvio Calabi writes in the foreword to the 1988 edition of Marbury's *Favorite Flies and Their Histories*.[1]

Recognized throughout the world as the second most prominent woman in fly fishing today, Maggie Merriman is a

58-year-old wunderkind who is particularly amazing for the fact that she did not begin her career in the sport until she was in her mid-30s. Yet once out of the chute, there was no stopping her. In 1978, she pioneered the first fly-fishing schools for women in the western United States. In 1981, she became one of the first women employed as a product consultant for a major rod company. And in 1982, she introduced the first fly-fishing vest designed by a woman for women — to mention but a few of the ways the sport has felt Maggie's indelible imprint.

Indisputably, Joan and Maggie are the charter members of that elite club of women who have worked their way to the top of the oldest branch of fishing. Indeed, Pam Montgomery, writing in the industry's leading trade journal, *Fly Tackle Dealer*, has called them "the greatest modern role models for women in both the sport and the business of fly-fishing."[2] Both continuously broke new ground — long before women's participation in the sport was recognized by the media — and both are busier than ever today as fly-fishing celebrities, instructors, and passionate promoters of this branch of angling that has been in their blood since childhood.

Like many of the women who have achieved prominence in all branches of angling, Maggie was raised in a family that loved the outdoors. The daughter of a Pasadena, California, horticulturist, her initiation into fly fishing came at the age of 10, during the first of many annual fishing pilgrimages, this one on the North Umpqua River in southern Oregon. While her father went after steelhead, Maggie, her sister, and her mother concentrated on trout. Two years later, the family switched its annual destination to the 9 Quarter Circle Ranch in the Gallatin Valley of Montana, a place which would later serve as the catalyst to her career as a fly-fishing professional.

At one time Maggie was headed into a career as an artist. After obtaining a bachelor of fine arts degree from the

University of Arizona, she subsequently studied commercial art at the highly regarded Art Center of Los Angeles. But she also quickly realized that to succeed in commercial art, she would have to move to New York. When she assessed her chances of reaching the top in that highly competitive male field, along with the sacrifice of leaving her beloved West Coast, Maggie opted instead to work in the wholesale furniture industry in San Francisco, where her talent as a painter supplied much of the art for her company's showroom. Meanwhile, she continued to fish at the 9 Quarter Circle Ranch during her vacations.

In 1972, when the ranch decided to host the Berkley Fly Fishing School for a week, one of the owners — by now a good friend — called her to suggest she attend, then return the following summer to guide and run an annual school for them. Although she had been fly fishing for some 25 years, the week Maggie spent with the Berkley School was like a curtain rising on the rest of her life. Formal instruction was still a novel concept in the early 1970s, and few fly fishers thought about how they got the line out there. Certainly while Maggie was growing up "there was never any mention of the technique of casting, other than you were taught how to put the fly on and you kind of mimicked what the adults did around you," she says. When it was over, she was so inspired that she began thinking, "Wow, maybe this is something *I* can do." After returning to California, she found herself thinking about it more and more, "because there really weren't any women in the western states teaching and also serving as an example that women can be in this sport."

Beginning in 1973, Maggie ran the 9 Quarter Circle Ranch's annual schools each September for the next eight years. At the same time, she availed herself of every opportunity to study other instructor's techniques, to hone her skills, and to improve her own teaching methods.

By the mid-1970s, Maggie reassessed her career future and came up with the daunting realization that "there was a glass ceiling in the furniture business for women. The highest I would ever get would be *showroom lady*," despite the fact that she was running her company's entire West Coast operation, she says. "I saw a dead end, so I said, 'OK, what is it you really love to do in life?' And I thought, 'Well, I love to paint and I love to fish.' So I gave myself a five-year plan."

While supporting herself through her paintings, Maggie began aggressively promoting her skills as a fly-fishing instructor. She linked up with Ed Rice's International Sportsmen's Shows and demonstrated casting from Seattle to Denver to San Francisco each expo season under the billing of "The Fly Fishing Lady of the West." She also led schools for the American Sportsman Club and for six years served as the Director of Fly Fishing Schools for Bob Marriott at his huge outdoors sports outlet in Fullerton, California. Most important, she founded the Maggie Merriman Fly-Fishing Schools, for which she independently toured the western states, teaching classes and workshops for local tackle shops and clubs.

Today, women-only fly-fishing seminars and workshops sponsored by local tackle shops and clubs are not uncommon in most cities. But when Maggie held the first one on the West Coast in 1978, a two-day event at a regional conclave of the Federation of Fly Fishers in West Yellowstone, Montana, it would mark another first in the evolution of the sport as well as in her career. She mounted a second, one-day workshop in San Francisco in 1979 for the Golden Gate Angling Club — which, not incidentally, had opened its doors to women only a few years before.

In 1982, the third of these groundbreaking events occurred at a Federation conclave in Boise, Idaho. But this time, instead of the usual two dozen or so attendees, word spread rapidly and calls poured in from women willing to travel tremendous distances to participate. "We didn't know what the turnout would be," Maggie says. "Well, instead of a one-day school, we ended up with a two-day school with 144 women!" The enthusiastic response not only "blew everyone's minds," she recalls, but in her opinion served as a declaration of sorts to the industry that "yes, women were interested in fly fishing."

By the early 1980s, Maggie no longer had time to paint. With fishing now her dominant career, in 1981 she became a product-development consultant for three years for a leading rod manufacturer, resulting in the Maggie Merriman signature fly rod for women. In 1982, she permanently located her schools to West Yellowstone, Montana, where the fishing was superb and the cost of living was unbeatable. That same year she became the first woman to design a women's fly-fishing vest, and she hired a high-quality cut-and-sew company in Montana to manufacture it. Unlike standard vests on the market at the time, hers was the first with colored zippers, a paisley print lining, and a snap across the chest instead of a zipper for closure.

At the same time, she was also apparently the first woman to design a line of fishing-related products, and these were issued under her name as well: men's and women's poplin and polar-fleece outer vests, padded reel cases, line-leader-tippet pouches, tote gear bags, and map cases. After five years, however, although all of her products had been big sellers, she chose to suspend production when it was no longer economical to produce them in the United States where she could be assured of quality control.

Besides writing a product-review column for *Fly-fishing Heritage* magazine for three years, Maggie also served as a regional and national director for the Federation of Fly Fishers, as a regional director of Trout Unlimited, and as a member of the advisory board of the American Sport Fishing Alliance.

In 1994, she became one of several women invited to join the consulting teams of leading rod manufacturers, representing a major recent breakthrough for women in terms of acquiring the status associated with these coveted contracts. She also continues to manufacture and distribute the extremely popular Spec Socs eyeglass retainers, which she introduced to the market eight years ago, and she serves as an ongoing consultant to the Swallow's Nest Sporting Store in Seattle.

Like the popular Energizer Bunny, Maggie shows no signs of slowing down. Each summer, she continues to lead her Maggie Merriman Fly Fishing Schools in West Yellowstone. Each winter, she heads to her Southern California home base, but she spends most of her time on the road. As a role model and casting guru for thousands of men and women, she never tires of demonstrating casting at sports shows and for local clubs, as well as leading seminars and workshops. She is also often packing her bags to accompany a group to such places as Alaska, Mexico, Belize, or Costa Rica, at the invitation of lodge and resort owners, to fish for salmon, tarpon, bonefish, or trout.

Her busy schedule never keeps her from volunteering countless hours to bringing more women into the sport, however. At present, she is in the process of implementing her latest vision, a national outreach program for women through the Federation of Fly Fishers and other avenues. She particularly wants to wake up tackle retailers and manufacturers to a largely untapped segment of the market— female consumers. Considering what Maggie managed to accomplish decades before the label *fly fisherman* evolved into the gender-free *fly fisher*, she will undoubtedly be successful in all her efforts.

What leads women like Maggie Merriman to think beyond the obvious options laid out for them in our society?

Perhaps the truth lies in the message conveyed by her parents: "My mother encouraged me to try all sports and all endeavors. I never heard my mother or father say, 'Women don't do that.'" Hooray for them!

Cathy Beck PENNSYLVANIA

"With a fly rod, she has landed a 23-pound snook. I know few men who can say that. She's boated giant tarpon, a ten-pound rainbow, more Pacific salmon than she could count, and a host of other species.... I consider her to be a complete fly fisherman, and certainly one of the top lady fly fishermen I've met in my travels around the world," Lefty Kreh, one of the world's deans of fly fishing, has written.

Even though Cathy Beck has only been fly fishing since the late 1970s, she ranks today in the top echelon of instructors, destination angling guide/hosts, writers and wildlife photographers, and fly-fishing personalities at outdoors shows and fishing expos.

Cathy grew up in the Fishing Creek valley of northeastern Pennsylvania, near Benton. Her father worked as a coal miner, logger, and farmer. Her mother balanced an assumably chaotic household of seven children with a outside job as a factory worker while volunteering as a Sunday-school teacher for over 40 years. Home was a "farm with lots of cows, chickens, pigs, logging horses, and ponds full of trout, bluegills, and bass," Cathy fondly remembers.

It was the kind of idyllic childhood that usually happens only in the movies. "Every spring Mom would take us down the road to the general store, and my sister and I would each get a new cane pole and a spool of braided line. We just tied about nine feet of line on these long poles and went fishing. When the line got too short, we'd put on a new piece. We knew Dad

CATHY BECK HAS FISHED HER WAY
INTO THE RANKS OF THE WORLD'S
LEADING FLY-FISHING INSTRUCTORS,
DESTINATION GUIDES, WRITERS,
PHOTOGRAPHERS, AND SPORTS-SHOW
CELEBRITIES.

always kept hooks in his tackle box, so with a few worms from the garden and a bobber, we were set.

"One summer, Mom saved enough S&H green stamps to get my sister and me each a Zebco 202 spinning reel and rod. Boy, did we think we were grown up! We had the outfits for about two weeks when my brother used them to run a night line across the big pond." Oops! "The cows stepped on both of them the same night and it was back to the cane poles until the following year."

The only thing they weren't allowed to do, Cathy recalls, "is fish in the spring ponds that held trout. These were Dad's pets and he would get really mad if he caught us kids fishing in his trout ponds. On the other hand, he never hesitated to clean all the bass and bluegills we could catch."

Following high school, she took a job in New Jersey, but it didn't last long. During a visit back home in 1978, she fell in love with Barry Beck while he was teaching her to fly fish. After a year of practice sessions on the river—up to five evenings a week during fishing season—Cathy was not only able to hold her own with veteran fly rodders, but she also managed to catch herself a trophy husband as well.

A couple years later, they bought Barry's parent's sporting-goods business and within a year started offering fly-fishing schools. In 1988, *Town and Country* magazine profiled Cathy and their schools, giving the business such a boost that they were forced to relocate to larger quarters, this time closer to Fishing Creek, where they were already spending most of their time guiding and teaching. It also didn't hurt that then-President Jimmy Carter—an avid fly fisher himself, along with his wife, Rosalyn—invited the Becks to participate in a fly-fishing get-together outside Camp David.

By 1992, Cathy and Barry were so busy doing it all—running the retail store, guiding, teaching, traveling, writing, and shooting exquisite outdoors photos—that something had to give. By selling the store, they were able to concentrate on developing a fishing-related career that would allow them to travel the world.

It worked. They are now among the top names listed in the celebrity billings of major outdoors sports expos throughout the East; both are members of the advisory staff of a major rod manufacturer; they have achieved international fame for their breathtaking wildlife and angling photographs, which have appeared in numerous calendars and on periodical covers; and Cathy has been featured at least once on the cover of every major fly-fishing magazine in the United States. Furthermore, they are among a handful of fly-fishing personalities regularly featured on such television shows as ESPN's "On the Fly," and few are more popular on the speaking and seminar circuit.

The centerpiece of their efforts is a destination fly-fishing adventure service called Raven Creek Travel, which allows beginning to advanced anglers, many of them couples, to accompany them to some of the finest fishing spots in the world, including the Bahamas, Alaska, Montana, Mexico, and Labrador.

Whether she is fishing, teaching, photographing, or leading others into the pleasure of the sport, Cathy has certainly earned a spot among the world's top fly fishers today.

Rhonda Sapp and Donna Teeny COLORADO AND OREGON

"About six years ago, Donna approached me [at a trade show] and said, 'We've got to do something!'" Rhonda Sapp recalls with zest. "Well, Donna went back to Oregon and I went back to Colorado. Then five years ago, she said, 'Rhonda, we've got to do something! We really have to!' So about four and a half years ago, she and I went to the larger manufacturers and said, 'More and more women are becoming involved in fly fishing, and we need things for women. We need gear. We need waders. We need a vest.' And they said, 'Sure, honey. Yeah. Right.'"

And that was the beginning of a great partnership, which they named Dirt Roads and Damsels. It was also possibly an historic first, since there appears to be no prior instance of two women combining their skills in a professional collaboration in the fly-fishing field.

Over a period of 24 years, Donna and her husband, Jim Teeny, have built up one of the most respected fly-fishing manufacturing enterprises in the industry, producing the famous Teeny Nymph fly patterns, fly lines, and other specialized products. In 1982, Rhonda Sapp and her husband, Ray, founded The Colorado Angler in Denver, which ranks as one of the leading fly-fishing specialty shops in the country.

Certainly, if they didn't understand the women's market, it's hard to imagine who would. Both had endured years of wearing pinching, ill-fitting men's waders in boys' sizes along with wading boots that took "five extra pairs of socks" to ensure a tight fit.

They weren't even looking to make a profit by bringing women's gear onto the market; they just wanted *somebody* to do it. So they worked with one company for over a year, only to be jolted when they saw the finished product at a fly-tackle dealers' show. "That's it?" Rhonda remembers asking the sales rep. "They said yes. So I went into the bathroom and tried it on and would not walk out [wearing] it. I said, 'This has got to be a joke! Who designed this wader, and for *whom?*'" The wader was so low-cut, she says, that you'd inevitably get wet. "It was an absolute joke!"

Determined to get suitable women's fishing clothing on the market, they tried again with another company, again with no aim of seeing a dollar from their ideas. "We said, 'Please build us a wader,'" Rhonda recounts. "'Oh, yes, honey, we will,' they said. So a year later, they came out with this wader. And we looked at it and said, 'Well, it doesn't look too bad. Looks very small, but it doesn't look too bad.'" They both went into the bathroom to try it on, and again they felt they couldn't walk out. "It wouldn't come over my boobs," she says. Donna adds: "I was so mad! *We* were so mad!"

"I was fighting back the tears," Rhonda continues. "And Donna was kicking me, saying, 'OK, now be cool.' So we walk over and we're trying to talk to the owner of the company about these waders. And we said, 'Well, they're bad. They're not good. Women have hips. Women have breasts. Women have small waists.' And the owner of the company looked at us and seriously said, 'But they look so good on Heather!' Can you imagine Heather? And then he turns around and says again, 'They looked so good on Heather that I wanted to take her to bed!' Our mouths dropped. We couldn't even speak. We turned around and walked out and said, 'That's it! We're manufacturing our own waders. We're doing our own vest. We're doing our own gear!'"

They got together at Donna's Oregon home and "created the vest over two bottles of wine at midnight," says Donna. "She's a trout fisherman. I'm a salmon/steelhead fisherman. We pooled our ideas of exactly what we wanted, so it took us two hours tops. We knew all this time what we wanted to have."

"It's like the ideas had just marinated for years," adds Rhonda. "We designed our entire line out of necessity, pure necessity."

"And frustration," chimes in Donna.

The resulting vest has seventeen pockets, including one for a camera and another to hide a self-protection device. They chose a soft nylon fabric for the outer shell, not unlike some-

RHONDA SAPP (LEFT) AND DONNA
TEENY, BOTH AT THE VANGUARD OF
WOMEN WORKING IN THE INDUSTRY,
WERE THE FIRST TO DESIGN AND
PRODUCE A FULL LINE OF WOMEN'S
FLY-FISHING CLOTHING AND GEAR.

thing one would find on a higher-priced designer jacket. They quilted the shoulders so the weight of the garment, when laden down with tackle and tools and other items, would be evenly distributed. They made it water-resistant, machine-washable, and stylish to a feminine sensibility, with a range of rich, stunning colors from fuchsia to emerald green. Their vest is definitely unlike anything on the market today.

The only problem was getting it manufactured. Donna had tried once to get a women's vest on the market 10 years before, using the same supplier that produced the popular vest designed by her husband under the Teeny Nymph company label. "They made me *one* in blue. That's all they would do. And I got so many compliments on it, but they would not make a run in blue. Absolutely not!" she says.

The two of them drew up a detailed illustration, took it to a patternmaker and had a prototype constructed, then began approaching wholesale sewers. For a while, it looked like they'd have to go overseas, but they finally found one in the United States. Then Rhonda and Donna launched into the rest of their product line: neoprene waders contoured to a woman's body, a combed-cotton turtleneck, a fleece pullover jacket and matching pants, and an authentic Australian-outback hat.

They're both self-admitted workaholics, putting in 16-hour days on their primary endeavors, plus daily phone conferences on future products and other Dirt Roads and Damsels endeavors. In addition, Rhonda teaches classes on rod building, entomology, fly tying, and other aspects of the sport.

Donna and Rhonda first met about 15 years ago at a sports show. At the time, they say, there was hardly another woman in sight on their side of the aisle. Donna can remember her first sports show in Spokane in the early 1970s, when she was "the only woman in a booth." The aura of a woman shilling tackle was not lost on the other manufacturers. Within two years, women were no longer an endangered species in these giant arenas. But unlike Donna, the others were models hired for their looks, not for their knowledge of tackle and fly-fishing tips.

So it's been a long, frustrating journey, both behind the scenes and on the water. "I mean, I could write a book on bad experiences that you just had to ignore," says Rhonda. On one particular occasion about 11 years ago, while she was fishing a local Colorado river run, two men walked up behind her and muttered, "*I* was going to fish where she's standing!" She says, "It was as if I wasn't fishing, but just standing in his spot. Well, as they stood behind me and made comments, I caught and released a fish. As they started to walk off, I caught and released another fish. As they rounded the bend, one of them turned around just as I was hooking another fish.

"And it was funny, about a week later, one of these men came into my shop. I was sitting there tying flies, and he walked by and he looked at me. He turned around and looked again, then he got rather embarrassed and he walked over and said, 'Were you fishing the Platte [River] last Sunday?' I said yes. He said, 'I think I recognize you.' And I said, 'I *know* I recognize you.'" Then he asked what pattern she was using, which happened to be exactly what she was tying at the moment. "The man was just in disbelief. How could I know this? I was a woman!"

One of the tenured female veterans in the industry, Donna got into the wholesale side of fly fishing in 1973, when she went to work for her future husband's fledgling company as a fly tier. Jim Teeny had already introduced his revolutionary Teeny Nymph pattern onto the market, but Donna gave it an immediate makeover, dressing it up and making it more marketable. A spin caster her entire life, Donna also switched over to fly fishing.

The first years for the company were rough. Jim hired a jobber to get the flies into stores, but he "had to go out and blow the dust off of them because salesmen don't go out and sell a product like you'd sell your own product," Donna says. More than 20 years, two children, and many 24-hour workdays later, the Teeny Nymph Company today produces an assortment of world-class fly lines, backings, tapered leaders, tippets, fly patterns, and other items.

Rhonda got into fly fishing in 1970, a year after moving from Kansas to Colorado and meeting her husband—who grew up on the sport. In 1981, they both quit their jobs and opened The Colorado Angler, which at the time was only the third fly-tackle store in Denver. "Went up against the big boys," Rhonda declares proudly. "Everyone said we couldn't make it. We've been there 14 years."

From the beginning, Rhonda made sure the shop was a place where novices and women, as well as advanced anglers, would want to congregate. She not only runs the guide service—originally taking out clients herself—but also leads an assortment of classes. Six years ago, she introduced the first of a series of women-only workshops that now occur annually.

Anyone who has had the good luck to attend a fly-fishing class or workshop led by Donna and Rhonda inevitably walks away muttering something like, "It's really so simple. How come I thought it would be so complicated?" They distill the mystery out of this intimidating science, giving their students the rudiments necessary to catch fish.

What makes it all work for Donna and Rhonda is a deep mutual respect and enviable friendship, despite the several thousand miles that separate them when they're not together working on another facet of their Dirt Roads and Damsels clothing line or some other way of bringing more women into the sport.

Jennifer Olsson MONTANA AND SWEDEN

The great success of Jennifer Olsson (formerly Smith) success can only make us wonder what lasting effect the presence of Joan Wulff, Maggie Merriman, Kay Brodney, and all of those who preceded them would have had on succeeding generations of young women in this country if these female legends had simply had equal time in the media.

Jennifer is certainly living proof of the critical importance of female role models on the lives of young girls. As a teenager, she can vividly remember thinking, "There's *the* woman who does this for a living," every time she gazed upon the autographed photo of Joan and Lee Wulff that hung on the wall of a Montana fly shop. And many were the occasions when someone would tease, "Oh, it's another Joan Wulff," about her or her girlfriends because of their uniquely intense interest in fly fishing.

"We had this sort of image that there was a place for a woman on the river, because of her," Jennifer recalls of Joan, who she says was "definitely! absolutely!" an early influence. Joan can be proud of what happened to this early admirer. Jennifer, now 36, grew up to become one of the most prominent women in the sport today—an internationally recognized guide, instructor, and speaker, as well as one of the few women making a living in the sport, partially from representing a major rod company.

Though she was raised in Long Beach, California, Jennifer's roots in Montana date back to the turn of the century, to the birth of her maternal grandmother, Erie McLaren, in Livingston. Because as a girl Erie had known Norman Maclean, who wrote the classic, *A River Runs Through It*, Jennifer once approached the author at a book reading, introducing herself as Erie's granddaughter. According to one account, "Maclean's eyes brightened. 'Oh, the McLaren girls,' said the old man, with relish. 'Weren't they a handsome group!'"[3]

Besides ultimately becoming her chosen home, Montana would be the place where a 13-year-old Jennifer discovered the joy of fly fishing while recovering from the profound loss of her mother to cancer. Her father, Jack Miller, had taken Jennifer and her brother to a gathering of several families in which the women minded the camp and the girls were expected to go horseback riding or wander down to the river "to throw rocks" while the boys got to go off fishing with the men. "I was having a really hard time," Jennifer recalls, "because I felt abandoned on all fronts." At the end of the first day of watching her father drive off, she burst into tears and said she wanted to go with him the next morning. Unaware of her interest, he naturally told her to collect her gear and join them the next day. She did and a passion was born.

Thereafter, the Millers' visits to Montana became an annual tradition. Her father built a place in West Yellowstone, and Jennifer would come out for extended periods of time during the summer months, working for Bud Lilly's Trout Shop when she turned 18, and fishing with the guides as well as her father the rest of the time.

After high school, she deliberately headed east to attend college, out of a desire to try something completely different. Four years later, in 1981, she graduated from Vassar with an English degree, then returned to Montana to vagabond around for a year to "sort of get that out of my blood. Then I'd go get a real job. It was a great place for a 20-year-old to run loose. It was a big open space," she says.

She eventually settled in Bozeman after being stranded there by a snow storm. She began writing advertising copy for a local radio station, and before long she had talked her way into a deejay job on the midnight shift. But the hours wreaked havoc on her social life, since everyone else was working while she slept, and vice versa. So she devoted herself to fishing, and eventually she met her first husband.

By 1984, she had passed the exam and put in the three years of apprenticeship required by the state of Montana to receive her guide's license. In 1985, she and her husband opened a fly shop and she "started taking this fishing thing more seriously." Not surprisingly, selling tackle was not enough. Though she was doing fine as a guide and free-lance fly-fishing writer, she wanted to take teaching to a higher level.

That's when she "realized, OK, if I want to teach, if I want to be Joan, then I've got to get some good information." Instead of turning to the local guides in the area, she decided, "I'm going to the source. She's lived this. She knows this. Don't waste your time with anything else." And she went to see Joan. She flew back to the Catskills for one of the Wulffs' weekend schools and stayed a couple of extra days to interview Lee Wulff for an article she was writing for *Fly Rod & Reel* on streamside fly tying.

From Joan she gained new insights into how to teach the mechanics of casting—things like, Why is it a tailing loop? How do you get rid of that? "Those kinds of questions were answered in a way that I could not only practice it, but I could impart that to students. It would be like a doctor being able to diagnose an illness," she explains.

Jennifer calls Joan's book, *Fly Casting Techniques*, "the primary work" on the subject, even though she's studied a number of other casting books and watched the numerous videos that eventually flooded the market. "They all believe in the same God, but [have] a different way to get there," she laughs.

In short order, Jennifer had a son, got divorced, and closed the fly shop. With a new state outfitters' license under her belt (again acquired after an arduous three-year apprenticeship and tough exam), she became possibly the first woman in Montana to use her license strictly for fishing, rather than as a lodge owner.

Over time, Jennifer built up an enviable reputation as a walk/wade guide, primarily on the Madison and Gallatin rivers as well as on the Spring Creeks of the Yellowstone. In 1990, she met the man who would become not only the second most important influence on her career but also her second husband, Lars Olsson.

A renowned Swedish fly-fishing author, conservationist, and the riverkeeper for a section of the River Gim near the village of Gimdalen in Sweden (which he had personally leased from local landowners and restored to the famous fishery that it is today), Lars Olsson had decided that a woman's touch was needed to introduce the sport to a wider audience in his native land. Because there were no accomplished Swedish female instructors, he recruited Jennifer through a mutual friend to develop schools for women. They now spend October through May in Montana and June through September on the River Gim in Sweden, guiding, teaching, writing, and serving as leading advocates for the preservation of both countries' endangered fisheries.

Meanwhile, in the early 1990s, Jennifer decided she had a lot to offer a major rod company and pursued a sponsorship with a vengeance, including talking her way into an annual fly-tackle dealers' trade show in Denver. At the time, there were no women on the pro staffs of any of the major tackle manufacturers. And, she admits, she pounded on a lot of the wrong doors before talking to Scott Rods. They turned out to be the most receptive from the moment she introduced the idea. In 1994, Jennifer became the first woman ever to join the pro staff of this highly regarded company, for which she now serves as a technical advisor and sports-event personality to help bring more women into the sport.

She continues to write, too, and has contributed pieces to the books *Uncommon Waters*, *A Different Angle*, and *The World's Best Trout Flies*, as well as numerous fly-fishing periodicals.

Would we know about Jennifer Olsson today if there had never been a Joan Wulff? Yes, probably so, because she is so intelligent and ingenious—like the rest of the women who've achieved recognition over the years. But there's no doubt that a spoonful of inspiration from someone like Joan Wulff can go a long way. And Jennifer is living proof.

Christy Ball and Lori-Ann Murphy WYOMING AND IDAHO

Destination angling adventures have been around for decades, if not longer. Christy Ball and Lori-Ann Murphy, however, were the first to establish a business offering such trips exclusively for women.

Combining fly-fishing instruction with travel to world-class fishing hotspots, their Reel Women Fly Fishing Adventures (no relation to this book) promises something you won't find in most brochures: "You will leave with rich memories and new friends!"

Indeed, their multiple-day trips to such places as Deep Water Cay on Grand Bahama Island for bonefish, the Crane Meadow Lodge in Montana, the Swan Valley Bed & Breakfast on the South Fork of the Snake River in Idaho, and horseback pack-in trips to alpine lakes in the Wind River Range of Wyoming for trout are booked well in advance. In fact, anyone hoping to sign up will have to get in line: 90 percent of their bookings in 1995 were from women who had joined them in 1994, the company's inaugural season.

Christy and Lori-Ann are on the cutting edge of the recent explosion of interest in fly fishing among women. They were included in a front-page *New York Times* article on the topic in August 1994 and were featured in *Mirabella* magazine the following month. Considering that Christy didn't even take up fly fishing until 1982 and Lori-Ann until 1983, their present success is nothing less than phenomenal.

In 1989, Lori-Ann became the first Orvis-endorsed female guide in the history of that 139-year-old company. When they're not escorting women on one of their Reel Women Adventures, both are Orvis guides during the summer months for Bressler Outfitters in Jackson, Wyoming. Together they pioneered Orvis's first women-only classes, in Jackson and Manchester, Vermont, which led to their unique partnership for Reel Women Fly Fishing Adventures. They also designed Orvis's first line of fly-fishing clothing and gear for women, in collaboration with Nancy Zakon, which debuted in the spring of 1995.

As the only girl in a family of two brothers, two step-brothers, and one half-brother growing up in Muncie, Indiana, "no one encouraged me in any way, shape, or form that I could be competent in the outdoors," Christy, 37, says of the transformation she would later make on her own. There was also nothing about her childhood that could have served as a precursor to her present-day career. "I don't remember ever seeing my father fish. My mom bought a cane pole every once in a while and put a bobber and some baloney on it and put us out on a dock, but I certainly wasn't raised fishing," she recalls.

After graduating from high school in 1976, Christy followed her future husband to Northern Wisconsin, where he was attending college. Though they could afford better, they deliberately chose a rugged rural lifestyle and built a house out of telephone poles and plywood. It had no indoor plumbing. "I scraped ice off the outhouse seat when it was 80 degrees below zero," she laughs.

Two years later, they moved to Boulder, Colorado, where she spent a year at the Boulder School of Massage Therapy, then several more years studying at the Rolf Institute, ultimately setting up her own practice both there and in Northern Michigan, where they finally settled.

In 1979, they began making annual months-long sojourns to a rustic home owned by her husband's family on Little Cayman Island, which lies directly south of Cuba in the Caribbean. Only ten miles long and one mile across, the island was "extremely underdeveloped," Christy says of their tropical paradise. It was also about as far from civilization as one could get, with limited electricity, no grocery stores, and only a dozen or so inhabitants at one time, most of them there for the local scuba-diving school.

Scuba diving was in fact Christy and her husband's chief amusement for the first several years. But that would change when her sister-in-law (and best friend) Nancy returned from her own visit to the island, having been initiated into the rites of fly fishing by the handful of professional guides from Montana and Wyoming who had started coming to the place. As Nancy waxed on about her new obsession, Christy listened in disbelief. "I just thought that she had lost her mind," Christy now laughs. "I remember thinking, 'Fishing! You like to fish? Why would anyone want to go out there, get devoured by bugs, spend eight hours looking around for a fish with the best end-results being catching this slimy thing that you couldn't eat anyway?' I couldn't see the lure. I'd rather sit home and pinch myself or something!" But she vowed to give it a try, just "to see what it was that captivated Nancy so much in this sport."

PROFESSIONAL FLY-FISHING GUIDES CHRISTY BALL (LEFT)
AND LORI-ANN MURPHY WERE THE FIRST TO ESTABLISH
WOMEN-ONLY DESTINATION ADVENTURES. IN ADDITION,
THEY CO-DESIGNED THE ORVIS COMPANY'S FIRST LINE OF
WOMEN'S FLY-FISHING CLOTHING AND GEAR.

On her next visit to Little Cayman, Christy hung around with the visiting guides for a while, then decided to give it a try. Grabbing her rod, she ventured down to the island's airstrip for an hour or two of practice-casting, then went fishing, convinced that it couldn't be that hard.

The only problem was she couldn't catch a fish, no matter how hard she tried. First of all, she couldn't "see" them—a must in saltwater-flats fishing. Second, she couldn't get the fly to them, because she didn't know how to cast properly. It was a rude awakening for someone who had always regarded fishing as a "dweebie thing to do." "I was terrible," she laughs, noting that fly fishing then became a challenge she was determined to conquer.

Talk about patience and tenacity! It would be *three years* before Christy caught her first fish, despite countless attempts. "That really changed something in me. I became completely obsessed with it. Completely went off the deep end," she says. After that, however, she was regularly landing bonefish, tarpon, and jack just like a pro.

But the Holy Grail of them all, permit, was still outside of her grasp. "Permit is the fish that sort of pushed me over the edge," she confesses with amusement. "At the time, it was sort of the prized catch, and I decided that was the fish I needed." Before long, she was dreaming about them at night, then getting up before sunrise and walking the island with her rod. "I got to where I could spot a permit tail seemingly half a mile down the beach."

After a while, she began driving to areas where she knew they fed, discovering one spot in particular that always held permit. But that didn't mean she could catch them. "Every time I'd pull in to check it out, I wouldn't see any fish, and I'd turn around and start backing the truck out of this little road and a tail would pop up. So I'd pull forward, get out and walk down there. No fish. And sometimes I'd do this like three or four times. And it was always at this one spot."

Determined to outwit them, she began staking out the spot, bringing with her a folding chair and a cooler filled with food and soft drinks for fortification during the long waits. "I'd have a rod rigged up for bonefish and one rigged up for permit, and I'd take my book." And about every 10 minutes, she'd see a tail pop up, grab her rod, and make a few casts, only to watch them vanish again.

Seven years after Christy took up fly fishing and four years after she caught her first fish, she finally hooked and landed her first permit. "I was so glad when I caught it and it was over with!" she exclaims. "I tell you! I mean, I was obsessed with this thing!" She had heard that "it takes 2,000 good casts to a permit to catch one, and I easily did that."

In 1981, Christy met guide Joe Bressler, then 17, on the island and often hired him to take her out. In 1987, she overheard him telling another guide about a school for professional guides he would be starting the following summer in Jackson, Wyoming. Intrigued, she asked him if she could attend, just to learn more about this sport that had gradually taken over her life. "Well, sure, you can sign up for it if you want, but I just want you to know up front that I'll never hire you and I'll never help you get a job," he hedged. She quickly responded that becoming a pro was hardly her ambition.

The following summer she was there in Jackson for the intensive two weeks of classes, which included sessions on the water learning how to row and control a drift boat against the river current. She did so well, in fact, that three days into the school Bressler invited her to join his blue-ribbon staff of professional guides the following summer.

At first she wasn't going to take the offer. Her family and friends, she says, thought she "had flipped out!" They cautioned her to think about the idyllic lifestyle she was about to forfeit, which included a devoted husband and the luxury of four homes, along with their own private plane to transport them on a whim. "I went for four years without being in the same place for more than 10 days," she relates of her once-cushy life. After giving it a lot of thought, she concluded she'd always "been doing things to make other people happy, and it was like, 'This is what I want to do, and darn it, I'm going to do it!'" There were other, less obvious reasons as well. "Looking back, it was just a pot that was waiting to boil over," she says.

So she headed to Wyoming and the job Bressler told her was waiting. "It was the most difficult thing I could think to do. I mean, there was nothing more foreign. I couldn't have been more out of my element than when I decided to be a fishing guide."

It was a summer filled with challenges, starting with the simplest: learning how to back up a boat trailer, which she practiced in her driveway first so she wouldn't embarrass herself down at the boat ramp. She also became adept at rowing over long distances and learning every inch of the waters she would later drift with clients. "Fortunately, I'm very coordinated, so I took to rowing real easily. But every day that first summer I was out there working for Joe, I'd come in and he'd say, 'I don't think you can handle it. Are you sure you want to do this?'" But she kept at it.

The following summer she began taking out clients. By then, Bressler had quit trying to talk her out of it, and of course, she wasn't going to be deterred anyway. She knew she had found her calling in life. "I really enjoy taking people fishing," she says, "because I get so excited about it. I mean, I [even] get excited about walking up and down the river in my waders." These days, it's caddis cases (the little houses bugs build, found lodged under the bottoms of rocks) rather than permit that "push me over the edge," she laughs.

Her final transformation to self-sufficient outdoorswoman came during her first trip alone to Little Cayman. During the months that followed, out of necessity, she learned to reckon with the elements and her latent instincts of survival as her surrounding physical environment deteriorated. The generator had broken down, so there was no electricity. The rats were making so much noise at night that she had taken to sleeping with ear plugs. Finally fed up, she went on the offensive. After getting rid of the rats by cleverly drowning them on little trays, she launched into "fixing the generator, and working on the outboard, and dealing with the water pump, and crawling underneath the truck."

It was a major turning point, even for someone who had previously chosen outhouses over marble-lined bathrooms. "There were so many things I'd never ever done before, and it was like, 'Not only can I do this, I can do it pretty good.' It's given me a new outlook. I don't approach things assuming that I can't do them anymore," she shares. It's a mystical lesson she also tries to impart to the women who join her and Lori-Ann on their Reel Women Adventures, so they too can acquire a sense of "confidence and competence."

Lori-Ann, also 37, grew up in Venice, California, just a few miles south of Santa Monica near Los Angeles. Summers were spent in the Sierra Nevada mountains, a day's drive away. "My mom and dad had seven kids in five and a half years [including two sets of twins], so the easiest thing to do was line us all up on the bank and have us fish. So we grew up fishing, mostly with worms and hooks, cheese and corn and stuff like that. And it was always a big topic of conversation," she says.

One of Lori-Ann's fondest childhood memories is of the time her father took her deep-sea fishing in San Diego when she was 12. For whatever reason, the charters didn't allow women or girls aboard, so they agreed she would be known as "Louie" that day. "I'm six feet now, but when I was growing, I was just this stick," she explains of their successful deception. While her father was gone to the head, "Louie," who was strapped into a harness with her rod out, hooked into a large yellowtail tuna. The fish was so large that the only thing that kept her from going into the drink was the firm grip that some of the other passengers had on her harness. "I was so scared," she says, "because [there were] two big blue sharks circling the boat and I just thought I was going to be eaten alive!"

At the age of 19, Lori-Ann moved to Coeur d'Alene, Idaho, with her boyfriend and spent the next six years working in a health-food store and playing college basketball and volleyball while obtaining an associate degree from North Idaho College. In 1983, she moved to Seattle to acquire a bachelor's degree in nursing, where she spent her spare time racing sailboats. Fishing was the furthest thing from her mind when a friend from Oregon's Columbia River town of The Dalles suggested she meet him at the Deschutes River, which is world-renowned for its steelhead runs. Always game for adventure, she accepted his offer, unaware that she was about to meet up with her destiny.

"The first day out, at four o'clock in the morning, I got my first steelhead on a fly. *That* was really amazing. When I look back on that, I realize that it was complete beginner's luck. And I just became obsessed. I started going down every other weekend. On the other weekends, I'd usually drive towards the Yakima and fish dry lakes," she says. Meanwhile, while managing low-income clinics in Seattle, she found herself doodling pictures of fish all over her desk calendar while talking on the phone. So when a friend called to see if Lori-Ann might be interested in taking her job as the director of public health, which she would soon be vacating, in one of the country's fishing hotspots, Jackson, Wyoming, Lori-Ann quickly responded, "I'm there!"

Since the job in Jackson didn't start until November, Lori-Ann decided to spend the summer in Driggs, Idaho, a tiny town in the Teton Valley, less than an hour's drive away. When a nursing position opened up at Driggs's 13-bed hospital, she decided to stay, admittedly seduced by the cafeteria's "incredible cinnamon rolls" and the place's friendly atmosphere. "Every day at lunch the doctor and everybody gets together at this big family-style sort of dinner," she says. During the winter months, she also worked part-time as a ski instructor.

Within months of landing in Driggs, Lori-Ann also met her future husband, Gary Bebe, who made his living as a professional fly-fishing guide. "He had just gotten off the Big Horn, and of course, I was completely enamored," she says. She attended a slide show at his house the next day, then he took off for a three-month kayaking trip in Costa Rica. But he called her on Valentine's Day, opening the door to a romance that bloomed upon his return. Soon after, he suggested she accompany him to the annual Orvis Rendezvous in Livingston, Montana, and check out guiding as a career. "I said I really didn't want to mix my work with my passion, but I'd check it out," she says.

The year was 1989. Lori-Ann was the only woman among 16 prospective guides. "You go through all kinds of different workshops put on by experts. And at the end of those two days, you take out an expert fly fisherman," she explains. As luck would have it, Lori-Ann was assigned Leigh Perkins, the owner of The Orvis Company, as her "client." "I had *no idea* who he even was," she laughs. Everything likely would have been fine if one of the men in her class hadn't informed her of Perkins's importance. Who wouldn't be intimidated about taking out one of the world's top fly-fishing experts. "I was sick to my stomach and it was awful," she vividly remembers.

Naturally, being that it was Leigh Perkins, they got the dubious distinction of going first while everyone else watched. Lori-Ann remembers that the fish were rising and she "was tying on the tippet and it took me forever! It was not working! And I stood up, thereby spooking all the fish, and I said, 'Mr. Perkins, it's making me too damn nervous knowing you're the owner of Orvis. I'm just going to pretend you're one of my regular fishing buddies and we're just going to have a fun day.' And when you know this man, he just loves to laugh and chuckle. And he just said, 'That's a lovely idea!' And we did. We fished until eight o'clock that night. We had a great time! And we've since become very, very close friends. He's a regular fishing pal of mine."

Though it was not her aim to snag a job, by the end of the Orvis Rendezvous weekend Lori-Ann had three offers: one from Canada, one from Elk Trout Lodge in Colorado (where Gary, her boyfriend, was the fishing director), and one from Bressler's Outfitters in Jackson.

Gary's offer prevailed. "I was actually petrified, because this [meant] the big 'C' word [commitment], in terms of relationship stuff. But I went down there and had a great time, and I worked at Elk Trout for two years, and we did mostly wade fishing. Then when Gary and I got married, I said I really wanted to stay home [in Driggs]. I really liked the fishing here." So they started working for their good friend Joe Bressler in nearby Jackson, "and I learned how to guide out of a drift boat."

In 1993, Lori-Ann was selected to serve as the fly-fishing technical advisor to Meryl Streep and Kevin Bacon on the film,

A River Wild. In 1994, Reel Women Fly Fishing Adventures was launched and Lori-Ann quit her position as director of a home-health program in Driggs, marking her retirement from nursing after 15 years, to concentrate on her quickly expanding fishing career.

How Lori-Ann and Christy met is another interesting story. After teaching Bressler's first women-only class, Lori-Ann was telling Leigh Perkins, by now a close friend, of the great response the class had received, when he suggested she repeat the course at the Orvis headquarters in Manchester, Vermont. Realizing she would need help, she turned to Christy, a fellow guide for Bressler's, who immediately signed on. Their Manchester clinic was so successful that it has become an annual event, along with their women-only classes in Jackson.

When they discovered early on that their students "were having a hard time saying goodbye," Reel Women Fly Fishing Adventures was born over a beer. At first they envisioned a "small, funky business. Take a couple of fishing trips [a year] and no big deal," Lori-Ann says. Then *A River Wild* came out, giving Lori-Ann additional recognition. Leigh Perkins announced their new enterprise in one of his Orvis newsletters, which goes out to some two million readers, and the *New York Times* and *Mirabella* pieces appeared. Before they knew it, the phones were ringing off the hook. "I feel like I'm just now getting caught up," Lori-Ann told me just prior to their second season of scheduled trips.

Partnerships are always a delicate balancing act. What makes theirs work, says Lori-Ann, is "a mutual respect for each other." They also share the same sensibilities and concerns about the quality of their company offerings. "We both have the same ideas when it comes to our clientele and how we want to take care of them, how we want a trip to be. We're both into having a good time," she enthuses.

Kelly Watt WASHINGTON

Imagine making your living traveling the globe in search of the ultimate fly-fishing adventure. Or having your own fishing show on the granddaddy of sports cable networks, ESPN. Certainly, many men have aspired for a career in which their days are spent on the water in exotic angling locales, but few have ever been able to make it work. Then again, being able to catch fish is but one of the key ingredients necessary to reaching the pinnacle of success enjoyed by Kelly Watt and her partner and husband, Jim.

At 34, Kelly not only possesses the on-camera charisma necessary to keep viewers entertained, but she can also run a sophisticated $60,000 video camera, record network-quality sound, and produce a shoot down to the fine details. And, yes, she catches fish. In fact, she has caught more sailfish on artificial flies than any other woman in the world, even though she did not pick up a fly rod until the mid-1980s.

Since 1987, Kelly has not only become a household name in the angling world, but together with Jim, she is the largest producer of fly-fishing videos in the world. Their "Fly Fishing Video Magazine" airs weekly on ESPN between October and December each year, and their library of home-video titles now includes some 40 different adventure and 25 how-to cassettes (all available by mail order). Last year alone, they brought 21 new releases onto the market.

But producing, directing, shooting, and editing their highly successful television and video series is only half of what keeps this tireless couple on the road about 70 percent of the time. Under the auspices of their Seattle-based independent production company, they're also on-call to all three of the major networks to shoot fast-breaking prime-time news stories on such subjects as earthquakes and other worldwide natural disasters, the Summer Olympics in Korea, and even Tanya Harding during her pre-Olympic legal travails.

Their pieces regularly appear on such shows as CBS's "60 Minutes;" ABC's "20/20," "World News Tonight with Peter Jennings," and "Nightline;" and NBC's "Nightly News" and "The Today Show." "Basically, our lives are controlled out of an assignment desk in Los Angeles or New York," Kelly says. "They call and say, 'Are you available for these days? And we either say yes or no, and *then* they tell us what the story's about."

Kelly's television career began straight out of college, when she got an entry-level job at KOMO-TV in Seattle, her hometown. From the station's veteran cameramen she learned how to become a sound technician. It was—and is—a field in which you'll find few women, which is not surprising considering the personal sacrifices required by the job. "Whether you're [working on] the local or national level, it's tough on your family life," Kelly explains. "You're traveling all the time, and you're on call all the time. It's just hard to plan a dinner party or anything."

Jim, meanwhile, had earned his stripes as a producer, director, and cameraman covering the Vietnam War for NBC News in 1967, then serving as an NBC staff cameraman until 1978 on jaunts to Cambodia, Laos, and Japan. He also accompanied President Nixon on his historic trip to China in 1971, and Secretary of State Henry Kissinger on an around-the-world mission in 1972. Ready to march to his own drumbeat by 1978, he relocated to Seattle and began free-lancing for the networks as well as producing the series, "The American Frontier."

Fate brought them together in 1985, when they were paired on an assignment. They joined their skills in business and married a year later.

In 1987, they decided to relaunch the concept of the "Fly Fishing Video Magazine," which Jim had tried in 1981 but couldn't make successful because the VCR explosion was still a few years in the future. This time it worked, although Kelly admits that in the beginning "it took a lot of explaining what a video magazine was. That was at least half of our marketing battle."

For their ESPN show, they produce a 20-minute version of each trip, then expand it to 60 minutes for the home video series. Both of them produce and shoot, then Jim does the editing and Kelly designs the packaging.

What has made the series so popular, Kelly believes, is the fact that most people can only afford a major fishing vacation every couple of years, and "this is a way of doing research on where they really want to go without spending a whole lot of money to find out the hard way whether this is what they thought it was going to be."

Besides the kind of fishing available in an area, each adventure video also shows the quality of the accommodations, including the interiors of the guest rooms and main lodge buildings. "We try to do a whole picture whenever possible, because going on a fishing trip is a lot more than just the fish," she says.

There aren't many marriages that could survive so much togetherness. But the Watts wouldn't have it otherwise. "It works out so well. We spend 24 hours a day together, and when we're apart, it's like we don't know what to do," she laughs.

CHAPTER 6

More Patterns of Excellence: Fly Tiers Today

MEGAN BOYD

HELEN SHAW

WINNIE AND MARY DETTE

JUDY LEHMBERG

PAGE ROGERS

AND OTHER SIGNIFICANT FIGURES

The great fly tiers will always be regarded as artists more than artisans. Their canvas is what might seem like an unremarkable hook to the casual observer. But every wind of the thread represents another brush stroke. And every adornment—whether fur, feathers, tinsel, or other ordinary and exotic materials—is studiously applied much like a sculptor adds and shapes her clay.

It's little wonder that their tiny works of art are collected and framed, and rarely if ever fished—especially today, when most flies sold in fly-fishing shops or through mail-order catalogs are mass-produced by overseas factories.

Among those to be admired for their mastery and dedication to perfection today are ...

Megan Boyd SCOTLAND

When the late author Joseph D. Bates polled the world's leading fly anglers for their opinion on who should be rightfully acknowledged as the master of fly tying today, the response was over-whelming: "The best are in Scotland and of course Megan Boyd is the best in Scotland."[1] During the six decades that Megan Boyd created her magical concoctions out of feathers

and fur, she did indeed produce flies that many regard as the Tiffanies of the 20th century.

The most important of the many accolades she received during her active years was the British Empire Medal, bestowed upon her by the Queen of England in 1971—making her the only fly tier to receive that loftiest of recognitions. (Notoriously reclusive, Boyd refused to travel to London to attend the ceremony. "Her eccentricities are surpassed only by her talent," one of her American customers told Tena Robinson, who profiled her for *Fly Rod & Reel*.[2])

How such perfection could emerge under the primitive circumstances in which she worked is a testament to the fortitude of this single-minded Scot. Her studio was nothing but a drafty old wooden garage which she had pulled onto the property next to her bungalow overlooking the North Sea in the Scottish Highlands. Spending between 14 and 16 hours a day, six or seven days a week at her bench, she didn't even have electricity until 1985, having relied solely on one gas lamp that served both as her light and single heat source!

By the time of her retirement in 1988, Megan's flies had reached fame of such mythical proportions that she had orders stacked up dating back to 1973. Even so, she never hiked up her prices, which were always just under an American dollar per specimen—despite the fact that wealthy anglers from around the world were begging to pay more if she would simply supply them. "I had masses and masses of letters from people who wanted to buy flies to frame," she told Judith Dunham for *The Atlantic Salmon Fly*. "As long as I was tying flies for the fisherman—which I started off doing to earn my daily bread—I kept doing it. All the other orders had to go to the bottom of the pile."[3]

Born in 1915, Megan got the inspiration to tie flies at the age of 12, after her father brought home a couple he had found along the riverbanks. "Flytiers were few and far between then, and I thought tying would be a good job to do," she recalled for Dunham. The riverkeeper on a nearby estate taught her the craft by having her disassemble a finished fly and then reconstruct it on a smaller hook.

At the age of 20, in 1935, Megan moved to the bungalow in Kintradwell, where she spent the next 53 years. She "had hoped to die making flies out there," she told Robinson. "That didn't quite come off... so I did what I never thought I possibly could do. I shut my hut door and walked out." The reason for Megan's retirement? Every artist's worst fear: failing eyesight. "I knew that my eyesight was going because I was making bigger heads on the flies," she said to Dunham, "and once you start to do that, it's no use."

Today, Megan's flies fetch as much as $1,000 each at collector's auctions. She's not impressed, however. "It's an awful waste of money," she insisted to Robinson, although she is apparently pleased that some of the flies have ended up in the protection of institutions like the American Museum of Fly Fishing in Manchester, Vermont.

Even though Megan did her best to pass on her skills — she gave fly-tying lessons to hundreds over the years — she lamented to Robinson that she was not able to find a suitable heir. "There is only one man I taught that could tie a decent fly. He is dead now. The modern ones just want to tie something quick and scrappy and sell it."

Perhaps the most amazing detail about this complex woman's life was the fact that Megan Boyd did not fish. "I was certainly invited to fish here and there," she explained to Robinson. "But I've never fished in my life. And I wouldn't kill a salmon if I got one. That part of it's the only thing I didn't like about my work."

Helen Shaw

In a 1989 *American Angler & Fly Tier* profile of Helen Shaw, author Dick Talleur recounts a story which so aptly sums up the reverence in which fly-fishing connoisseurs regard this extraordinary woman's life work that it bears repeating:

"Arnold Gingrich, the renowned editor of *Esquire* magazine and an inveterate angler and flyfishing writer himself, was presented with a special collection of one hundred of his favorite flies tied by Helen, in commemoration of the magazine's fiftieth birthday," Talleur relates. "It is a matter of record that upon opening the box, he tearfully remarked, 'I never had a Helen Shaw fly; now I have a hundred. Nobody's worth that much.'"[4]

Helen not only ranks among the greatest fly tiers in the history of the sport, but she was also the first to demystify this arcane skill with her 1963 landmark book, *Fly-Tying*.[5] Rather than another weighty dissertation on fly-tying techniques that only an expert could dicipher, Helen's was ingenious for its deceptive simplicity. Through it, armchair fly tiers everywhere were suddenly given a rare chance to observe a master at work—with step-by-step photographs of Helen's hands in action demonstrating the entire construction process, accompanied by succinct explanatory captions and an enlightening introduction to the essential elements of a tier's treasure trove.

"Now that everyone else has had a run at paying superlative homage to Helen Shaw for her picture book on fly-tying," *The New York Herald Tribune*'s Art Smith wrote in 1963, "I should like to weigh in with a flat appraisal of its value: It is the best fly-tying textbook that ever has been published, and anyone seeking to master the craft of fashioning trout flies without this illustrated guide propped open before him is simply cheating himself.... The book, as Mel Ellis of the *Milwaukee Journal* has said before me, is a must."[6]

Helen once said that when she glimpsed her first trout at the age of three, it was "love at first sight." Born in Madison, Wisconsin, she learned to fish from her father and began tying flies as a youngster. Though no one in particular influenced her style, she absorbed the techniques of local tiers, thus refining her skill so early that she was already producing flies for a growing clientele by the time she graduated high school.

At 20, her business had flourished to the point that she was able to set up a shop in Sheboygan, initially with a partner, producing flies for such notables as President Herbert Hoover, among others. Fly-tying materials were obtained either by mail or by foraging such places as the Chicago stockyards for calf tails. And according to Talleur, she was "an active and enthusiastic flyfisher" who often joined some of her customers out on the water.

If Helen was unaware of the oddity of her profession, especially for a young woman, she was made aware of it during an emergency visit to the hospital for a chronic kidney infection. As she humorously related to Talleur: "A young intern, while doing a work-up of my case, asked me what I did for a living. I told him that I dressed flies. He turned to the nurse and said, 'How long has this patient been delirious?'"

Surprisingly, she was not the only woman tying in the Midwest prior to World War II. "There were a fair number of female commercial tyers," she told Talleur, "but they didn't operate as individual professionals. They tied on a piecework basis for large distributors, principally the Webber Company, which had ninety to a hundred women tying all the time. They would start a week with a huge pile of materials for a single

AMERICAN FLY TIER HELEN SHAW
REVOLUTIONIZED THE CONCEPT OF
HOW-TO BOOKS WITH HER 1963
LANDMARK TOME, "FLY TYING," CON-
CEIVED AND PHOTOGRAPHED BY HER
LATE HUSBAND, HERMANN KESSLER.

pattern. The Monday-Tuesday flies were pretty fair, but by the end of the week they had gone far down-hill, as the materials got picked over and fatigue and tedium set in. Webbers' offered me the head job once, but I wanted no part of it. I was always a meticulous tyer, and speed and production are contrary to what I do."

One of the most significant unions in the fly-fishing world was formed when Helen met her future husband, Hermann Kessler, already the art director for *Field & Stream*, a position he would hold for some 25 years. (Hermann would also later conceive and serve as the founding president of the American Museum of Fly Fishing.) During a visit to Milwaukee to fish, Hermann stayed with one of Helen's friends, who introduced them. During subsequent visits and a flow of correspondence, a romance blossomed. "Helen told me with a coquettish smile," Talleur wrote, "'When the letters started coming Special Delivery, I knew Hermann was serious.'" They married in 1953, and she closed up her little shop in Sheboygan and moved to New York to join him.

Working out of their Manhattan apartment, Helen was immediately deluged with orders from the city's corps of discerning fly fishers, particularly members of the New York Angler's Club. Her flies also began receiving deserved publicity in publications like *Field & Stream*, and she occasionally demonstrated her fly-tying prowess to enraptured audiences at expositions throughout the city—although she found these exhibitions less than ideal as a teaching tool since only those standing closest to her could get a full view. "To be watching anyone working with something as relatively small as a trout fly hook can be frustrating to a learner, since most of the details are necessarily obscured by the tyer's own fingers. It is certainly entertaining but not instructive," Helen says. "Hermann realized this and was entirely responsible for the idea of organizing and presenting my work photographically."

Hermann, who was an accomplished photographer but not a tier himself, envisioned a book illustrated with photographs that a complete novice like himself could follow with ease. Thus, *Fly-Tying* was born out of a collaboration in which Hermann composed and photographed each step of the process and Helen supplied the editorial contents.

Fly-Tying was an instant best-seller upon its publication in 1963, even though it appeared "at least five years before the beginning of the tying/fishing boom," Talleur notes. As important, writes Talleur, it "lifted Helen Shaw out of virtual obscurity and secured for her a well-deserved niche in the top echelon of the world's fly tyers." Though it hardly seems possible, especially considering the proliferation of fly tying how-to books over the last 32 years, Helen's book has never been out of print except for one brief period. "Those instructions are still fundamental today," she explains with obvious pride of its enduring relevancy. "Tools, vise and materials may differ somewhat, but the process of binding those materials to a hook has not changed."

Helen and Hermann collaborated twice more: once for her second book, *Flies for Fish and Fishermen*, which was published in 1989, and also for a third volume, which remains incomplete due to Hermann's death in 1993. Through the years, Helen also wrote numerous magazine articles and contributed to other books on the subject, among them Art Flick's *Master Fly-Tying Guide*. Two examples of her stunning handiwork are also featured in Judith Dunham's *The Art of the Trout Fly*.

Surprisingly, almost nothing has been written about Helen herself and her remarkable life, except for the excellent profile authored by Talleur in 1989, in which he respectfully dubbed her "the Greta Garbo of fly tying." Perhaps Art Smith best explained in his glowing 1963 review why Helen's name does not readily roll off the lips of the latest generation of fly fishers: "I think that it is typical of Helen Shaw, whom I know and greatly admire, that she should have produced a book so utterly devoid of pretense or condescension, because this is exactly the sort of person she is. There is about this tall, attractive woman with the broad-spaced brown eyes something that suggests abhorrence of ostentation. In going through *Fly-Tying*, I found just three uses of the pronoun 'I.'"

We can be grateful to the late Hermann Kessler that he recognized Helen's immeasurable talents and guided her to her rightful place in fly-fishing history.

Winnie and Mary Dette NEW YORK

Since the late 1800s, the Catskills region of New York has served as a popular mecca for both fly fishers and city-weary tourists, thanks to its rural beauty and trout-rich rivers, including the Beaverkill and the Neversink. There is also a fly-tying tradition in the Catskills, born out of the growing demand for the magical imitations that were meticulously tied by a dozen or so of the finest tiers who have ever lived. In a class of their own, however, are what are known simply as the Dette flies, produced for over 65 years by Walt and Winnie Dette.

Born in 1909 in Roscoe, New York, in a 36-room boardinghouse on the Beaverkill River built by her grandfather, Winnie grew up around many of the world's fly-fishing notables, including famed hotelier Charles Ritz, who took up seasonal residence at the Ferdon's River View Inn during the 1910s and 1920s.

Winnie actually had her heart set on a career in journalism, for which she was awarded a one-year scholarship to Cornell University upon graduation from high school at the age of 15. But her mother would not hear of it. "Young ladies simply were not supposed to consider careers other than teaching, nursing or secretarial positions," explains Eric Leiser in his indispenable book, *The Dettes: A Catskill Legend*, "and Winnie was forbidden to pursue her course. In short, she was grounded." On hindsight, Winnie related to Leiser years later, "I guess I wasn't so smart after all. I should have told them I was going for a teaching degree and then gone on to journalism at a later date."[7]

Instead, Winnie stubbornly refused to go to college at all. At the age of 16, she took a job at the local bank and remarkably worked her way up to assistant trust officer by the time she was 21.

In 1928, at the age of 19, she married Walt Dette, a local boy who worked down at the drugstore. An avid fly fisher — Winnie would become one as well — he had already gotten one foot into the fishing business by convincing the owner of the store to let him set up a tackle shop in one corner. He also had the inspiration to learn how to tie flies himself and offered Rube Cross, one of the premier tiers in the country, $50 to teach him. But Cross turned him down flat. "The art of fly tying was a highly guarded secret in those days," Leiser notes.

Undeterred, Walt rented a room on Main Street for $12 a month, and he, Winnie, and a friend, Harry Darbee, began teaching themselves. "Learning to tie flies was one of their first priorities. That was accomplished by taking apart various Rube Cross, and other, patterns to see how they were constructed," Leiser explains. "As Walt carefully unwound each turn of thread, Harry and Winnie would watch and take notes. Then all three would try to put one together again."

While all three held down their full-time jobs, Walt and Harry started a sideline business repairing and wrapping fly rods, and Winnie tied the first Dette flies, which were sold out of the cigar counter in her father's inn for a quarter apiece. In 1929, Walt and Winnie moved into the inn to help run it and set up their fly-tying operation in an upstairs room. They also put out their first mail-order catalog, which offered 100 different dry-fly patterns—25 of which were their own designs or modified versions of old standards. Walt also began raising chickens to supply them with their fly-tying feathers.

During the next two years, "the legend of the superb Dette flies was born," Leiser writes. "Those who gathered at the inn soon spread the word that this was the place to be and that the patterns tied by Walt and Winnie were among the best in the country.... It became a mark of distinction among anglers to say, 'I have my flies tied by the Dettes.'" Orders began pouring in from members of elite angling clubs, and it was all Walt and Winnie could do to keep up while working their full-time jobs, a problem which continually plagued them over the years.

For whatever reasons, the devastating effects of the Depression had not yet hit little Roscoe by 1931, when Walt and Winnie took out a bank loan to purchase the inn from her parents and had their first child, Mary. A year later, however, the anglers suddenly stopped coming, forcing them to deed the property back to the bank and move to a small house owned by Winnie's grandfather, where they attempted for the one and only time in their lives to support themselves entirely from their fly-tying labors. To carry them through the winter months, they began tying for wholesale companies. "Feather and fur flew in all directions and work ceased only for meals, sleep, and taking care of the new baby," Leiser reports.

In 1933, Harry Darbee returned to the area and signed on as a partner to help out with the escalating workload. Winnie was pregnant with her second child, Walter Clay, but continued to put in long hours at her bench. A year later, they were so desperate for help that they hired a young woman, Elsie Bivens, to sort hackles and other materials. But Harry and Elsie eloped in 1935, and the partnership came to an end as the Darbees lit out to set up their own fly-tying business. But somehow Walt and Winnie survived, even filling one wholesale order of over 12,000 flies of various patterns. That same year, they put out their second and last catalog, offering tools, hooks, assorted fly-tying materials, and their trademark flies.

During World War II, Walt worked a job in a Brooklyn defense plant and ran his friend Jim Deren's Angler's Roost fly-fishing store. Unfortunately, he never received a dime for the latter, which would have taken some of the pressure off Winnie, who remained in Roscoe with their two children. Besides her full-time job and household chores, Winnie was "tying flies every waking hour, including weekends. Though rationing was a way of life during this period, it did not dampen, nor diminish, the enthusiasm of anglers willing to make a trip to the Beaverkill," Leiser writes. But the orders that arrived by mail from all over the country did allow them to quit supplying to wholesale houses.

In 1946, the Dettes were among those profiled in a *Fortune* magazine article about the Catskill tradition. It only added to their legend. Over the years, other newspaper and magazine articles followed, although the Dettes never sought out the publicity.

"As their reputation grew, the Dette home became the hub around which fly tyers and anglers would gather, not just to buy flies or garner information, which was always freely given, but to belong and perhaps by being there become part of the tradition," Leiser writes. "Both novice and expert never ceased to marvel at the precise maneuvers the Dettes' fingers made time and time again, turning out one exquisite pattern after another. The flies of a pattern, when individually examined, seemed identical and perfect, almost as if cloned."

In 1955, soon after having her first child, their daughter, Mary, approached her father about learning how to tie. Three children later, she was still at it. "While kept busy pinning diapers and warming bottles, Mary was also busy tying flies to make spare money. Once the children were grown, fly tying had become too much of a part of her life to be abandoned.... Today she ties most of the flies bearing the Dette brand and style," Leiser reports. Ironically, the Dettes' son, Clay, showed little interest in fly fishing and none in fly tying.

Their good friend Joan Wulff notes in her book, *Joan Wulff's Fly Fishing*, that "the flies of all three [Walt, Winnie, and Mary] are exactly alike and the flies are simply 'Dette flies.' The mother-to-daughter tradition has only a slight chance of being carried on by Mary's daughter Linda, but it would certainly be nice for the Catskill school of fly tying to have a bloodline continuity."[8] It's hard to fathom that in 1992, when Leiser published his chronicle of their lives and success, Walt and Winnie had been tying flies for six and a half decades.

Walt passed away in 1994 and Winnie is now retired. With the Darbees' deaths in the early 1980s, this great tradition is now literally in the hands of only one person, Mary Dette.

Eric Leiser's book, *The Dettes: A Catskill Legend*, contains color plates of their exquisite handiwork as well as tying instructions. A superb color photograph of their flies is also included in Judith Dunham's *The Art of the Trout Fly*.

The art of tying the intricate Atlantic salmon fly "has been lauded as the pinnacle of the craft of flytying, the zenith of the angling arts, the ultimate test of a flytyer's ability," author Judith Dunham writes. It's little wonder, considering that Judy Lehmberg, one of the world's leading practitioners of this revered craft, spends between three and six hours tying just one of these intricate specimens.

Spend a few minutes browsing Dunham's highly praised book, *The Atlantic Salmon Fly*, which features glorious photographs of what she calls the "crown jewel of flies," including one of Judy's finest, and it's not hard to understand why these museum-quality tiny works of art are collected more than they are fished. Those produced today are one-of-a-kind expressions of their tier, in which exotic plumage splays from a hook lavishly wrapped with silk and tinsel in a configuration reminiscent of the splendor of the Victorian Age from which it hails.

One would think a background in art might be more suited to such a hobby than Judy's bachelor's degree in wildlife management or her master's degree in biology. More surprising, she has never even fished for Atlantic salmon, a prohibitively expensive sport for most, involving travel to the salmon's home waters in Norway, Scotland, England, Ireland, Iceland, or Canada, along with the substantial fees charged by private landowners who generally control access to the rivers.

A college biology instructor, Judy did not fish until she met her husband, Verne, a college environmental sciences instructor. Even then, the actual act of casting a fly at the end of a line would not come until after Verne had taught Judy how to tie flies. It seems that she was immediately taken with the plethora of natural materials in Verne's fly-tying kit.

Growing up, Judy's favorite toy was a microscope and her favorite pastime was exploring the outdoors near her Fort Worth, Texas, home. "I have loved nature since I was a child," she told Dunham. After obtaining her bachelor's degree, she taught high school biology before heading to South Africa to teach at a private all-boys school for six months. While there, she spent several weeks touring Kenya and Tanzania before returning to Texas to start graduate school. Judy loves to teach, which shows in the "Teacher of the Year" awards she received from Phi Theta Kappa in 1987 and the Southern Council of the Federation of Fly Fishers in 1990.

Teaching certainly has its advantages as well. Based in Dayton, Texas, just outside of Houston, Judy and Verne are able to spend their entire summers fishing for trout in Montana and Wyoming. "Judy thinks nothing of a day-long, 20-mile, belly-boat float down Montana's Bighorn River all alone," Chuck Tryon, an admiring friend, says. "She's quite a singular lady!"

A tireless advocate on behalf of conservation, she has also served in elected positions on the board of the International Federation of Fly Fishers, which honored her with their "Woman of the Year" award in 1993. "My interest in wildlife motivates me to be environmentally conscious," she relates in *The Atlantic Salmon Fly*. "In my flytying, I don't want to use materials from endangered species. Many tyers do, and that aspect of tying Atlantic salmon flies bothers me."

It's not so much the amount of time it takes to tie one Atlantic salmon fly as the years involved in mastering the technique. Perhaps more than anything, this particular breed of tiers seems to derive their satisfaction as much from the challenge of achieving perfection as from the stunning finished product that results. "I know what I am seeking to achieve in a salmon fly and I haven't been able to create the right one yet," Judy has explained of her driving passion. "One of my earlier flies is framed and hanging in my home. Every morning I look at it and think that I should throw it away. It makes me mad to see it. There are a dozen different things that I do not like about that fly. I go through the same thought process every day, and I guess I keep the fly to remind myself that I can do better."

She already has.

Page Rogers CONNECTICUT

When saltwater fly rodding took off like a rocket in recent years, Page Rogers was there with her series of original imitations designed to lure striped bass, Atlantic bonito, blue fish, and many of the other coldwater species that can be found on the flats between Maine and North Carolina.

Thanks to a revolutionary concept in the fly-tying world called product licensing, Page's feathery creations are now reproduced and distributed by Umpqua Feather Merchants, a highly regarded wholesale supplier. Only a short year ago, however, Page was spending most of her spare time trying to keep up with an overwhelming number of orders from the five tackle shops which she had been supplying exclusively. And with her full-time career as an Episcopal minister, she was growing increasingly frustrated that her fishing—which has always served her as a source of spiritual renewal—was quickly drifting away.

Aggravating the problem, of course, was the deluge of publicity Page's popular inshore saltwater patterns have received. She has been featured in almost every leading magazine, including *The Fly Fisherman*, *Saltwater Sportsman*, and

Saltwater Fly Fishing, as well as in the following books, just since 1994: George V. Roberts's *A Fly Fisher's Guide to Saltwater Naturals & Their Imitation*, Ed Mitchell's *Fly Fishing the Coast*, Bryan Peterson's *Modern Saltwater Fly Patterns*, and Deke Meyer's *Saltwater Fly Patterns*.

Nothing, however, tops the recent honor of having her collection of patterns exhibited with those of Carrie Stevens and Helen Shaw at the Peabody Museum of Natural History in New Haven, Connecticut. It is a remarkable distinction for this former art major who has been tying for only about a dozen years.

A fly fisher for over three decades, Page was raised in rural Durham, Connecticut, in a family in which her mother, sister, and brothers all fished. "I grew up fishing and singing in the church choir," she once joked. It was during a vacation on Martha's Vineyard soon after graduating from Yale Divinity School that she discovered her passion for saltwater fly fishing. She now spends up to eight weeks a year there, staying in the family home and exploring her favorite waters, always with the possibility that she will come home inspired to create a whole new pattern. "I've spent hours in my kayak on a saltwater pond watching the bait fish. I observe the colors of the fish. I watch how they swim, their shape in the water. Many people who make flies get the colors wrong, because they look at bait fish out of the water, and the fish are a different color than when they're in the water," she has said.

As Page exemplifies, great artists have always derived their inspiration from the science of life as filtered through creative eyes.

Other Significant Figures

One of the most celebrated fly tiers working today is Bonnie Harrop, who with her husband, Rene, established the

House of Harrop in Idaho in the early 1970s. Two of the last of a disappearing breed of commercial custom tiers in the United States, their artificials are renowned for their precision and consistency of quality.

There's nothing ordinary about Ruth Zinck of Canada, who has made an art out of tying flies with common materials like velvet ribbon and wrapping foam, all easily obtained through hobby shops and yarn and fabric stores. For natural materials, she scans roadsides for dead animals or birds and has been known to talk a zookeeper into gathering up the feathers from an emu cage. In 1988, she became one of the first women invited to demonstrate tying for the membership of the Federation of Fly Fishers and has appeared on their program every year since. An often-published fly-fishing writer as well as a tireless advocate for conservation, Ruth has also had the distinction of serving as an international director of the Federation for six years. And, yes, she fishes. As her friend Chuck Tryon recounted to me in a letter: "Ruth is as grand a lady as ever cast a fly. Probably somewhere near or in her seventies, she still wades her Canadian rivers and outfishes most men."

Fly Fisherman magazine calls Torill Kolbu "the first lady of fly tying" in Norway.[9] Only 31 years old, she has already achieved worldwide acclaim, including the honor of a front-page feature story in *Fly Fisherman*, for her innovative technique of crocheting her flies with a standard crochet hook. After taking first prize in a Norway competition in 1990, she won a bronze medal at the Quebec Atlantic salmon fly-tying world championships in 1991, followed by a silver medal in 1992, and four first-place awards in 1993. As the president of Quebec's competition noted in a letter to her: "Your technique of weaving the hair wing to the body is a great innovation that has not been seen in the last 25 years of fly tying." Since 1992, over 50 of her salmon and sea-trout patterns and more than 30 of her trout and grayling patterns have been reproduced by a major hook company through a Philippine factory, which allows Torill to concentrate her artistic attention on other revolutionary designs.

PART II

Women's Legacy in Big-Game Saltwater Angling

On the way up [to Nova Scotia, in 1936] I was told about fabulous Jordan Bay, the ladies' tuna fish pond. It was practically land locked, was only forty feet deep, and held many tuna, averaging from five hundred to eight hundred pounds. One had been caught by Faith Low a few days before weighing 749 pounds, which was then the world's record. This was something. Exactly one year ago I had caught the first tuna ever to be taken by a woman on rod and reel in Nova Scotia and now they were catching them over seven hundred pounds. In those early days the record kept changing every little while. I remember the former Mary K. Whitney had it for three days, then Mrs. Bill Chisholm from Cleveland broke it. The former Mrs. Kenneth Jenkins also caught a big tuna, although when I had seen her four months previously she had been in a cast because of a broken neck. The sport of deep-sea fishing took hold as quickly with women as with men.

—CHISIE FARRINGTON, *Women Can Fish*[1]

For most people, the phrase *big-game angling* conjures up one classic image: an angler buckled into a fighting chair at the back of a bobbing boat in the middle of a rolling sea, braced and tugging against the strength of a leaping marlin or some other exotic billfish or giant tuna in a quintessential contest of wills, native cunning, and dwindling patience. Invariably, that daring soul is assumed to be a man—rarely, if ever, a woman, as if women could not handle the mammoth tackle or possess the brute strength so often associated with pulling in the *big* fish.

But we now know that women were there all along. In fact, they were there before big-game angling officially became a sport in 1898:[2] On May 2, 1891, Mrs. George T. Stagg landed a 205-pound tarpon, measuring seven feet, three inches long, a feat she recounted in a little-known anthology of women's writings on angling, *The Gentlewoman's Book of Sports I*, published around 1892.[3]

"He was mounted, and Dr. Henshall, who has the fishing exhibition for the World's Fair, to be held in Chicago in 1893, has asked me to let him be placed in the show," she wrote, which certainly indicates it was a rare feat for the time.

For those thinking that Mrs. Stagg's remarkable catch was little more than a fluke, she had also brought in a 102.5-pound tarpon earlier that year. Furthermore, according to Mrs. Stagg in her essay, she was not the only female out trolling the high seas. Three other women had also taken tarpon exceeding 100 pounds each in 1891!

Four years later, in 1895, Lady Orford of England became the first woman of record to take two large tarpon in one day, each weighing 128 pounds, off the coast of Florida.[4] In 1900, Mrs. Jim Gardner, who was married to a popular Southern California guide, caught a 136-pound bluefin tuna unaided.[5]

We'll never know exactly what possessed these courageous women to venture out in those early years, even on a calm sea. We can only imagine how many days they drifted their baits waiting for a bite. Or how many tugs-of-war it took before they landed these notable catches. Or what must have been going through their minds as they stepped into their shallow wooden rowboats—hardly seagoing crafts by today's standards—in their ankle-length, long-sleeved dresses, with such an unorthodox mission in mind. Or how many of them never came back because a sudden storm turned a tranquil sea into an inevitable deathtrap.

Now figure in the fact that women were not allowed to join the Catalina Tuna Club or any of the other private angling enclaves created by men, no matter how many record-breaking fish they caught, and it's nothing short of miraculous that women toughed it out on rough seas to fish at all.

Yet they did. And at least by the 1920s, they had their admirers, if what happened to Mrs. Keith Spalding, the wife of a Catalina Tuna Club member, is any indication. There's no reason to believe that Mrs. Spalding set out to break anybody's record or that she intended to set off a furor which would reverberate throughout the big-game world. She merely went fishing, but she inadvertently got snagged in the "vanity [that] riddled big-game angling society in the early decades," as former *Field & Stream* saltwater editor George Reiger labels it in his book, *Profiles in Saltwater Angling*.[6] Reiger provides us with this rib-tickling account.

It seems that best-selling Western writer Zane Grey, also one of the most celebrated anglers of all time, had the biggest ego as well. "ZG permitted his obsession with swordfish and his boastfulness to lead to a grave indiscretion—an indiscretion that eventually cost him many friends, his reputation, and changed his personal life forever," Reiger writes. In 1920, Grey caught a

418-pound broadbill swordfish, then the most coveted of big-game fish. As a result, he "quickly became a nuisance around the club house as he recounted, over and over again, the minutest detail of his fight.... It got so bad that most Tuna Club members tried to avoid him, ducking down behind newspapers when he entered a room, or excusing themselves to run an errand in town when he sat down on the arms of their chairs.

"The following summer, 1921, Mrs. Keith Spalding, who never weighed more than 100 pounds in her life but was one of the finest anglerettes ever associated with the Tuna Club, landed a 426-pound broadbill," Reiger continues. "That evening nearly every TC member lined up in the vestibule of the clubhouse to call Zane Grey's home on the hill.

"They gave him the business — asking how far did he think Mrs. Spalding had rowed the winter before; suggesting that ZG should use Jergen's Lotion rather than saltwater on his hands; pointing out that Mrs. Spalding's fish had been hooked even farther from the heart than his had, and so forth.

"Zane Grey blew his cool. He declared that Mrs. Spalding could not have landed such a big fish by herself. She must have had help.

"That kind of angry comment was exactly what some club members had been waiting for. Ray R. Thomas, vice-president of the club that year, notified Grey that he must apologize to the club in writing or resign. Zane Grey did both," Reiger states.

Grey subsequently defended his honor in print in various wide-ranging journals, thus blowing this incidental dispute into a stormy issue within the entire saltwater world.

But, notes Reiger, "Zane Grey wasn't the only Tuna Club member plagued by Mrs. Spalding's proficiency." After spending several seasons going after a bluefin tuna on regulation light tackle, club member Jimmy Jump finally achieved his goal with a 101-pounder, only to be outdone a short time later by Mrs. Spalding with a 103-pounder on the prescribed 9-thread (27-pound test) line.

"Mrs. S. was one of the outstanding lady anglers of all times," Reiger declares. "Only nine Tuna Club members (including her husband) ever won as many as five buttons [then the highest distinction] for trophy fish. Had she been permitted to join the club, she would have been the tenth."

If only we knew more about these ace female anglers. But, unfortunately, those were the days when few journalists thought about profiling the men whose feats made it into the pages of angling history, much less the women whose feats didn't.

At least we have more than a glimpse into the lives of the women who fished during the Golden Age of big-game angling—the 1930s and 1940s—thanks to Chisie Farrington, who chronicled her own and her friends' big-game angling exploits in her book, *Women Can Fish*. And George Reiger's indispensable tome, along with more recent sources, finally allows us to recognize these women who set world records no one assumed possible, snatched away the most prestigious of tournament titles, pioneered revolutionary techniques on behalf of the sport, or simply committed their angling skills to progress marine science.

Whether they fished at the turn of the century, in the heyday of the sport during the 1930s and 1940s, or during the last few decades of dwindling stocks, women have always been able to bring in the big fish. And to their credit, women were also among the first to preach the wisdom of catch-and-release on the high seas, or there wouldn't be a sport called big-game angling today.

May we never again think of the angler at the back of a bobbing boat as only a man. Chances are, it was and is a woman.

CHAPTER 7

"The Anglerettes" of the 1930s and 1940s

CHISIE FARRINGTON

HELEN LERNER

AND OTHER SIGNIFICANT FIGURES

At a time when nothing more was expected of them than planning menus, playing bridge, and accompanying their wealthy husbands on around-the-world fishing expeditions, dozens of women eschewed their traditional roles as socialites in favor of trolling the high seas in pursuit of fish that routinely weighed between 600 and 900 pounds.

It was the Golden Age of big-game angling, when the oceans were flush with billfish and giant tuna. "These were wonderful years," Chisie Farrington, one of the premier anglers of this period, notes in her delightful 1951 book, *Women Can Fish.* "People were still experimenting, but big-game fishing was really coming into its own."[1]

It was also an era in which the big-game fraternity commonly referred to the women who brought in the big fish as *anglerettes*—"Mrs. Farrington's one of the finest anglerettes I've ever seen," guide Johnny Cass once told author George Reiger[2]—or simply by their married names. However dated such designations may seem today, these women were universally admired and even envied by those with egos healthy enough to withstand the competition, including their friend Ernest Hemingway. (Fortunately, Zane Grey was no longer around.)

What made them great—in fact, extraordinary—were several things. For one, they defied the prevailing mystique of the sport: that it took brute strength, more than endurance and finesse, to land fish many times an angler's own weight—especially since most of these women barely tipped the scales at 100 pounds themselves and were handling Paul Bunyan–sized tackle.

They invariably exhibited the patience of lacemakers in their pursuit of these marine trophies. "Don't think that you catch fish every time you go out," Chisie recounts. "One year I trolled twenty-one days from 8:30 A.M. until 6 P.M. for blue marlin. During that time I had only one blue marlin strike. I hooked it and lost the fish when the leader wire was out of the water."

They also never surrendered in the midst of a battle, no matter how long it took or the physical miseries they endured, before boating a fish. If they didn't make it back to shore in time for cocktails and dinner with their husbands and friends, so be it. If the fish broke off through no fault of their own, it happened to the best of anglers. But cutting the line just to end their physical distress? Inconceivable, as exemplified by Chisie's recollection of her doubts midway through the day of her most challenging encounter—a 10-hour and 25-minute fight with a 493-pound tuna:

At this point I thought I was crazy. What would I have if I landed this fish? Nothing but a cold, tired, dead fish that was not nearly as large as the one I had caught two days ago. Then why didn't I give up? I guess there was a certain amount of pride. I thought of all my friends who had built up my fishing and I didn't want to poop out on them. I thought to myself I will keep on going until I faint. I can't keep on going forever, eventually I must faint. But that cold air blowing in my face wouldn't let me faint, so I just kept on reeling the skiff up to the tuna and then the tuna would pull out more line. I could do nothing at all with him; then why didn't I give up? I thought of all the letters I could write, the Red

Cross work I could do, the things I could accomplish in the hours spent battling this d—n tuna. Then why didn't I give up? It was no crime to give up. I was a fool not to, but the longer I kept at it the madder I got, and the madder I got the more determined I got to boat the tuna if it [was] the last thing I ever did!

Indeed, what truly made these women remarkable was their dedication to the ethics of the sport, as established by the Catalina Tuna Club in 1895, wherein no part of the tackle except for the leader wire could be touched by anyone but the angler. And while there was certainly no way to prevent cheating, with only the angler and the crew in the boat, there was also no way that any of these women would have handed the rod over to someone else to finish their fights. They played by the rules because the rules made it a level playing field between the angler and the fish. But not everyone did, as Chisie recited in one telling account about an incident that took place in the early 1930s:

When I was at Palm Beach a group of us went sailfishing and as I was the only person on board who had ever caught one I felt like a maestro. We had been out about an hour when we ran into a school of them. The captain saw it, hooked one, and handed the rod to a man on board. I had heard this wasn't ethical but no one seemed to care. The man fought it for a while and got tired of it. No one else wanted to try his hand. I was very pleased, offered to take over, and after a little while brought the fish in. To this day it hangs in the man's office and he shows everyone the sailfish that he caught. I don't really think he knows the difference, but thank goodness there are not many who fish that way today.

Collectively, the anglerettes produced one of the most dazzling chapters in the legacy of women and angling. Individually, the two highlighted here, Chisie Farrington and Helen Lerner, were unequivocally the best of the best the sport has ever seen.

"Perfection! The real record is to take the first one, because if you catch the biggest fish, someone eventually is going to catch a bigger one," read Ernest Hemingway's congratulatory cable to his friend Chisie Farrington when she became the first woman to catch a broadbill swordfish off the coast of South America.

And indeed, establishing *firsts* would become the hallmark of Chisie's angling career in which she ultimately secured 11 world records (one men's and 10 women's).

In 1935, she was the first woman to catch a tuna on rod and reel in Nova Scotia, followed a year later by her "first really big fish," a 720-pound bluefin tuna in Nova Scotia's Jordan Bay. In 1939, she became the first woman to catch two marlin in one day off the coast of South America. That same year, after a five-hour and 40-minute fight, she brought in the 584-pound swordfish that produced Hemingway's accolade and broke Mrs. Keith Spalding's 426-pound broadbill record of 18 years before (the one that drove Zane Grey crazy).

Broadbill swordfish were in fact regarded as the ultimate saltwater challenge from the 1920s through the 1940s. Once dubbed "the greatest gladiator of them all" by Zane Grey, the broadbill was so difficult to catch that Grey himself landed only two during nine years of aggressively pursuing them. Chisie's husband, Kip, another top-flight angler, spent six years before getting his first one, and numerous others chased them for up to 15 years with no success. "Even Ernest Hemingway could be shaken in his devotion to giant blue marlin when conversation turned to the legendary broadbill swordfish," Reiger recounts in his book, *Profiles in Saltwater Angling*.[3]

The fact that Chisie caught *five* in just over a decade made her a legend in her own time. The fact that she was the

BIG-GAME "ANGLERETTE" CHISIE FARRINGTON ESTABLISHED
11 EXTRAORDINARY WORLD RECORDS DURING THE 1930S AND
1940S. SHE IS PICTURED HERE IN 1936 WITH HER "FIRST
REALLY BIG FISH," A 720-POUND BLUEFIN TUNA.

only female angler along with eight men to take two in one day—then considered the greatest saltwater feat possible—deserves Hall of Fame recognition. (It stretches the imagination to even picture this petite sliver of a woman hauling in a 396-pounder and a 659-pounder within hours of each other during a 1941 outing off the coast of Chile.) Not to be overlooked, Chisie was also one of only two women—Helen Lerner was the other—to take swordfish in both the Atlantic and Pacific oceans; only two men had done it. If Zane Grey had not died in 1939, he surely would have been green with envy!

How Chisie managed to do it all while plagued by a physical handicap is a testament to her fortitude. Born in 1908, the former Sara Houston Chisholm grew up in moderate circumstances, though there was apparently enough money for a trip abroad in 1925 at the age of 17. While in Paris, she contracted infantile paralysis (a polio-related virus) and was confined to bed for several months. "In the acute stages of infantile paralysis all I could move was my head from side to side, but I couldn't raise it from the pillow nor move my arms nor shake hands," she writes in *Women Can Fish*. For the rest of her life, Chisie coped with only partial strength in her right leg and hand, which made her long angling battles excruciatingly painful.

Chisie's first encounter with fishing occurred the same day she met her future husband, Kip Farrington. Kip was already well entrenched in the sport as both an accomplished angler and a book author. (He later became the saltwater editor of *Field & Stream*.) So important was fishing to their lives that Chisie and Kip married in 1934 only 10 days after announcing their engagement, "because the tuna would then be due in Ogunquit, Maine," she writes. Because of the times, such a whirlwind ceremony raised more than a few eyebrows. "My family were a bit amazed at having to set the date of our wedding according to the tuna and that Christmas every leading obstetrician sent us a card," she relates with amusement, "but after we produced nothing but tuna they finally gave up."

Though they had spent much of their four-year courtship bouncing around on churning seas, handling slimy fish was not exactly what Chisie had envisioned for her honeymoon: "Kip suggested we go chumming on our wedding trip. This sounded very romantic to me, but I hadn't caught on that it would mean grinding up mackerel off the Portland Lightship at 4 A.M. in a very rough sea." Another "fatal error," she wittily recalls, was presenting her new husband with a pair of Zeiss 7/50 binoculars: "On our drive up the Connecticut coast he spent most of the time looking out to sea over at the Montauk Light instead of looking at me." And then there was Kip's unusual wedding gift to her: "A fishing harness, which some of my friends didn't think a very appropriate gift."

But Chisie also knew she was fortunate to have a husband who treated her as an indispensable companion on his worldwide big-angling quests and who admired her remarkable angling skills. Even so, she couldn't help jesting that Kip's gifts over the years were exclusively fish-related, including two pins marking spectacular records, one of which was a diamond swordfish-shaped brooch. "These two pins are my favorite pieces of jewelry and I almost always have them on. Kip never forgot my first broadbill and ten years later he gave me an anniversary dinner for it. I was greatly touched but I told him I wished he could remember the date we were married as well as he could the dates we caught fish," she writes good-humoredly.

So prevalent was Chisie's presence in the sport that she appeared in 11 big-game angling films and authored stories for *Harper's Bazaar*, *Vogue*, and *Mademoiselle*. Despite her extraordinary angling achievements, her greatest enduring accomplishment was probably the publication of her 1951 book, *Women Can Fish*, mostly because it created the only extensive record of women's participation at that time, supplemented by long-lost photographs of many of the anglerettes with their mammoth catches.

Significant of the regard in which Chisie was held are the words that Francesca LaMonte, the Associate Curator of Fishes for the American Museum of Natural History, wrote in the foreword to *Women Can Fish*: "I am sure no one would dispute the statement that Chisie Farrington is the world's outstanding woman angler. But I am also sure that Chisie wouldn't want me to say so. However, anyone who reads this book cannot fail to see what those of us who know Chisie realize so well: she is a true sportsman, generous, unassuming, enduring, and an expert in her field."

Helen Lerner NEW YORK AND BIMINI

"Mrs. Lerner was the best anglerette I ever knew, and one of the best fishing people — man or woman — in salt water. I used to put the spyglasses on her while she was working a fish," Johnny Cass, one of the sport's renowned guides, told author George Reiger.[4]

Few women could shine on their own in the long shadow of Mike Lerner, whose personal legacy includes the designation of founding father of the International Game Fish Association. The only possible exception is his wife, the inimitable Helen Lerner.

The Lerners were considered Bimini's foremost angling couple at a time when that exotic Caribbean island was crawling with the sport's wealthiest and most glamorous angling gentry. Yet Helen was hardly your typical socialite wife. "She always had, and still has, house guests and household duties to attend to," Chisie notes in her book, "so she only fishes part of the day. She used to take a run out to the concrete ship, which is an old wreck not far from shore, where you can count on getting a boatload of small fish. On the way home she would make a circle out into the Gulf Stream and invariably pick up a blue marlin."

Although no account exists of how many records Helen set or how many fish she caught, her feats were clearly the measuring stick by which many anglers gauged their own performances. Over the years, she became the first woman to take a bluefin tuna on the European continent, the first to take nine tuna in one year, the first to catch a broadbill in both the Atlantic and Pacific oceans, and the first to take four different species of marlin. And she did it all while plagued with overwhelming seasickness.

Most telling of her prominence in the big-game angling world is the gold medal she received from France's Academie des Sports after World War II for catching the first giant tuna on rod and reel ever taken off the coast of Brittany. Only one other female had received this prestigious honor: Gertrude Ederle for becoming the first woman to swim the English Channel.

Anyone who came within casting distance of Helen's regal personality was inevitably swept up into her huge fan club. "Every guide who fished with her speaks of Mrs. Lerner with admiration," Reiger writes, "and on [one] occasion, she hooked a large marlin in midmorning and fought it skillfully for over seven hours. It grew dark, but still she kept on. Suddenly the fish rushed to the surface and in a final leap, threw the hook — as simple as that. Helen was perfectly calm. She just turned in her fighting chair and smiled at the others aboard."

Superseding Helen's phenomenal angling career, however, was what she and her husband, Mike, did to progress science. Beginning in 1936, setting world records for them was incidental

to a greater mission: providing the means and opportunity for the scientific community to conduct the first comprehensive field research on the diet and migratory patterns of the ocean's grandest game fish.

Their odyssey began the year before when Mike showed up on the doorstep of the American Museum of Natural History in New York with a large fish to donate for research. It was the beginning of a long association with the museum, resulting in seven major expeditions all over the world and the accrual of an unprecedented foundation of scientific knowledge, all financed and organized by the Lerners. During each months-long trip, Mike and Helen daily hauled in the specimens, all caught solely by rod and reel, which the museum's scientists (including Francesca LaMonte—see Chapter 13) subsequently spent much of the night dissecting on the spot or at a nearby makeshift laboratory. It was the first time that scientists had been given access to such prime specimens, since commercial fishermen always brought in their fish minus the head, fins, tail, and innards in order to conserve boat space.

The Lerner's many donations to the museum included mounted specimens for display in the galleries (which also served as teaching aids for succeeding classes of marine scientists before World War II) and a state-of-the-art marine laboratory they had constructed in Bimini ("something approaching a marine biologist's Shangri-la," notes Reiger), which became the museum's Caribbean field station. The laboratory allowed scientists from all over the world to study fish in their natural environment and share their findings with scientists in other fields, including human cancer research, which benefited from their observations of malignant tumors in fish.

In 1939, Mike embarked on an equally ambitious project: He created the International Game Fish Association, served as its president from 1940 to 1961, and underwrote its sizeable budget. It's not clear to what extent Helen was involved in the IGFA during those years, as it would have been inappropriate for the president's spouse to serve on the board of trustees. But, based on their other endeavors, she was undoubtedly assisting in some capacity. Far more important is the fact that the IGFA ranks today as the standard-bearer of the sport's integrity — including being the official arbiter of all world records — and a world leader in the conservation movement.

During World War II, the Lerners also toured the war front on behalf of the USO, screening their fishing films and staying up many a night until dawn talking fishing with the troops, who zealously welcomed the distraction from the harsh realities of their immediate future. And after the news spread that many downed pilots and crews stranded at sea were dying of starvation or thirst while safe on their rafts, Mike designed and financed a survival kit that included emergency fishing tackle.

Indisputably, no one has had a more profound or enduring impact on the sport of big-game angling than Mike and Helen Lerner.

Other Significant Figures

Sadly, little is known about the rest of the anglerettes of the 1930s and 1940s, except for their following moments of greatness:

Denny (Mrs. Ben) Crowinshield, who established the record for the biggest fish caught by a woman by 1948 (an 882-pound tuna), was renowned for her speed at pulling them in. She once boated a 601-pound tuna in one hour and 10 minutes and a 300-pounder in 10 minutes, although the leader broke on the latter when it reached the boat. But like a trooper, she apparently "laughed it off, saying she didn't want any midget anyway and shortly afterward had a 635-pounder in the boat in seventeen minutes flat!" recounts Reiger in his book. He also notes: "Whether she is rigging the baits, rigging the leader, running the boat, gaffing the fish, or just fishing herself, Mrs. Crowinshield is tops at it all. When Kip [Farrington] went fishing with her and her husband Ben off Palm Beach, Mrs. Crowinshield was already on the boat when the men arrived. She had fixed the baits for them and was ready to cast off."

Jo (Mrs. John) Manning caught more tuna off Nova Scotia than any other woman, including a 782-pounder, in fights that averaged six to seven hours. Her largest tuna, a 585-pounder and a 751-pounder, were taken in the very same day on rough seas! As Chisie raves in her book: "In 1946, at Nova Scotia, [Jo] had a tuna, which was thought would go over eight hundred fifty pounds, up to the boat in about an hour and forty-five minutes on 24-thread line [72-pound test]. Maybe it was over nine hundred pounds."

Additionally, Mrs. Henry Sears established a women's world record for a 704-pound blue marlin on 24-thread line. Mrs. Maurice Meyer held the women's world record for many years for an 818-pound tuna, which also happened to be the largest taken off the coast of Maine. Margot (Mrs. Bill) Lawrence, the wife of the well-known outdoors artist and illustrator, caught the largest fish in U.S. waters by a woman, a 499-pound tuna, in 1937. In 1950, Mrs. Eileen Brownson, then New Zealand's leading female angler, established the world record for the second-largest fish ever taken by a woman with a 846-pound black marlin caught off the coast of her native country. Mrs. Oliver C. Grinnell contributed the introduction to Connett's *American Big Game Fishing* and became the first woman to take a broadbill swordfish in the Atlantic.

Also of note on the international scene were Mrs. Nathan of Australia; Mrs. Enrique Pardo of Peru; Mrs. Carlos Badaracco, Mrs. Herberto Bohtlinck, Mrs. Pablo Bardin, and Norah Bohtlinck of Argentina; and Laurette Llavallol, Mrs. Jorge Prado, and Betty (Mrs. Mario) Osward of Brazil ("the only woman to have competed in the International Tuna Matches," according to Chisie).

In the United States, there was Mrs. Al Pfluger (wife of the well-known Miami taxidermist), Mrs. A. M. Whisnant, Mrs. Joe Gale and her daughter Miss Jane Gale, Mrs. John H. Egly (wife of the head of the Penn Fishing Tackle Manufacturing Co.), and Roma (Mrs. Frank) O'Brien, Jr. (wife of the president of Tycoon Rod & Fin-Nor Reel Co.).

CHAPTER 8

The Grande Dames of the Sea from the 1950s through the 1970s

EUGENIE MARRON

ANN KUNKEL

HELEN GRANT

AND OTHER SIGNIFICANT FIGURES

The 1950s in many ways marked a new era for women's legacy in big-game angling. Women streamed into the sport as an explosion of interest occurred particularly as a result of the formation of the International Women's Fishing Association (IWFA) in Palm Beach, Florida, in 1955. Many women also began fishing alone or in the company of other women, rather than solely with their spouses. And they were possibly the first voices in the crusade to end the recreational pillage of these great species, which were being decimated by a tournament world that refused to adopt catch-and-release policies.

Aside from their individual achievements, however, was the enormous prestige that accrued to women's place in the sport as a result of the exemplary ethical standards embraced by the membership of the IWFA, regardless of whether they were fishing their own women-only tournaments or others. Like The Women Flyfishers Club in the Catskills, the IWFA has fostered a unique camaraderie and pride of accomplishment among its members—in this case through a handful of competitions each year, the sharing of skills and knowledge, and a variety of special recognition awards. Admirably, among its other efforts on behalf of conservation, the group also maintains a scholarship fund to assist needy graduate students who are pursuing advanced degrees in the marine sciences. The IWFA is celebrating its 40th anniversary in 1995, and it's significant that the three revered women profiled here have all been active members most if not all of that time.

I believe you will agree that the regal presence which women brought to the sport during the 1950s through the 1970s makes them the grande dames of the sea. Certainly the women portrayed here are symbolic of the spirit and integrity of the many women who fished during that prolific era.

Eugenie Marron FLORIDA

"The sport of big-game fishing holds a dangerous fascination that has only one parallel elsewhere in life. Getting involved in it is like falling into the clutches of a jealous lover. From the day the involvement starts, your time, your thoughts, your energy and your money must all be dedicated to a single consuming cause," Eugenie Marron writes in her 1957 autobiographical book, *Albacora: The Search for the Giant Broadbill*.[1]

"Once I devoted years to mastering techniques in painting and sculpture. Today I am a painter who does not paint and a sculptor who does not sculpt. I fish," she continues.

"'It's terrible,' insist my friends, and even my mother. From the walls where they hang, the characters in my pictures seem to point accusing fingers at me. But I am very happy. My husband, Lou, and I have found a way to follow our first love, the sea, not idly or wastefully, but for a purpose. Together we fish for science."

Almost two decades after Mike and Helen Lerner facilitated the first of seven groundbreaking oceanic expeditions for the American Museum of Natural History, Eugenie and Lou Marron began dedicating their angling services to science by

EUGENIE MARRON, HERE IN 1954 WITH
A WORLD-RECORD 772-POUND SWORD-
FISH, DEVOTED HER ANGLING SKILLS TO
SCIENCE BY SPONSORING AND LEADING
A NUMBER OF MAJOR MARINE-RESEARCH
EXPEDITIONS WITH HER HUSBAND, LOU.

escorting the University of Miami's Marine Laboratory to a first-ever field study of the intriguing Humboldt Current in the Pacific Ocean in the early 1950s. Their mission not only opened the doors to unraveling the inexplicable mystery of El Niño (a sudden recurring warm current with a catastrophic effect on both climates and fish populations), it also allowed their guest scientists the opportunity to investigate such unknowns as the life cycle, migratory patterns, and historic evolution of billfish.

In addition, they were able to collect giant squid for a critical study on the chemistry of nerves being conducted by a professor of biology at the Massachusetts Institute of Technology. With Lou and Eugenie doing most of the fishing, the expedition yielded 41 striped marlin, 26 black marlin, and 11 albacora (broadbill swordfish) for dissection. They were also able to ship vast quantities of plankton to the University of Miami, air express central nerve columns from giant squid to MIT, and gather enough data on the Humboldt Current to serve the needs of oceanographers. "As a layman, I can hardly attempt properly to evaluate the scientific work which we have done, but of all the accomplishments of Lou's life and mine, this is the one of which we are most proud," Eugenie shares in her book.

Long before Eugenie and Lou set out to progress science, fishing had become the most important facet in their lives. It would lead them to many world records, including four for Eugenie in 1954—a 772-pound swordfish among them—and Lou's history-making achievement, a 1,182-pound swordfish, taken off the coast of Chile in 1953, which at that time was the largest game fish ever taken on rod and reel.

The Marrons first met at Columbia University, where Eugenie was working on a master's degree in fine arts and Lou was majoring in business administration. Both were raised in

New Jersey, where they continued to live after they married. Starting out as a real-estate developer, Lou was immediately successful in business, which allowed them to buy a secondhand Chris Craft. "The fishing bug first infected us in those early days, when moonlight fishing was satisfying in more ways than one. It was romantic and it was cheap. A big thrill for us then came on the night we caught a 91-pound shark, but the real transformation from normal girl to dedicated angler occurred in the middle of a party," Eugenie writes.

Eugenie always loved a good party, and at this one she was in the midst of belting out a tune while perched on the piano in her best black-velvet dress when a local New Jersey skipper waltzed into the room and announced that there were "tuna off to the nor'east." Lou got so excited that he turned to his wife with the proclamation, "Sounds great. Come on, Genie. Get down off the piano and get a move on." But it didn't sound so great to her. "If you think I'm going to go fishing at twelve o'clock on a Saturday night, Lou Marron, you can start thinking all over again," she retorted. But when he bid her a good time and said he would be back in the morning, Eugenie quickly leaped off the piano and shouted, "Wait! I'll finish singing on the ocean. Wait for me."

Once on board, Eugenie immediately went down to the cabin to find something more suitable to wear, but she found only a pair of dungarees. "So off came the dress and on went the pants and with that single speedy change of costume my whole life turned around," she writes. "I did not know or even suspect it at the moment, but from that time forward I was always fated to be more at home in jeans on a wildly tossing boat than at the finest party in the smoothest silks."

And what a night it was! Lou managed to bring in a 577-pound bluefin—which would have counted as a world record if the crew hadn't inadvertently touched the tackle—and Eugenie got a solid 430-pounder. "I was a sorry sight, with matted hair and a broken rib caused by the shoulder harness that we used in those days. But I had my fish! The State of New Jersey arranged for my fish to be mounted and soon began using it to attract tourists. It was the first giant tuna landed by a woman off the coast of the United States. 'See,' men in the state Chamber of Commerce proclaimed proudly, 'this is what a little woman caught. Can you imagine what a man can do, fishing off the Jersey shore?'" To Eugenie, however, "catching that first tuna was only the beginning of a long fishing career which led ultimately to our search for the giant swordfish."

While serving as the chairman of the board of the Coastal Oil Company in New Jersey, Lou had a severe heart attack at the age of 37, which would ultimately change their lives for the better. Four touch-and-go months of recovery followed, in which the Marrons were forced to reassess their priorities.

Wondering what he could and couldn't do under these new circumstances, Lou asked his doctor, "Suppose I play a quiet game of golf from time to time?"

According to Eugenie, the doctor earnestly replied, "Then I won't be responsible for what happens to you."

"What about fishing?" Lou then asked.

"The doctor undoubtedly thought of catching sunfish from a rowboat or sleeping near a lazy country stream," Eugenie recounts in a humorous passage.

Instead, as we now know, she and Lou set out on an odyssey that would take them all over the world in pursuit of giant tuna and their beloved albacora—a physically strenuous activity if ever there was one. "For whatever medical significance it may have, Lou's heart has been fine ever since," Eugenie happily reports. "In fact, several years ago when the physician finally learned what Lou had meant by fishing, it was he who almost suffered the coronary."

Around the late 1920s, Eugenie—like everyone else— began fishing with big tackle. But somewhere along the way, she sorted the whole thing out in her mind and decided that it wasn't a fair matchup between angler and fish unless she shifted to light tackle. "Some lines can stand 200 pounds of pressure before they break. Using them against fish has always struck me as being only one degree away from using depth bombs. Six-thread [18-pound test] line is more sporting," she explains in the book. It was so unique a departure from the norm that Chisie Farrington would note it in her 1951 angling memoir.

Eugenie and Lou also developed a predilection for the broadbill swordfish, which Eugenie equated to "the most involved, complex and intricate feat in the whole sport of fishing.... It is a humbling thing to consider the tenacity and the courage and the brave hearts that albacora show in mortal battle. My ribs have been cracked and my hands have been rubbed raw in fights against them. Without a doubt they are king of all the deep-sea game fish."

The Marrons also became avid conservationists, clearly a pioneering concept in the early 1950s. "Neither Lou nor I ever kill a fish unless it is to be used for food or for scientific examination. After enough years of catching everything that swims, the edge of excitement that comes from indiscriminately hauling in fish has been dulled."

So strong was the bond of big-game angling between Eugenie and Lou that they apparently harbored a fantasy of catching the biggest fish in the sea, which they privately dubbed "Bosco." In fact, when they returned from that first historic expedition to the Humboldt Current, Eugenie recounts that within "forty-eight hours out of the jungle of Ecuador, Lou climbed into white tie and tails and I squeezed into a tight, off-the-shoulder evening gown. Then we went to a charity ball at the Hotel Plaza in New York City. My hair was frizzled and my skin was blotched with flea bites, and some people close to me at dinner seemed to be staring in surprise. Only when Lou explained that I was suffering from a rare and virulent South American disease, closely allied to bubonic plague, did most of them turn away.

"Even in the bright and formal atmosphere of the Plaza, it was hard for either of us to put Bosco out of our minds. 'He's still roaming off Iquique,' I said abruptly, 'daring us to go back after him.'

"'Well, let's go back, then,' Lou said. 'Let's go back damn soon.'

"There was champagne in front of us and we lifted our glasses.

"'To the day we find Bosco,' Lou said."

To which, Eugenie whimsically concluded: "I hope the old bones hold out."

Indeed, they did. Before Lou Marron passed away in 1966, there were so many expeditions that today, at age 95, Eugenie has lost count.

And significant of her honored place within the sport, she was inducted into the International Women's Fishing Association's Hall of Fame in 1988.

Ann Kunkel FLORIDA

In 1994, Ann Kunkel became only the second woman in the 56-year history of the International Game Fish Association elected to its board of trustees. (The first was Francesca LaMonte, the organization's founding secretary in 1939 and a trustee from 1973 to 1978.) Ann's appointment represents one of the most prestigious honors bestowed upon a woman by the angling world in recent memory, and one that had been rightfully earned.

In 1983, she became only the eighth woman inducted into the International Women's Fishing Association's Hall of Fame. She was also a founding member of this exemplary nonprofit organization in 1955, served as its president twice, and currently sits on its board of directors.

As an angler, she has landed nine swordfish and 110 giant bluefin tunas, all but five of which were tagged and released. Of her swordfish catches, two were taken on the same day, which has long been regarded as one of the sport's outstanding feats. Ann has also fished all over the world, including for salmon in Canada and Norway (as a fly fisher) and for billfish in the Bahamas, Mexico, Panama, and Ecuador, as well as for bonefish, tarpon, and bass.

Perhaps the greatest contribution Ann will make to the IGFA's continuing efforts to save the world's fisheries will be as an ardent defender of catch-and-release. "I am rabid on the subject of conservation," she says of her conversion after putting five giant tuna on the dock at one of the first tournaments she fished. She still shudders at the thought of the waste she witnessed in Acapulco in 1957, when she watched the boats taxi in from a sailfish tournament and one by one dump their booty on the dock, then hang each one up to be photographed with the lucky angler. Ann remembers thinking that one fake fish would serve the same purpose. "Why kill all those good fish, just to have your picture taken? Really, I got incensed. I was so horrified and so shocked. There must have been thirty or forty fish piled up like cordwood." She just happened to be there with the IFWA, which had just held its own event. "We were the first group ever to fish Acapulco and demand that we release the fish. They'd never heard of it, *catching and releasing fish.*"

One of the first practitioners of tag-and-release, a cooperative effort between scientists and anglers to chart the oceanic wanderings and growth of billfish and tuna, Ann bursts with pride about the bluefin tuna she tagged four years ago which was subsequently caught by a Japanese longliner off the coast of Uruguay. Frank Mather of the Woods Hole Oceanographic Institute in Massachusetts, a leading sponsor of the program, called her up with the news. "He said, 'Annie, it's the first time we ever knew that [these tuna] went down there,'" she proudly reports.

Ann grew up in New York and settled in Palm Beach in the 1960s. She is a passionate outdoorswoman, and golf, tennis, and horseback riding have also always ranked high in her life. In addition, she is a licensed pilot accomplished at landing on the sea as well as land.

In the early 1950s, she began vacationing in South Florida and got her first taste of big-game angling, going out with a friend several times a week for what she calls "fun fishing." Then one day she ran into her friend Ginny Sherwood, who asked her to join the newly formed International Women's Fishing Association. And through the IWFA, Ann discovered her passion for giant tuna, which has given her "a feeling of accomplishment." Tuna are known for testing an angler's patience and skill, but this five-foot, five-inch angler insists that "it's not muscle" that counts; it's "knowing how to do it. You've got to have good legs, because you have to pump the fish up."

Ann was widowed twice, and her second husband did not fish. In fact, he was bewildered by her fascination with the pastime. "He was a golfer and tennis player," she says, noting that he did give it a try once or twice. "But he didn't like it. He said he didn't have the patience. 'I don't know how you can stand there and not do anything, not get anything. Nothing happens. You just drag bait around.' And I said, 'But it's exciting *when* you do,'" she recalls with a gleeful laugh.

Undaunted, Ann began hiring charters on her own or with friends. "Very often, I'd call up a boat and go on out. Then it cost only $65 a day." But times have changed, she notes. Now it costs $400 or $500 a day and "the fish aren't there. You pay that for a lousy little bonito!" On occasion, she would also take off for extended trips on a rented charter by herself while her husband waited patiently at home.

Although many of her friends had their own boat and crew, Ann shrewdly decided she didn't want the responsibility or the expense. "This way, if I went over to the islands [Bimini or the Bahamas] and something happened to the boat, I could just get off and say, 'Sorry,'" she laughs. "[Then] it wasn't my expense if they blew an engine or something happened."

When asked if she had children, Ann is quick to respond with a laugh, "*Fortunately*, I do not. I said fortunately, not *un*fortunately." As she explains, "I've done so much in my life. I'm always interested in doing something new. When I was young, all I wanted to do was fly. Well, I got my pilot's license and I was licensed to land in sea. And I used to ride horseback four or five hours a day. And I played golf and tennis. I just love sports and the outdoors. When you've got children, you can't be doing that."

Twelve years ago, Ann took up fly fishing, which she learned from her good friend Joan Wulff, who once led classes on various kinds of fishing for the IWFA membership while Joan was living in Miami during the 1960s. "She's a fabulous teacher! I can't say enough about her," Ann enthuses, adding, "A lot of people know how to do things, but they can't teach it to someone else. Joan can."

Ask Ann Kunkel why fishing has been a foremost priority in her life for so many decades and she responds with an answer as simple as a Zen Buddhist riddle but no less complex in its meaning: "When I go fishing, I leave my troubles behind me."

Legend has it that Herbert Hoover once grumbled, "She always beat me," in reference to Helen Grant's towering skills behind a saltwater rod. Helen, however, modestly insists that she did nothing more than knock Hoover off the big board (where the members' records were posted) outside the Angler's Club in the Florida Keys when she bested his bonefish catch in the 1950s. "I was half sorry and half excited," she chuckles of the occasion, adding that Hoover took to calling her "*that* woman. He didn't cotton to me much after that."

Actually, this is not entirely true. On at least one occasion, during a dinner party in his honor, Hoover insisted of the seating arrangements, "Have *that* woman come sit by me." And why not? Hoover fished every chance he could get and undoubtedly saw an opportunity to pick the brains of one of the best.

At 78 years old, Helen Grant still plays tennis three times a week, but she doesn't fish anymore. When she did, particularly in the 1960s and 1970s, no one topped her, at least not for long, in the big-game tournament world in Palm Beach, the Florida Keys, and the Bahamas.

"Because of her enduring fishing career and her unparalleled angling feats, Helen Grant has long been recognized as the 'queen' of tournament fishing," notes *Motor Boating & Sailing*[2] magazine in 1992, the last year that Helen competed in the Gold Cup Invitational Billfish Tournament in Palm Beach, representing the Key Largo Anglers Club with her son, Richard Grant, Jr. (Naturally, no one was surprised that the Grants came in second, despite the fact that Helen was already in her 70s.)

Helen is honestly stumped when asked how many tournaments she's won over the years. Query her about her winning secrets, and she's quick to say, "I just happened to fish so many that I won a lot." Win a lot she did, as evidenced by the barrels of trophies stored in her basement, along with the engraved silver trays, bowls, and Steuben crystal displayed in the sitting room of her South Florida home. And those are only the ones she got to take home. Others are still hanging around the sponsoring clubhouses or on view in public places like the Miami International Airport—home, allegedly, to a large trophy she was once awarded by the prestigious Miami Metropolitan Fishing Tournament.

According to Dade Thornton in *Tournament Digest* magazine, "Her log of first places is astonishing."[3] Among them are her prizes in Jo Jo DelGuercio's short-lived Women's World Championship in 1970, the World Championship Billfish Tournament in the Keys in 1971, the West Palm Beach Silver Sailfish Derby in 1971 and 1976 (in which she was twice designated as "Overall Winner"), and the Chub Cay Blue Marlin Tournament (since known as the Club Championship) in 1972. In the latter, she won with the 643-pound *remains* of a marlin that sharks had decimated after a five-hour battle.

And the list goes on: In 1973, she took home the "Beiniche Trophy" for catching the most sailfish in one day and became the High Point Lady Angler in the Big Game Club's White Marlin Tournament. In 1976, she became the only woman with the distinction of earning a spot in the top 10 and the designation of "World Class Angler" in the annual World Release Championship, as well as first place at the all-important Sailfish Tournament in Palm Beach. She got top honors at the Chub Members Tournament in 1981 and 1983, bringing in 15 of the 30 fish caught in the latter. Fishing with her son Rick, she also won the famous His and Hers Tournament in 1976, 1980, 1985, and 1988.

And, adds Thornton, "The coveted Chub Cay Individual Championship Trophy 'belongs' to Helen also. [It is] given to

PRESIDENT HERBERT HOOVER
ALLEGEDLY ONCE GRUMBLED OF
HELEN GRANT'S PHENOMENAL
ANGLING SKILLS: "SHE ALWAYS
BEAT ME."

the member who scores the most points for the year in all the Chub Cay tournaments. Helen's name is on the carved Marlin Perpetual that stays in the bar five times—in 1972, '76, '80, '81, and '83. The closest to that record is DelGuercio, who won it three times. Helen also won the Chub Cay Grand Slam Award so many times—three in 1970—that Henry Bryer had to quit giving away Fin Nor reels every time she won it."

In fact, it was at Chub Cay that "her reputation as Queen of Anglers was carved in marble," states Thornton. "Helen was and is a superb tennis player, golfer and skeet shooter and Cat Cay, with all of those amenities, was a frequent stop. At the Cat Cay Tri-Lympics (which unfortunately had a very short tenure) she won both the skeet and the golf but wound up with the Hard Luck Trophy overall because of a miscue in the fishing division."

Though billfish would become her passion, Helen grew up fly fishing for trout in Wyoming with her father. "I loved it. We always went to a ranch for the summers. My brothers liked the wrangling and all that, and I liked the fishing," she says. She started "serious" fishing in the 1950s in the Florida Keys at the invitation of a friend from the Key Largo Club who took her out for what would become a memorable day. She not only caught a sailfish and "loved it, [but] from then on I was just hooked. And then I did more and more."

Helen and her husband, Richard, joined the Key Largo Club, bought a 34-foot Hatteras, and hired a well-regarded skipper, Earl Smith. "Helen had a good teacher. Earl had worked as mate for the legendary Tommy Giffard and passed many of the innovative techniques he learned from Tommy (including kite fishing) on to Helen," writes Thornton.

But fishing would never grab hold of Richard like it did Helen. "Richard was a good angler, he didn't want to pursue it all the time like I did. He was a sailor," she explains. On the other hand, Helen "didn't like sailing, and I would go, but I felt sort of guilty about it [for not going more often]. But, then, I didn't. I think it's boring as anything," she lightheartedly admits.

It was obvious almost from the start that Richard was never going to be her fishing pal, though they otherwise had a wonderful marriage. "His idea of fishing was to go out late in the morning and come home early in the afternoon," she reflects fondly. "That didn't fit well with me. My idea was to go out early and come home as late as they'd allow me, 'till dark. Oh, I loved it!" Richard was also often detained in Dayton, Ohio, managing the family business. But, she says, he "didn't mind" that she fished all the time. "He was proud of my fishing."

Multiple-day tournaments, Helen soon realized, gave her an excuse to fish more "because you have to go and you have to stay, unless you're deathly sick or something. And then, of course, I got the bug and wanted to go anyway." As luck would have it, Helen's son, Richard Jr., inherited her angling gene and grew up to become a frequent tournament partner, and for at least a decade they became the team to beat.

When Helen wasn't caught up in the heat of competition, she often fished with her female friends, including Ann Kunkel and Faith Igleheart. Mostly, however, she fished solo with her own crew. All in all, she says, she can count on one hand the number of days she did *not* fish in a year's time. "I never got scared and I never got sick, so I really fished more than I should have," she reflects with guilty delight.

Like so many of the other women who devoted their lives to big-game angling, Helen is tiny — only five feet, four inches tall and about 110 pounds. "People ask, 'How can you catch these big fish?' Well, you don't have to be big. You can be small but coordinated."

Her longest struggle behind a rod was 11 hours with a big blue marlin that she ultimately lost in the dark just before midnight. "That happens. And if you don't expect it, you're going to be mighty disappointed," she says matter-of-factly.

Besides her other herculean feats, Helen has also set two world records on mere 12-pound test: an 83-pound Atlantic sailfish in 1965 (a record that stood for 17 years) and a 148-pound mako (which she landed in five minutes) in 1969.

Today, Helen is an ardent believer in catch-and-release. "In the early days, we kept our fish and put them on the dock. And I shudder now when I think about it. But nobody thought of the results. Nobody thought about conservation. We just gradually eased into that. And now, of course, we don't kill *any* fish unless it's for a [world] record."

Returning for a moment to that time, some four decades ago, when Helen broke Hoover's standing bonefish record: It seems she dashed off a letter to her father ("He was proud of all the things I did"), who sent back his congratulations with a check for $1,000. And Helen would have us believe it was no big deal!

Other Significant Figures

As a way of honoring all those women who went after the big fish during the 1950s through the 1970s, following are some of the phenomenal world records established during this era — all of which were still standing at the end of 1994!

Black marlin: Mrs. Charles E. Hughes's 1,525-pounder on 130-pound line in Peru in 1954; Kay Mulholland's 874-pounder on 50-pound line in Australia in 1976; and Georgett Douwma's 1,323-pounder on 80-pound line in Australia in 1977.

Blue marlin: Marguerite H. Barry's 406-pounder on 20-pound line in Mexico in 1972 and Carmina Miller's 401-pounder on 20-pound line in Puerto Rico in 1975.

Mako sharks: Audrey Cohen's 911.75 pounder on 130-pound line off Palm Beach in 1962 and Florence Lotierzo's 880-pounder on 80-pound line in the Bahamas in 1964.

Thresher sharks: Mrs. V. Brown's 729-pounder on 130-pound line in New Zealand in 1959.

Tiger sharks: Mrs. Robert Dyer's 1,314-pounder on 130-pound line in Australia in 1953 and June Irene Turnbull's 1,173-pounder on 80-pound line in Australia in 1963.

White sharks: Mrs. Robert Dyer remarkably still holds four of the five line classes with a 912-pounder on 80-pound line in 1954; and a 369-pounder on 20-pound line, an 803-pounder on 30-pound line, and an 801-pounder on 50-pound line, all in 1957. All four were taken in Australia.

Swordfish: Mrs. D. A. Allison's 759-pounder on 130-pound line in Chile in 1959; Dorothea L. Cassullo's 492.25-pounder on 50-pound line off Montauk Point, New York, in 1959; and Eugenie Marron's 772-pounder on 80-pound line in Chile in 1954.

Bluefin tuna: Mrs. Phyllis Bass's 518-pounder on 50-pound line in the Bahamas in 1950; Patricia M. Kuhnle's 884-pounder on 80-pound line in Canada in 1977; and Colette Perras's 1,170-pounder on 130-pound line in Canada in 1978.

CHAPTER 9

A Living Legend: Marsha Bierman

FLORIDA

If big-game angling were an Olympic event, Marsha Bierman would have a fistful of gold medals. But then, where would she find the space to display them? The den of her South Florida home is already chockful of towering trophies, silver trays, and engraved plaques, all signifying her place as the preeminent billfish angler in the world. Indeed, these symbols of her success eventually might have taken over the house if she hadn't retired from tournament competition in 1984 out of concern for the impact that these events were having on an ever-scarcer resource.

From the moment she burst upon the tournament scene as the first woman ever to win the prestigious Bahamas Billfish Championship in 1977, there has never been a time in Marsha's two-decade career in which she wasn't making angling history. To date she has over 2,000 billfish catches to her name. Of the highly prized blue and black marlin, few have topped her current tally of over 280. She has also tagged and released all nine of the billfish species and all three of the major tunas on standup tackle, making her the first and only angler ever to do so.

More importantly, with the exception of the fish she caught prior to 1985 and her world record established in 1986,

Marsha has released every one of these majestic creatures back to the sea. It is an unparalleled feat made possible only because of her revolutionary short-rod standup technique, which allows her to bring these mammoth fish to the boat within 15 to 30 minutes of hookup, greatly enhancing their chances of survival over traditional hours-long battles.

She is also the only angler to date to catch and release two "granders" on standup 50-pound tackle: a blue marlin estimated at just under 1,300 pounds in 1991 (which she landed in only 18 minutes) and a black marlin weighing approximately 1,100 pounds in 1992 (which she brought to the boat in only 23 minutes). Both would have qualified for IGFA world records if she had opted to kill them for the necessary official weigh-in back at the dock.

Exemplary of her unwavering commitment to protecting our future stocks of these great game fish, Marsha has received dozens of honors over the years, including five from the Billfish Foundation. So it came as a surprise to no one that when the International Game Fish Association created its annual Conservation Award in 1992, Marsha was in the original group of five selected to receive the sport's equivalent of the motion-picture industry's Academy Award.

Between 1986 and 1993, the last year of the list's existence, Marsha Bierman was named the number one offshore angler in the world on *Power and Motoryacht* magazine's annual Top Ten list for an astounding six out of eight years, the last five consecutively.

And that's only the short list of what this dedicated angler has achieved.

In a sport in which boats cost upwards of a million dollars — not counting the yearly expense of a captain and crew and everything else — it is no less remarkable that Marsha has been able to participate at all, much less fish her way to the top.

It hasn't been easy, requiring her to hold down a full-time job as a stockbroker until 1989, when she became the first and only offshore angler in the history of the sport with major endorsement contracts and paid speaking engagements all over the world.

Hard as it is to imagine, Marsha had never fished, even for trout, until the late 1960s when she met her husband, Leonard Bierman. Lenny not only introduced her to big-game angling but has also served as her technical wizard and indispensable crew member from the beginning.

"It was certainly nothing I planned for early in life," she says of her present career, which has her jetting regularly between continents as an ambassador for the sport. In fact, until 1971, it seemed like Marsha would be trapped in a succession of secretarial jobs forever.

Few would guess that this sophisticated woman spent her childhood on a 380-acre working farm in the Catskill Mountains of New York, a place so remote that she was one of only 18 in her high school graduating class. She had neither been to a city nor known anyone who had lived in one until she went away to college eight miles away.

Like a lot of young women in the 1960s, she obtained a two-year degree in the secretarial sciences, her only ambition being to find a decent paying job. After graduation, she headed to Rochester, New York, with several of her college chums and began working in the secretarial pool of a major corporation. "It was a horrible experience," she laughs. "I was a little too flashy for the place. My skirts were too short. My earrings were too long. I wore too much lipstick. I didn't walk right. You were supposed to be in the secretarial pool from two to eight weeks. I think I was there eight months. Then they put me in industrial relations where I worked on death certificates."

After spending a week vacationing in Florida with some of her girlfriends, Marsha returned to submit her resignation—"probably right before they fired me," she laughs again. "I think it was a neck and neck race"—and relocated to Fort Lauderdale. But work was hard to come by, so she returned to New York state and ultimately headed to the Big Apple, which she had visited only once.

It was the scariest thing she had ever done, she says. Mustering up her small-town courage, she turned to the want ads with the aim of finding a "glamour" job. Amazingly, she did, as the secretary to New York Jets head football coach Weeb Ewbank and his staff—even though she had seen exactly one football game in her life.

Two years later, in 1966, she moved to Florida to take a similar position with Miami Dolphins' head coach George Wilson, where she remained another three years. During that time she also met Lenny, who would serve as the catalyst towards her new destiny.

Finally, in 1969, she took her last position as a secretary, this time working for a stockbroker at a large firm. Notably, two years later when he quit, Marsha obtained her license and took over his accounts, working as a stockbroker herself until 1989.

Meanwhile, Marsha and Lenny began spending all of their spare time acquiring, restoring, and selling boats as a means of financing their quickly consuming passion for offshore angling. On weekends, they cruised over to Bimini, 46 miles away, to participate in tournaments—but not, surprisingly, to fish themselves. For the first six years, Marsha served as the captain and Lenny as the crew, with various friends filling in as the angler. With Marsha responsible for finding the fish as well as servicing the engines and preparing and cleaning the boat, and Lenny in charge of preparing the baits and tackle, they usually returned home each Sunday night with at least one marlin, and each season they usually won one or more area tournament titles.

In 1975, they were finally able to hire a captain, and Marsha moved over into the fighting chair. "Lenny never cared about being the angler," she explains, although he has certainly caught his share of the big fish, particularly tuna, over the years. By the end of her first season, Marsha picked up a special recognition trophy from the Bimini Big Game Club for the most outstanding fishing season ever recorded by an individual in the Bahamas. By 1976, she had landed some 60-odd marlin, but she still did not regard herself as "an accomplished angler"— although the rest of the world soon would.

In 1977, on a lark, Marsha entered the Bimini Blue Marlin Tournament, the fourth tournament of the five-leg Bahamas Billfish Championship, the most prestigious of the tournament circuits at the time. Of course it was with no presumptions of winning, since the title was awarded on the basis of cumulative points from all five week-long events, and most of the other contenders had fished the first three legs. But, with Lenny as her crew, Marsha fished all week and came in first place on that leg. One can only imagine the talk at the awards banquet that night about how this virtual unknown seemed to have all the luck.

Two weeks later she entered the final leg, the Chub Cay Summer Blue Marlin Tournament, and brought in an astounding three marlin on her first day, throwing a pall over the event for everyone else. Then someone else caught a single fish that outweighed all three of hers, pushing Marsha into second place. The third day another contender came in with two, and she was bumped down to third place. But on the last day, Marsha caught one more, a catch that was enough to hand her the tournament title. What's more, in spite of participating in only the circuit's final two events, she also won the Bahamas Billfish Championship crown—making her the first woman ever to win that most coveted of titles. Suddenly the name of the Cinderella angler, who had delivered two back-to-back knockout punches against the crème de la crème of the tournament world, was being wired around the world. It was the kind of story that sports editors lap up: something like a player from the minor leagues who somehow gets himself into the World Series, then amazingly bats the home run that secures the pennant.

A lot of people would have stayed at that victory banquet after picking up their trophy to bask in the limelight. Instead, Lenny and Marsha left right away to join the group they considered their peers—the contenders' captains and crews, who were dining nearby. As the Biermans walked into the room, those hardy veterans rose in a spontaneous ovation; after all, this "Rocky" was not that long ago one of their own. "To this day, that was one of the highlights of my life," Marsha says, still moved by the tribute.

During the next few years, while the Biermans continued to hold down full-time jobs, Marsha kept up her winning streak with major victories at prominent events like the Hemingway Tournament in 1983 as well as the International Gold Cup Tournament in Palm Beach and the one-time Bum Phillips Celebrity Invitational All Billfish Tournament in the Bahamas in 1984. Also in 1984, she caught her 100th marlin in Bimini, a feat which has never been surpassed, even by Bimini's adopted son, Ernest Hemingway. Not surprisingly, this big-game champ with working-class roots was suddenly being profiled on national television shows like "P.M. Magazine."

And 1984 was also the year that Marsha exited the lucrative arena of offshore tournament fishing after she and Lenny began

INTERNATIONAL ANGLING CELEBRITY MARSHA BIERMAN
HAS LANDED (AND RELEASED) OVER 2,000 BILLFISH—
TWO OF THEM OVER 1,000 POUNDS EACH—USING HER
REVOLUTIONARY SHORT-ROD STANDUP TECHNIQUE.

searching their souls about the depleting populations of billfish throughout the world. Never again, they vowed, would they kill a fish intentionally. And since all of the tournaments required contenders to deliver their catches to the dock, they felt they had no choice but to depart from competition. It cannot be overstated what a conscientious, leading-edge decision they had made. It would be years before a mass consciousness about conservation would ultimately permeate the sport. And Marsha's winnings had been important to financing her big-game angling passion, which remains out of reach of the middle class because of the exorbitant expense involved.

"They're so majestic," she says. "Once you've seen a marlin come out of the water and realize the power involved to get something that massive out of the water just by wiggling its tail, to me it's just breathtaking. I don't know anybody who's ever caught one that doesn't feel that way. But why that same person can kill them in this day and age, I don't know. I guess it's called bragging rights. I guess they don't think people will believe them if they don't."

Only once since that momentous decision has Marsha breached her "no kill" policy: in order to establish an IGFA world record for a 218.5-pound blue marlin on 16-pound test. And, she says, she's regretted it ever since. "It didn't make me feel warm and fuzzy at all," she declares. "Afterwards, it was like, 'For what? For my name in a book?' The record was quickly beaten by somebody else and by somebody else again." There's no doubt, says Mike Leech, the president of the International Game Fish Association and one of her ardent admirers, the official record book would be filled with Marsha's catches if she had not opted to let them go.

Leech, in fact, can remember one occasion when both he and Marsha were participating in a tournament in which a $90,000 Mercedes was at stake for the biggest fish. Much prestige would also accrue to the winning crew that brought it in. "Marsha said, 'If I catch one that big, there's going to be a fight on the boat, because I'm going to release it and the crew is going to want to keep it.'" No matter where she went, the temptation was always there: kill the fish, take home the booty. But she stood her ground.

It's hard to say how long Marsha would have been able to maintain her stature in the sport without the limelight of tournament victories if she hadn't read a magazine article in 1986 describing the short rods that had been developed for the long-range charters working out of San Diego. Only five feet long versus the traditional 7½-foot "sticks" used by big-game anglers, these short rods had been designed to maximize the rod leverage needed to boat tuna in a matter of minutes so that 40 or 50 anglers could fish for these notorious fighters at one time. But no one had ever thought of applying the same principle to billfish.

Inspired, Marsha bought a couple of short rods at a Florida Keys tackle shop, then headed with Lenny to St. Thomas for a test run. But she had never seen one in action, so it wasn't a very successful trial. The gimbal belt—a hard plastic apron that cradles the rod butt, allowing the angler to stand rather than sit—didn't fit. The pumping action she had always employed from the fighting chair was not only ineffective, but it actually put more stress on her lower back, leaving her in excruciating pain. "I got my technique pretty early on," she says, "because I hurt myself." But she didn't give up.

After having the rod butts shortened, she returned to St. Thomas for another trial run, still with less than satisfactory results. Clearly in physical agony, Marsha was asked by a female friend why she continued. "Well, I was doing it because at that point it had become a challenge," Marsha recalls. *A real challenge. I wanted to conquer it, I guess, because I'm not a quitter. I see* things through, if I can. I didn't want it to get the better of me. When we had a captain, his way of getting me to do things was to say, 'Well, a man can do it.' And I could do anything if he said that, which generally had to do with varnishing or sanding or some kind of manual labor."

She had also grown tired of fishing from a fighting chair. "I had found that it didn't have a lot of challenge, and that is the end result of what I'm fishing for," she says. "The sport, to me, is testing myself." Now, if she were to sit down, "I'd feel like I was cheating," she laughs.

In the end, Lenny designed a special line of short rods and Marsha developed her now-famous standup technique including her "pelvic tilt," adapted from the stance that weight lifters have long used to protect their backs. And she began training like an athlete to build up her body strength, running or speed walking eight to 12 miles a day for endurance, supplemented by low-impact aerobics and weight lifting. Notably, the late Jo Jo Del Guercio is the only other offshore angler known to incorporate a body-building regimen into his fishing. "I've gone fishing with guys in their early 20s who run, and they'll say to me, 'My God, you're in good shape,' after they've been huffin' and puffin' 10 or 15 minutes into reeling in a fish on the standup technique," she says.

Marsha also switched to lighter tackle, exclusively employing 50 pounds or less (versus the more common 80 pounds or higher), which she manipulates by manually applying additional drag with her free hand. Not only does it enhance the challenge for the angler, she says, but it also seems to induce the fish to surrender more quickly, thus improving its rate of survival upon release.

Within a couple of years, the name Marsha Bierman was synonymous with the short-rod standup technique. Without intending to, the Biermans had revolutionized a sport which had remained largely unchanged for half a century except in terms of boat innovations. The woman who had previously made her name pulling in tournament titles was now pulling in huge fish in 15 to 30 minutes without the aid of a fighting chair. Anyone doubting her standing in the sport only had to turn to the annual Top Ten list released by *Power and Motoryacht* magazine.

In the late 1980s, the Biermans produced the first how-to videos for the sport, featuring Marsha demonstrating her technique. In 1989, she received the first endorsement contract, with one of the world's leading offshore rod manufacturers, which also issued a short-rod design onto the mass market that Lenny had been instrumentally involved in designing. And as she traveled the world sharing her standup secrets at packed seminars in places like Australia, New Zealand, Singapore, and South America, short-rod sales surged to nearly 70 percent of the offshore rod market.

Her star rose even higher when, in 1991, Marsha became the first angler to catch a grander on 50-pound standup tackle — a Pacific blue marlin estimated at just under 1,300 pounds, which she brought to the boat in 18 minutes flat. A year later she did it again off the Great Barrier Reef in Australia with a black marlin weighing more than 1,100 pounds. Of course, both fish were tagged and released, for which the IGFA honored her with a special commendation in lieu of the official world records she would have had if she had killed them.

She also began her television career, appearing as a guest host on the Nashville Network's "Celebrity Outdoors" series for one season. At the same time, she was being profiled on ESPN's "Tournament Trails" and other shows.

Throughout it all, Marsha has kept up her crusade on behalf of conservation, preaching the need for catch-and-release through her seminars, videos, and television appearances. In

1993, she finally achieved one of her longtime goals by capturing, tagging, and releasing two swordfish off Venezuela, thus giving her the distinction of releasing every one of the world's billfish species on standup tackle. It has been occasions like this, which are certain to garner international media attention, that have probably done more to convert trophy hunters into enlightened preservationists than the steady stream of pamphlets and mailings put out by nonprofit organizations—though both efforts are crucially needed.

It seems truly symbolic of the paramount role that women have taken on behalf of the preservation of our future fisheries that Marsha Bierman was one of three woman out of a total of five people selected to receive the International Game Fish Association's first annual Conservation Award in 1992.

Also, like Kelly Watt in fly fishing, and Linda England and Fredda Lee in the bass world, Marsha has joined an elite group of women who have their own televised fishing series. Since 1994 she has been co-hosting "Blue Water Challenge" with veteran actor Robert Fuller, allowing viewers to witness Marsha in action with her standup technique while visiting such billfish hotspots as Venezuela, St. Thomas, Cozumel, Puerto Rico, Australia, Costa Rica, and Panama.

Preparation has always been the backbone of Marsha's success. Long before there were video cameras, Lenny filmed her in action so she could analyze her own technique, a learning tool she picked up from her years working for professional football teams, which have traditionally relied on training films. Both perfectionists, she and Lenny also leave nothing to chance when it comes to her baits and tackle. Throughout the year, they stock their freezers with mackerel, mullet, and ballyhoo which they've either caught themselves or acquired from local commercial fishermen. They also keep an ongoing computer log of when the line on each reel was changed, how much was spooled on, and what action it has seen. Each reel is also numbered so the log can reflect what fish were caught on each. Prior to each trip, old line is stripped off and new line is tested for its breaking strength before being spooled on, hooks are modified and sharpened, leaders constructed, and rod guides checked to make sure they are turning smoothly, along with the endless other details that the average angler takes for granted when they stock their tackle box and head for the water.

"I'd have to say that most of my successes were indirectly reflective of Lenny," Marsha insists. "It has been his attention to detail and his coaching and teaching as we went along that led to my successes. I mean, I certainly didn't do it all by myself."

Even with Lenny's indispensable assistance, however, it is Marsha alone who races against the clock as she makes hundreds of quick decisions in the heat of the confrontation about when to pump and how much drag to apply before she's reached the limits of her tackle. In the end, all the preparation that goes into the complex equation called big-game angling comes down to only one thing: the test of wills between a woman in physical and mental fighting shape and a fish weighing as much as 10 times her own weight.

Even so, Marsha cannot remember the number of times she's been asked over the years, "Who helped you?" It's a question that has faded away as her reputation has soared. Well, almost. She still laughs about an encounter in South America several years ago at the end of a two and one-half day fishing trip. She, Lenny, and a male friend had just arrived back at the hotel, where they were introduced to a press entourage from a local angling magazine who were apparently unaware of Marsha's eminence in the sport. "How many marlins did you catch?" one of them asked Lenny. "Fifteen," Lenny answered.

The questioner then turned to Marsha and asked in a patronizing tone: "And did *you* get to catch one?" "Yes," she responded, trying to keep a straight face, "all fifteen."

When I think of what Marsha Bierman has done on behalf of women and conservation, I also can't help thinking how proud the "Anglerettes" would have been to know that their deeply held principles and passion have survived to the present generation.

CHAPTER 10

Women Making Big-Game History Today

Deborah Maddux Dunaway

Terri Kittredge Andrews

Sandra Storer Donahue

AND OTHER SIGNIFICANT FIGURES

We can exult in the prominence that women have achieved in the world of offshore angling today. In a sport in which perseverance and dedication are as essential as skill and stamina in bringing in the big fish, scores of women have excelled in the global arena of world records and tournament victories.

Among those to be praised for their profound impact on the sport are ...

Deborah Maddux Dunaway TEXAS

Imagine tangling with a 303-pound blue marlin for five straight hours with only 12-pound test line between you and the fish. Or struggling to hold on to a 381-pound black marlin for nine hours and 45 minutes with only 16-pound test. For a petite 45-year-old angler named Deborah Maddux Dunaway—who also catches her fish standing up with only a gimbal belt on which to rest her rod butt—the only challenge in angling is the one in which the odds favor the fish.

On April 10, 1993, Deborah became the first angler in sportfishing history to hold all nine IGFA billfish world records, one for each species in both the Atlantic and Pacific oceans. Suddenly this former Houston legal secretary, who had never fished for big game prior to 1985, had accomplished what no other angler had done in a lifetime of fishing. She had scaled the Mt. Everest of the offshore world, a feat for which the International Game Fish Association presented her with its loftiest of distinctions: Angler of the Year.

By the end of 1994, Deborah had acquired an astounding 30 world records, 22 of them for billfish. She is unquestionably one of the most extraordinary offshore anglers of all time—and not just for the fact that she has apparently set more billfish records than any other angler, but also because all but two of these records were for fish taken on two- to 16-pound test—an incredible 16 of them on two- and four-pound test line! Anyone not familiar with line classes need only know that two-pound test is the equivalent of a couple strands of hair, and four-pound test just slightly thicker. One false move in a multi-hour tug-of-war and that fish will be gone as quickly as it hooked up. Even for trout or bass, few anglers employ line as delicate as the two- to four-pound test on which Deborah pulled in a 102-pound sailfish and a 142.8-pound striped marlin, respectively!

"The best coach, the best cockpit crew in the world won't enable just anyone to catch fish twice her weight on line that isn't strong enough to make good dental floss," Ken Grissom of *The Houston Post* wrote in 1993 of Deborah's rare skill. "You have to be a world-class angler, with lightning reflexes and a deft touch."[1]

There's no doubt that Deborah discovered what was apparently her destiny in life when she met her husband, Jerry Dunaway, an offshore billfish angler since 1969 and a leading world-record-holder himself. Through Jerry's astute counseling, she was out of the gate like a thoroughbred, catching a 300-pound blue marlin on 130-pound test in just her first season. A year later she switched her allegiance to light and ultralight tackle and began her personal quest for world records—garnering five in 1986.

In 1987, she produced two records: a 239-pound black marlin on eight-pound test line in Panama, "a record which will be hard to beat,"[2] announced *Motor Boating and Sailing* magazine at the time, and a 273-pound blue marlin in St. Thomas on 16-pound test. There would have been a third blue marlin for the record books, too, if she hadn't intentionally broken the line after six hours of excruciating pain. "That was the last fish I have ever broken off," she says, resolutely. "Everybody [her husband and crew] was extremely upset with me. And, of course, I immediately regretted it. Just maybe I could have taken a little more pain." When she grabbed five more records in 1988 off Africa's Ivory Coast and Senegal as well as the Cape Verde Islands, *Motor Boating & Sailing* magazine named her its "Rookie of the Year."[3] Then came the distinction of having accrued more billfish world records than any other single person in the history of the sport, with a 109.75-pound sailfish in Costa Rica in 1989.

Some people would have relaxed at that point and rested on their laurels, but not Deborah. In 1991, she racked up another three records, one of them a 303-pound Pacific blue marlin on 12-pound test caught in Costa Rica after a five-hour struggle, a feat which led the IGFA to hail the event as a "milestone in angling history. With this catch, Deborah has become the only person in history, man or woman, to simultaneously hold world records for eight of the nine billfish species. The only one to escape her is the spearfish."

She established seven more records in 1992, but it was not until she caught her 26.5-pound spearfish on four-pound test in Kona, Hawaii, in 1993, at the end of a three and one-half hour fight aboard the *Humdinger* with Captain Jeff Fay, that Deborah had reached the pinnacle of offshore achievements. She not only

IN 1993, DEBORAH MADDUX DUNAWAY BECAME THE FIRST ANGLER IN SPORT-FISHING HISTORY TO HOLD ALL NINE IGFA BILLFISH WORLD RECORDS, ONE FOR EACH SPECIES IN BOTH THE ATLANTIC AND PACIFIC OCEANS.

had all nine billfish records, but all were current (although several have been broken by other anglers since).

Once again, a lot of anglers might have stopped there. But even today Deborah shows no signs of slowing down. In 1994, she added two more records. The most significant was for a 381-pound black marlin on 16-pound line, a world record she had tenaciously chased for eight years and had many times come close to setting. Determined to finally succeed, Deborah gave it everything she had and more during the relentless nine-hour, 45-minute fight. It was "the most exhausting and nerve-wracking thing I have ever done in my life," she shared in the IGFA's membership newsletter, *The International Angler.* "I got so tired I believed I couldn't go on.... I went from standing up for 5 hours, to the chair for a couple of hours and then to sitting on the foot rest of the chair so I could stand up faster when the fish got close." By the time it was landed, she recounts, "I was just crying. I don't know if I was crying because I thought the fish had got away, because I was happy, or because I knew I wouldn't have to try for this record any more.... After reflecting on why I was crying that night, it was because I don't have to do it again!"[4]

Contrary to the popular belief that serious record contenders like Deborah simply go fishing a lot and just happen to catch a record-breaker, the Dunaways plan out everything at least two years in advance. Deborah and Jerry set goals of the records they hope to establish. Once on-site, multiple rods are rigged up with different line classes, depending on which records they hope to secure. And only after their captain gauges its size from the bridge to ensure that a particular fish is a record contender do the Dunaways grab a specific rod and attempt to hook up. "This is a team sport," Deborah insists of her success. "My crew is responsible for each one of these records in terms of doing their part. I believe that I have the finest crew and the best coach in the world." Besides Jerry's consistent support, Deborah is quick to credit Captain Trevor Cockle, who aided her in 24 of her world records, along with Captain Skip Smith, who skippers the Dunaways' 48-foot *Hooker* wherever they go.

Both committed conservationists, the Dunaways "do everything we can possibly do not to waste the fish," Deborah says of those which make the record books. "And [while] we personally may not eat that fish, we see to it that someone gets it." Most often, that means it will end up on the tables of an African village or other remote community where it will be most appreciated.

More than anything, Deborah says, her fishing has given her the confidence to believe in herself. "My husband has taught me you really can do anything you set your mind to. If you go after it, and you want it bad enough, you can accomplish it. You have to stay with it. It may not come easy. You have to work very hard for it. And you have to want it. But you can accomplish it."

Of course the same could be said about accomplishment in general. Deborah just happened to pick big-game angling as the focus of her life. "It's just something that I enjoy," she says, adding with a laugh, "I don't quilt."

Terri Kittredge Andrews PANAMA

In the late 1920s, big-game angler and best-selling author Zane Grey discovered one of the mother lodes of the world's billfish fisheries, Panama's Pinas Bay, along with its baitfish-rich reef which bears his name today. Since the mid-1970s, Terri Kittridge Andrews has served as the steward of its bounty, both as an ardent conservationist and proprietor of the world-renowned Tropic Star Lodge.

Running what many regard as the premier billfish fishing resort in the world is only one aspect of why the saltwater world holds Terri in high esteem. One of the most accomplished light- and ultralight-tackle anglers, Terri has set nine difficult IGFA world records, eight of them on 16-pound test or less, including an 83-pound sailfish on four-pound test line. And that's not counting the 450-pound marlin on 20-pound test line that never made the record books because she chose to release it instead.

The Darien Jungle of Panama is not the sort of place one expects to find an American woman, especially one with a small child, even with her husband right there to assist her in the complex operation of a resort boasting a fleet of boats and a staff of more than 60, many of them natives.

Located approximately 150 miles from Panama City — actually a one-hour plane ride, as there are no roads — the Tropic Star Resort sits smack dab in "National Geographic" country on a 1,500-acre spread facing Pinas Bay. Besides its fine, five-course cuisine and luxury accommodations, the primary draw, of course, is the more than 120 world records which have been established here by visiting anglers and the abundance of black, blue, and striped marlin as well as Pacific sailfish that make fishing its waters almost like throwing out a worm on a hatchery-stocked trout pond. Built in the early 1960s by a wealthy Texan, every board and stick of furniture was originally brought in by barge. Terri's father, Conway Kittredge, was actually the resort's third owner. "He just fell in love with the property when he first saw it," Terri told *Yachting* magazine in 1986. "He realized that a place like this could never be duplicated today. He knew that it wouldn't make a lot of money, but he couldn't resist it."[5]

Initially, Terri concentrated on bookings from her home base in Orlando, Florida, then took over the chore of managing the place on-site. Today, the resort is typically full, but it wasn't always so. Terri remembers too vividly their struggle to survive "the Noriega years," a fiscally dark time when the nervous political climate kept their regulars away.

Under Terri's watchful eye, the resort is run as smoothly as a Navy vessel. *Yachting* magazine has hailed it as possibly "the world's most extraordinary fishing resort";[6] *Marlin* magazine has called it "one of the touchstones of the international big game circuit";[7] and *Fly Fishing Saltwater* has equated its daily dinners, which are prepared by a native chef, as "rivaling those of some of San Francisco's finest restaurants."[8] There have also been recent profiles on such television shows as ESPN's "Walker's Cay Chronicles," "Jim and Kelly Watt's Fly Fishing Video Magazine," and "Mark Sosin's Saltwater Journal," as well as PBS's "Nature."

Also because of Terri, Tropic Star Lodge has been cited as a world leader in conservation by the Billfish Foundation for its aggressive tagging program, which aids marine scientists in tracking the migratory patterns of these magnificent species. Moreover, to encourage guests to get more individually involved in conservation, the resort offered to pay the foundation's membership dues for one year for each of their guests in 1995.

Terri herself has also served as a distinguished IGFA representative since 1981 and a delegate to the IGFA World Fishing Conference in France in 1984, and she has actively campaigned the Panamanian government about the need to regulate illegal commercial fishing within the 200-mile limit. And through her encouragement, her guests predominantly practice catch-and-release.

Clearly, if it wasn't for a caretaker like Terri Kittredge Andrews, the Zane Grey Reef and its renowned billfish fishery would exist today only as part of the folklore of the past.

"Ernest Hemingway would never have believed it. If he could gather one more time with the guys around the bar at the Compleat Angler and they told him one of the most prestigious prizes in the hairy-chested world of big game sport fishing had been won by a good-looking blonde with a dancer's figure and firey-red fingernail polish, he'd think they'd been too long in the rum punch," declared one sportswriter whose sentiments are right on the mark.

There's no doubt Hemingway would have been dazzled that a second woman had won the most prestigious title in tournament fishing, the 1985 Bahamas Billfish Championship, following Marsha Bierman's grab of the crown from left field in 1977.

But probably more than anything, Hemingway would have relished Sandy's photo-finish upset victory as the long shot that only a betting fool might have placed money on. After all, she was in seventh place going into the last day of the final leg of the five-tournament series. The night before, she had even told a fellow competitor that it would take a miracle for her to win, since the outcome of the event rested on bringing in a fish weighing over 400 pounds in order to best the front-runner. So sure was everyone that this event was as good as over that the officials began tabulating the results at 2 P.M., with two hours to spare. After 20 feverish days of tournament trolling without a marlin in sight, Sandy was convinced it was over too. She stood by that day thinking more about what she would wear to the cocktail party that night and what provisions she would need for her next fishing trip than about the tournament in progress.

And then, from seemingly nowhere, a blue marlin exploded from the water and grabbed her bait, just 20 minutes before the officials would have been announcing the winner. Like a prizefighter, Sandy leaped into action. Moments later, her son,

In 1985, Sandra Storer Donahue
became only the second woman in
the history of the Bahamas
Billfish Championship to win that
prestigious title.

Captain Scott Storer, radioed into the tournament headquarters that Sandy had hooked up and was still in the running.

And for the next four hours, it was a matchup of wit and stamina between this former high school cheerleader and a fish at least three times her own weight—even through a torrential downpour that would have sent saner souls fleeing into the cabin. At one point, the tournament officials radioed back, "We're all here at the cocktail party waiting for you. How much longer do you think it will take you to boat that fish?"

"Sorry, no way to know," Scott responded.

One can only imagine the cheers when Sandy's fish weighed in at 485 pounds, making her the overall victor. "I had fought that fish so long and so hard," she later laughed, "I had worn the seat out of my bathing suit."

Sandy had not only achieved every offshore angler's dream, but she could also dispense with another personal goal. It seems she had also told her fellow competitor the night before that she "was going to keep on fishing until I was 85 years old if I had to and that if it was the last thing I ever did, I was going to win the championship."

Determination aside, perhaps the most amazing part of Sandy's victory was the fact that she had been big-game fishing for only six years. A native Floridian, Sandy had grown up fishing from bays and bridges around Miami but didn't get bitten with the billfish bug until years later when she and her then-husband bought their first boat. While her husband's film-production company kept him too tied up to fish more than occasionally, for Sandy it became an obsession. "You don't wake up one morning and say I'm going marlin fishing," she explained of her unlikely career in an interview with *Motor Boating & Sailing* magazine in 1985. "You catch a sailfish and then another, and the next thing you fish a tournament and get a marlin on. And that's the ultimate."[9]

Having achieved her goal of winning the Bahamas Billfish Championship, Sandy switched to light tackle and began pursuing world records in 1986, beginning with one for a 231-pound blue marlin on 16-pound test that same year.

Today, Sandy doesn't go after the trophies like she once did, although she still turns out for the annual Hatteras-Bertram Shootout in the Bahamas. But with her second husband, fishing remains a major part of her life. This is, after all, the woman who once said, "It was as if I'd found what I'd been born to do."

Other Significant Figures

Also among the best the sport has ever produced are Barbara Immergut and Diane Mellish of New York; Pam Basco of Texas; Jocelyn Everette and Cherie Waroquiers of Hawaii; Marg Love, Liz Hogan, Christine Perez, Ruth Stoky, Cheri Ann Matthews, and Janeen Davis of Florida; Gene Duval of Virginia; and Carmina Miller of Puerto Rico, to mention but a few.

Among women's recent moments of greatness on the tournament scene ...

Susan Troubetzkoy won the 1992 Gold Cup Invitational Billfish Tournament in Palm Beach, Florida, after fishing for only two years. Combined with her string of wins in 1991, *Motor Boating & Sailing* magazine designated her the heir apparent to Helen Grant.[10]

In 1990, Sharon Torruella of Puerto Rico became the first woman in the 37-year history of the Club Nautico de San Juan's International Blue Marlin Fishing Tournament to win the oldest title in tournament fishing. Significantly, the feat landed her on *Power and Motoryacht* magazine's Top Ten list that year. It also marked the last time Sharon would kill a marlin.

In 1993, Myrtice Peacock won the Bahamas Billfish Championship, followed a year later with the distinction of catching the second-largest blue marlin ever in the history of that historic event — with an 885-pounder.

Also in 1993, Donna Robinson beat out 304 other anglers to win the Port Antonio Marlin Tournament in Jamaica. According to the IGFA's *World Record Game Fishes*,[11] she became the first woman to catch eight blue marlin in a tournament and to set a Jamaican record by releasing seven blues in a tournament. And she has twice caught four blue marlin in one day during a competitive event.

Sixteen-year-old Heidi Mason, who established her first world record at the age of 11, had a phenomenal 1993 as well. Besides establishing the standing world record for a 463-pound hammerhead shark on 80-pound line, she subsequently won a string of tournament titles, including the Miami Mini Met Tourney's release division and the designation of Met Master Angler for Women.

In 1994, Sue Stolzman of Hawaii became the first woman to win Kona's World Cup Blue Marlin Championship in its 10-year history, competing against many of the world's best anglers and captains. Also in Hawaii that same year, team leader Pam McLaughlin led the Hawaii Big Game Fishing Club to a first-place victory in Kailua-Kona's Record Setters Light Tackle Tournament; Pam herself won top individual angler.

And then there was Sandra (Honey) Beazley's 1994 spectacular win at the Lizard Island Black Marlin Classic in Australia, in which she tagged and released 10 black marlin.

Among the most significant world records set by women which were still standing by the end of 1994 are ...

Blue marlin: Marg Love's 295-pounder on eight-pound line in 1992 and her 266-pounder on 12-pound line in 1993, both in the Virgin Islands.

Black marlin: Kay Mulholland's 998-pounder on 20-pound line in 1982 and Jill Hooper's 814-pounder on 30-pound line in 1983, both in Australia.

Mako sharks: Cheryl Adams's 634-pounder on 30-pound line in Australia in 1992; and a tie between Joy Clements's 697-pounder in New Zealand in 1986 and Lesley Martin's 698-pounder in Australia in 1987, both on 50-pound line.

Thresher sharks: Jocelyn J. Everette's 302-pounder on 30-pound line in Hawaii in 1994 and Dianne North's 802-pounder on 80-pound line in New Zealand in 1981.

Tiger sharks: Leanne Grieves 1,208-pounder in Australia on 30-pound line in 1989.

Swordfish: Cherie Waroquiers's 267-pounder in Hawaii on 30-pound line in 1988 and Marg Love's phenomenal two-record whammy in 1993 within four days of each other in South Africa: a 283-pounder on 20-pound line and a 266-pounder on 12-pound line!

White sharks: Janet Forester not only bested Mrs. Robert Dyer's 1,052-pound record of 40 years before with a 1,164-pounder on 130-pound line in Australia, but it also ranked as the biggest fish caught by a woman in 1994.

PART III

Women's Legacy in Bass Fishing

My mom used to tell me when I was little, "Oh, honey, someday you're going to grow up and meet some dark handsome man, and he'll marry you and he'll love you so much and he'll put you on a pedestal." The joke around our house is that I didn't know the pedestal would be on the deck of a bass boat.

—KATHY MAGERS, ROCKWALL, TEXAS

For better or worse, fishing to me is what gambling is to many: I'm addicted. Often I don't hear what people are saying to me: I'm going fishing in my mind and have room for nothing else. Many times housework, dirty dishes, and dirty clothes pile up while I'm off on a binge. Sometimes my child has to find another way to get to football practice because Mom has succumbed and gone fishing, again!

—CAROL CRAUN, LOCKESBURG, ARKANSAS, QUOTED IN

Women's Sports and Fitness MAGAZINE, 1984

A lot of people read for relaxation. A lot of people love to swim. A lot of people [love] to travel. I love to fish. . . . I've heard that every day you fish, you add seven years to your life.

—LUCY LOWRY, PENSACOLA, FLORIDA

I raised three boys and they spent a lot of time fishing. My youngest thought our boat was a playpen. They're all grown and have their families now, and I believe the experience of quality time we spent camping and fishing contributed to make them all better family-oriented men.

—MARY LIPKA, HAZELWOOD, MISSOURI

When you encounter them delivering your mail, checking your groceries, doing your hair, or working behind a desk in some office, you would never suspect that these seemingly ordinary women haul bass boats thousands of miles, stampede across huge reservoirs with the throttles wide open on their sleek 200-horsepower chariots, or spend as much time shopping for fishing tackle as they do for clothes. Together with the women who have already shed their past occupations for careers as bass pros, they are the glorified Bass'n Gals.

Years before the creators of the motion picture *A Field of Dreams* coined the phrase, "Build it and they will come," Sugar Ferris did exactly that. In 1976, she created Bass'n Gal, the first and only national fishing organization for women. By early 1977, she had launched her acclaimed tournament trail, which for the last 18 years has pulled in up to 200 women to each event, as if they were following a pied piper from state to state. Indeed, the history of women and bass fishing is virtually synonymous with the history of Bass'n Gal, the dominant force for women in the sport then and now.

Today, Bass'n Gal ranks as one of the largest angling organizations in the world, with over 30,000 individual members, 100 affiliated clubs, and a national tournament circuit consisting of five invitational competitions leading to a Super Bowl–like season finale, the Classic Star world championship.

Sugar Ferris has said that it's important for women to create their own traditions and histories, and Bass'n Gal is a testament to the fact that she has. A religious-like fervor permeates the organization, from the national trail on down. For $18 a year ($15 for first-timers), members devour each issue of the organization's bimonthly magazine with a zeal commonly accorded a new Danielle Steel novel. They tune in to "The Bass'n Gal Tour," a cable-television series featuring tournament highlights, like it was a top-rated prime-time sitcom. They also turn out for Bass'n Gal club events, as well as other local tournaments, proudly touting their affiliation with the organization like it was a badge of honor. Similar to avid sports fans everywhere, they have also adopted their own set of heroines and role models: the women who have fished their way into stardom on Bass'n Gal's national tour.

Leading the list is Chris Houston of Cookson, Oklahoma, the unsurpassed champion of women's competitive bass fishing with 17 titles, all exclusively from the Bass'n Gal trail. Among the other distinguished female bass greats—each with multiple titles—are Burma Thomas of Scottsboro, Alabama; Linda England of Old Hickory, Tennessee; rising star Pam Martin of Bainbridge, Georgia; Betty Haire of Charlotte, North Carolina; and Lucy Mize of Ben Lomond, Arkansas. And certainly keeping everyone on their toes have been the likes of titleholders

Rhonda Wilcox of Malakoff, Texas; Vojai Reed of Broken Bow, Oklahoma; Jeanette Storey of Murray, Kentucky; Penny Berryman of Dardanelle, Arkansas; Sherrie Brubaker of Westlake, Louisiana; Mary Satterfield of Findlay, Illinois; Linda Hughes of Hixson, Tennessee; Joy Scott of Van Buren, Arkansas; Kathy Magers of Rockwall, Texas; and Mary Ann Martin of Clewiston, Florida. Notably, they are only some of the women who have excelled on the trail over the years. (See the Appendices for a list of Bass'n Gal All-Time Earners.) It is also important to point out that most of these women were simultaneously accumulating titles on a second all-women's professional trail called Lady Bass, which existed from 1986 to 1993.

The life of a national Bass'n Gal competitor is not all that different from the one a woman golf pro leads. They're both on the road a lot. They both spend a lot of time practicing between matches. And they both have to win at least some of their events, or their work quickly becomes an extremely expensive hobby. Many would say, however, that for a Bass'n Gal contender the commitment is particularly daunting.

Bass'n Gal events are scheduled at different major reservoirs and rivers throughout the season so that no one contender has enough of a home-court advantage to affect the final standings. The competitions are predominantly scattered throughout the South and Midwest, with an occasional visit to places like upstate New York, subjecting every contender to the long-distance drives—often 12 hours or more—required to fish the entire circuit, with a boat in tow. Any contender worth her weight in lures also averages between 150 to 250 days on the water, as practice is first and foremost the chief ingredient of winning.

There's also the universe of knowledge required to outwit one of the wiliest, moodiest, and most unpredictable game fishes in the world. Bass'n Gals need the equivalent of a master's degree in the science of lures to keep up with the hundreds of types and colors on the market, each with its own unique action and retrieval techniques. The bottom line, of course, is knowing how to cast and retrieve the lures, at what depths they work, and which baits to use for varying degrees of water clarity and under what weather conditions. If a Bass'n Gal doesn't know all of these things, she might as well stay home. Complicating the issue is the array of rods, reels, lines, and other paraphernalia she must acquire and tame in order to maintain a cutting edge while the clock is ticking down on any tournament day.

Winning an event, a feat which automatically endows the victor with a brand-new Ranger boat and trailer, is, of course, each Bass'n Gal's primary goal, along with making it into the Classic. But out of a field of 150 to 200 contenders, there is usually only one winner, so placing "in the money" is critical to offsetting the tremendous expense of competing. While entry fees are relatively modest, at only $200 or $300 per invitational, the cost of fishing the entire tour still costs $1,100 a season. If the Bass'n Gal doesn't have major sponsors, she will have to purchase a state-of-the-art bass boat equipped with a 150- to 200-horsepower outboard motor, aerated livewell, sophisticated electronics for gauging depths and locating fish, electric trolling motor, plus a trailer and other accessories—along with a reliable tow vehicle to pull it. Even without the vehicle, the package can easily run over $25,000. Add to that the additional expenses of insurance, ongoing maintenance, fishing tackle, and out-of-pocket costs of $600 to $1,000 per event for gas, motel, and food. If she "pre-fishes" the tournament location for additional practice time, which most competitors do, out-of-pocket expenses can easily double.

Then there's the weather! You'll never see a Bass'n Gal coming in early as a result of eight-foot swells, blistering heat, ice, snow, thunderstorms, pelting rain, or hail. Even when she's confronted with a life-threatening lightning storm or tornado, only with great reluctance will she abandon a honey hole of hungry big lunkers and seek safety.

Most amazing of all is the fact that the majority of Bass'n Gal contenders are over the age of 40. If she's done nothing else, Sugar has created a unique tradition for women in which age and physical prowess seem to have no bearing. Where else will you find women in their 50s to 70s, balancing themselves in a standing position on a rolling craft for up to eight hours, casting several thousand times in the course of a tournament day, trailering a boat alone on congested freeways and lonely back roads, or fixing a flat tire or motor in a pinch? Nowhere but on the Bass'n Gal trail.

Why do they do it? "Competing expands their horizons," Sugar Ferris proudly explains. "It also gives them time to themselves. I think we all need that. It's something they can do totally without any interference—you know, women all their lives have been told exactly what they need to do, until the women's movement came along. But when a Bass'n Gal is on the water, she has to make all those decisions herself. So it's really an expansion of her personality."

In 1967, when Ray Scott essentially invented the bass tournament fishing movement by creating a set of cheat-proof rules and founding his Bass Anglers Sportsman Society (BASS), women were never expected to invade one of the last bastions of male society: the megabucks world of professional bass competitions.[1] In fact, until 1991 women were excluded from the big daddy of trails, BASS's multimillion-dollar circuit, for reasons of "sexual privacy"—so its male competitors could answer the call of nature without the inhibition of female partners in their boats. Of course, women had been fishing local and regional co-ed tournaments since the early 1960s without complaints, so they were totally mystified by BASS's rules.

Chances are women would not be allowed on the BASS trail today if the Army Corps of Engineers had not issued an order in 1991 for BASS to either open its doors to the opposite sex or face a prohibition against holding its events on Corps-regulated reservoirs — some of the best bass-fishing waters in the South. BASS relented, and Vojai Reed of Broken Bow, Oklahoma, became the first woman to fish one of their events. Then 55, this Bass'n Gal world champion (1984) and Angler of the Year (1989) finished a respectable 58th in a field of 234, despite what must have been a very intense week.

A few months later, Conny Jenkins of Knob Noster, Missouri, then 36 years old and another Bass'n Gal veteran, became the second woman to compete in a BASS event. In reference to the age-old dispute that had kept women out of the tournament in the first place, one nationally syndicated writer mused at the time: "Conny Jenkins held it all day long. Her partner, Paul Elias, tinkled over the side one time. Jenkins turned her head. And there you have it. History."[2]

Since then, only Linda England and Fredda Lee have fished an entire BASS circuit, which they did for three seasons (1992–1994). But with the exception of a few others, women have not crossed over as expected. Certainly cost has been a major factor, since BASS's entry fees start at $600. Yet more than anything, many Bass'n Gal members say, it is the camaraderie and friendships they've developed over the years on the women's trail that they're reluctant to leave behind. "You can't hardly miss a tour," declares Illinois veteran Margaret White, 63. "I've *got* to see my fishing family!"

Undoubtedly Margaret represents the feelings of the thousands of women whose lives have been transformed by their involvement in Bass'n Gal when she says, "We were all wanting Sugar Ferris to do what she did so we could fish, because it wasn't easy for women to do this. We got a lot of criticism. But she was brave enough to start this thing and carry it through."

Our hats are off to Sugar Ferris and to all of the Bass'n Gals on the occasion of their 20th anniversary in 1996!

CHAPTER 11

A Living Legend: Sugar Ferris

FOUNDER, BASS'N GAL • TEXAS

In 1967, when Ray Scott, an insurance salesman from Montgomery, Alabama, created the Bass Anglers Sportsman Society (BASS) and organized the first professional bass-fishing tournament in the country, Sugar Ferris, a single mother who would later revolutionize the sport on behalf of women, had not yet tossed a bass lure for the first time.

In fact, until 1971 Sugar was not what you would call a serious angler, though she had grown up in a family in which fishing and hunting were a matter of survival. "When we talked about Crispy Critters at our house, we weren't talking about a breakfast cereal," says this aristocratic Earth Mother, whose laugh is as contagious as chicken pox in a kindergarten. Sure, she fished "off and on—I'd go here and there—but it was never anything that I was really particularly interested in."

So how did this Southern-bred bundle of nuclear energy become the galvanizing force behind women's professional bass-tournament angling and the head honcho of a league of her own? Certainly not as a result of hearing that women had been excluded from BASS's multimillion-dollar circuit for reasons of "sexual privacy." Sugar wasn't even within earshot of the complaining and groaning that was presumably going on at the time.

Like many divorced women attempting to stretch a pay-check from month to month, she was instead consumed with working a job she hated. And she might still be the head of the steno unit at a major oil company's data-processing center in Houston if she hadn't been told that her daughter would be bused 16 miles away, although they lived only two blocks from her school.

So Sugar packed up herself and her daughter and headed back to her tiny hometown of Livingston, Texas. In her absence, Livingston had become a recreational hotspot as a result of the creation of a giant reservoir known as Lake Livingston. Even so, there wasn't a lot of work around that paid a living wage, so it was fortunate that Sugar's destiny kicked into gear soon after she arrived.

While working in a marina, Sugar was arm-twisted into authoring an article on fishing — despite her own adamant protests that she didn't know a thing about writing or the sport. And within three weeks, she became one of the first female out-doors writers in America, as the editor of *The Lake Livingston Progress*, a weekly recreational supplement to the county's only daily newspaper.

And *that* was when Sugar Ferris and tournament bass fishing crossed paths for the first time — because if there is one thing that butters the bread of a small-town newspaper situated in a business community dependent on a bass-producing lake, it's reporting the final results of visiting tournaments.

So Sugar grabbed her notebook and camera and headed out to the lake. But instead of encountering a welcome mat, she ran right smack into the middle of that dispute about bathroom privileges. It didn't matter what she was doing out there; no man wanted to relieve himself with a woman in his boat, reporter or not.

After the competitors' boats roared off each morning, Sugar spent the rest of her reporting day milling away the hours playing bingo with the competitors' wives and girlfriends—in which *their* prizes were small kitchen appliances put up by the tournament sponsors—until the boats came back in. "Well," she notes, with a wry chuckle, "if you've been to one weigh-in, you've been to them all. The only thing that changes is the name and the number."

Not one to entertain boredom for long, Sugar soon wanted to "see what's so great about this sport. You know, everybody kept talking about it!" So she called up the BASS organization and talked to president Ray Scott about the possibility of getting into one of those boats. "And, you know, I got the same spiel about privacy and all that—which was OK with me. I never fought any of that stuff. Didn't make me any difference, you know," she says, without a trace of rancor.

Meanwhile, while making the rounds of the marinas to pick up the weekly fishing reports, Sugar became friendly with the local guides, then all male, who loved her for the fact that she never pretended to know a thing about fishing. In fact, when they were giving her the scoop on the latest fishing action, she often didn't have a clue what they were talking about. "One of the guides one day said, 'Well, they caught a gross on shimmy babes.' All I heard was gross and shimmy babes, and I said, 'I've been down to Junior's and I never noticed any female strippers or hookers,'" she recalls, in ripples of laughter. What he meant, of course, was a dozen bass caught on a specific lure. What Sugar thought he meant was Jimmy Gross's nightclub on Lake Livingston, the only haven for a good time in the midst of a region dominated by dry counties.

One day, one of those guides offered to initiate her into the arcane world of bass fishing. And wouldn't you know it, Sugar caught two fish—on her first try. That, according to Sugar, was the

In 1976, Sugar Ferris founded
Bass'n Gal with its own highly
celebrated professional
bass-tournament trail, thereby
giving women an opportunity to
compete on a national level.

moment that actually "changed bass fishing forever, because I loved it! I thought those bass were the most wonderful things that I had ever hooked into. Well, then I went every chance I got, because I had a lot of friends who were guides and they taught me a lot."

Sugar became so knowledgeable about her bass fishing that she was able to impress her future husband, Bob Ferris, by taking him to her favorite fishing hole, though with an admonition: "I would tie a piano wire and concrete to him and sink him if he ever told anybody where this hole was! Of course, I went back up there and his whole bass-club team was sitting on it!" she roars. It didn't matter, because his club won the Texas state tournament that year by weighing in a staggering 159 cumulative pounds.

Unfortunately, now that Sugar had taken a big drink of the forbidden nectar, what was once merely annoying had now become intolerable when it came to doing her job. "I was sitting at this bingo game and I'm breathing fire, because you want to be out there and nobody'll let you fish because it's all limited to men only," she recounts. And as she was waiting for them to call out E6 or F5 or whatever, one of the male competitors happened to float by and gallantly shout out, "My—aren't we ladies having fun!" Well, the effect was something like passing a lighted match a hair too close to a pile of waiting firecrackers.

Sugar says she yelled back, "I'd rather be fishin'!" She continues, "And some of these ladies around the table said, 'So would we!' So we forgot about the bingo game and I said, 'I know what let's do! Let's hold an all-women's bass-fishing tournament!' And they said, 'You think we could?' And I said, 'I've got a publisher who would probably think it's wonderful. He's 24, he owns five newspapers, and he's always looking for some new promotion.'" And, true to her word, Sugar's publisher did indeed come aboard.

Of course, the news spread like dust in a tornado. Between the guffaws and knee slapping, there was an awful lot of personal philosophizing on the order of "Aw-shucks, we know women can catch crappie—but *bass* fishin'!" "Well, of course, you know, all the good old East Texas boys thought I had two chances to succeed: slim and none," Sugar smiles coyly.

Little did they know Sugar would treat the challenge like a life-or-death mission. After naming it the National FEM (short for female) Tournament, she dug out all the wives' names and addresses she'd collected while accompanying Bob on his BASS tournament trail and wrote to each one. She also set the entry fee at a modest $5 and allowed competitors to bring a driver because, she recounts, "Some of these women couldn't run boats yet." She also got her publisher to put up a boat as the first prize—though it didn't come with a motor—and $600 for second place. And 96 competitors, mostly local, showed up. Which tells you how little those good old East Texas boys knew their own women!

That 1972 event was so popular that within two years Ranger Boats founder Forest Wood began putting up a brand-new metalflake boat each year thereafter as the first prize, just like the BASS boys got. And by its last year, 1976, 128 female competitors from eight states participated, and major press like *Sports Afield* covered it. It should also be mentioned that women no longer needed to bring a boat driver—they had not only learned how to run those big outboards by themselves, but now the titles on those vessels were often in their names only.

And that was the backdrop to the 1976 American Fishing Tackle Manufacturers' Association trade show in Dallas, which Sugar attended with her now-husband, Bob. Not surprisingly, the buzz of the event was Sugar's last hugely successful FEM tournament. "On the floor, all the men were saying, 'Boy, did you hear about that women's tournament down at Lake Livingston? We need to start something for women, because that's going to be the coming thing,'" she recalls.

"Well, you can imagine how that scared me. I'd sat on my behind for three years, too frightened to really jump in and organize a national women's fishing organization. I suppose I was afraid it wouldn't work, that there weren't enough women out there to support it. But it scared me even more that someone else, especially some man, especially one that wasn't attuned to the needs of women in the outdoors, would jump in and start one, and there would go my dream! At that particular moment in time, I knew it was time for me to move!"

Seizing her moment in history at a meeting of the Outdoors Writers Association of America on the last day of the convention, Sugar stood up and announced that she was starting a national women's fishing organization. And while the members present "just thought that was the most wonderful thing," her husband, Bob, sat next to her in a state of shock. "I'll never forget Bob's expression. Never in my life!" she laughs. Bob, who was clearly caught unprepared, quickly recovered and assured her, "'Well, honey, whatever you want to do, I'll support you.' And he did," Sugar says proudly.

"What's the organization's name?" someone called out from the floor. And for possibly the one and only time in Sugar's life, she was speechless. She truly hadn't gotten that far in her thinking. Then suddenly the name plopped into her head like a big bass lure landing on a glassy-smooth lake, inspired by an incident which had occurred only a few weeks earlier.

It seems that the Rebel Lure Company had sent her a free tackle box with an engraved brass plate that read: "Bass'n Man Sugar Ferris." Annoyed, she returned it promptly with a "smart-mouth reply." Before long, a new box arrived with the inscription: "Bass'n Gal Sugar Ferris."

So, with all the confidence she could muster, Sugar told that auditorium of press, "It's going to be called Bass'n Gal!"

After securing Rebel Lure's blessing (in fact, they later served as one of her tournament sponsors), she immediately filed for a trademark and incorporation papers.

And it can be said that during the next couple of years, Sugar's life changed dramatically. At the time she made the announcement, she had committed to taking a job in the state legislature, which she gave up; she moved the organization's headquarters from her home to a real office out of necessity, due to the volume of work and number of employees required to keep up with the growing membership; and, most important, Bob Ferris, once a prominent disc jockey in Amarillo, left a highly successful 20-year career as a state district sales manager for a major chemical company to become Bass'n Gal's much-revered vice president.

Sugar took a hard look at two tournament practices which no one else had either thought to question or had the courage to challenge. First was her adoption of a five fish per day limit per contender to reduce the impact of a large tournament on a particular body of water. It's significant that all the other trails were allowing ten or fifteen fish per angler per day and have only recently shifted to the five-fish rule. "Conservation is something that we owe to the sport, and five fish are a lot easier to keep alive in a livewell all day than 10 or 15 fish," Sugar explains of her visionary wisdom. "In tournaments, it's the sport of competition, and fishing is secondary. It doesn't make any difference if it's one fish or 15 fish, it's still a tournament competition. And those fish allow us to use them to win, so we need to make every effort that we can to keep those fish alive."

Sugar was also the first to institute a "paper fish" rule, which allows contenders to measure a fish between 12" and 15" with what is called the Golden Rule (estimating the fish's weight based on size) so that it can be calculated in the day's total catch. In this way, fragile stocks of younger bass can be released immediately back into the water to enhance their chances of survival.

In 1978 she set another precedent as well. She reorganized the affiliate-club program by removing club dues as long as 80 percent of their members belong to the national organization. (Even today, the cost is only $15 per person to join.) She also replaced the usual club entry fee for competing in the national Affiliate Club Tournament of Champions with the requirement that clubs submit a scrapbook of clippings and other evidence of their public-service projects within the previous year. Furthermore, they get to choose and implement whatever projects best serve the needs of their local communities, as long as they undertake one conservation and one youth fishing project per year.

"The most useful thing a person can do with a life is to use it for something that's going to outlast it," says this 58-year-old living legend of America's most popular branch of angling.

Not only has Sugar Ferris accomplished her goal, but without her extraordinary tenacity and driving passion to bring women into the spotlight, it's doubtful there would be a women's legacy in bass fishing to celebrate today.

CHAPTER 12

Top Pro
Bass Anglers

CHRIS HOUSTON

LINDA ENGLAND AND FREDDA LEE

PENNY BERRYMAN

KATHY MAGERS

During the 20 years since women's professional bass fishing debuted, those who have fished their way to the top have proven that women can flip a bass lure as well as an egg, handle a high-powered boat like it was the family car, and read a topographic map as if it were a recipe for a new dish. They've also shown that women can bring home the bacon, as in Linda England's $360,000 in career tournament earnings and Chris Houston's $260,000 in Bass'n Gal winnings to date, along with the free boats, tackle, and paid promotional appearances that come with being a recognized star.

Thanks to Sugar Ferris and her determination to give women a place in the sun, a galaxy of women have achieved prominence within the sport in the last two decades. So many, in fact, that they deserve a book of their own. I regret that each and every one of these women cannot be honored here, as all are fascinating—as much for the paths they took to their self-realizations as for their superior angling skills. Five of the top pro bass anglers today are presented here as examples of the diversity and inspired dedication that exemplifies the women who have devoted themselves to the spirit of competition through the least expected of avenues: fishing.

Chris Houston OKLAHOMA

She is the Chris Evert of bass fishing, the legend of the legends on the Bass'n Gal circuit. Each season's crop of new rookies watch her like a hawk, hoping to emulate her phenomenal success. Veterans, at least the ones I spoke with, regard her with the reverence and admiration normally accorded an elder statesman, a testament no doubt to her self-effacing manner as much as to her angling skills.

What has Chris Houston done to deserve so much respect? For starters, she currently ranks as Bass'n Gal's all-time money-earner and is in a league of her own in terms of racking up titles on a single circuit. Not only has Chris accumulated seven Angler of the Year awards, three Classic Star world championships, and seven national titles, she is also the only contender to take one of each within the same season. And she's done that twice, in 1977 and 1991! Like the great athlete she is, Chris has demonstrated remarkable endurance over the years, walking away with the Classic Star crown in 1990 after three dry and several marginal years, followed by a triple-threat win in 1991. She's also the only contender in Bass'n Gal's two-decade history to fish every tournament and qualify for every Classic.

Even if this 49-year-old thoroughbred never steps into the winner's circle again, chances are her 30-year-old daughter, Sherri Houston Combs, a Bass'n Gal contender since the age of 16, will be adding her own share of titles to the family's illustrious legacy in the sport in years to come.

Chris is typical of the women who've carved out careers as pro bass anglers in that she learned how to thread a worm onto a hook before she had mastered her ABCs. At the age of 14 she met young Jimmy Houston when his family settled in her hometown of Cookson, Oklahoma. Their dates consisted of late-

WITH SEVEN ANGLER OF THE YEAR
AWARDS, THREE WORLD CHAMPION-
SHIPS, AND SEVEN NATIONAL TITLES,
CHRIS HOUSTON IS THE LEADING
FEMALE CONTENDER IN THE PROFES-
SIONAL BASS-TOURNAMENT WORLD.

night fishing trips, concluding just in time to clean their mess and head to school. It was an unusual courtship, Chris muses, but going to the movies "was just a waste of money" since she always fell asleep in the middle of the show anyway.

Their marriage in 1963 was in many respects a match made in angling heaven. Jimmy, who would become one of the bass world's leading celebrities as a two-time BASS Angler of the Year and as a television fishing-show host, not only became her fishing partner for life but also her staunchest supporter. Years ahead of the trend advocating a more liberal interpretation of women's roles in the home, Jimmy came home one day after fishing in one of the first tournaments on nearby Lake Tenkiller with the suggestion, "You ought to fish one of these things. You really have as much skill as the guys I fish with." Chris did, and she took fourth place in her first, a state event.

He also talked her into competing in the husband-and-wife division at her first national tournament on Lake Texoma in the mid-1960s, a tournament which nearly turned out to be her last. Amazingly, there were enough women fishing those early local events that Chris drew a female partner for the morning sprint of the competition. And everything was fine when they set out in the Houston's aluminum runabout with its little motor. When a storm blew in suddenly, turning the glassy lake into a raging miniature sea, Chris aimed the boat at the nearest shore and they climbed a mountain in search of help, managing to hitch a ride back to the weigh-in area. "Of course, I was just ready to quit," she laughs now of her first harrowing experience. "I didn't want any more of this fishing." But Jimmy would not hear of it. He and another man fetched their boat. By then, everyone had headed back out, so he also ferried her to her next partner's vessel "and away I went again that afternoon." It hardly seems possible, but Jimmy and Chris won the couples division that day.

At around the same time, a new tournament circuit formed in which the top contenders from local bass clubs could compete. Since none of the clubs allowed women, Chris helped form the Tulsa Bass Belles, notably the first organized women's bass club in the United States. "We did have to really scrape to get enough women, but we finally wound up with probably a dozen or so as charter members," she recalls. Their logo featured a feminine-looking bass with large red lips and a bow in its hair. They also began holding tournaments of their own and inviting various experts to speak at their monthly meetings. Years later, Sugar Ferris would be one of those standing before them and, as a result, the Tulsa Bass Belles was the first club to affiliate with Bass'n Gal upon its inception.

In spite of their success, the Belles always had a dilemma: securing enough boats to accommodate their outings. Most husbands were reluctant to hand over the keys, Chris says, citing a popular cartoon to illustrate a typical attitude at the time: "There goes my two most-prized possessions, the wife and the boat." It didn't get much better out on the water. "I kid you not, people would go by and turn around and come back to see if what they saw was really what they saw," she chuckles, adding how "all of the gentlemen would come over to try to help you unload [the boat], and of course you sure didn't want a man to have to help you, so you did it yourself. We went through a lot of formative years there with all the girls and had a lot of fun teaching them to back up the trailers."

In the early 1970s, Chris, along with a half-dozen other women, also fished a new tournament co-ed trail. "Some of us made the money a few times. We were pretty well respected, but [we still knew] we were treading in a man's world," she says. It was always an uncomfortable situation when pairing time rolled around, she notes, "not knowing if [your male partner] was actually going to be upset." To cope with the bathroom problem, Chris abstained from drinking anything, including coffee, and always let her partners know, "If you need to go, just go. It won't bother me." Though they rarely did, she laughs, "I'd worry about them so much, pretty soon *I'd* need to go." When the first Bass'n Gal tournament started in 1978, more than anything, Chris welcomed the relief of never having to think about her bodily functions again, allowing her to concentrate solely on her fishing, which she regards as one of the reasons she did so well in the circuit's early years.

It's hard to believe that over a period of two decades there was not one mishap or family crisis that kept her away from her beloved Bass'n Gal tournaments. "Can you believe that I've never been sick?" she asks. Of course, her idea of sick may be a bit different from most people's. For Chris, it doesn't include, for instance, the time she severed a tendon in the thumb of her rod-throwing hand during a skiing vacation and refused to let the doctor perform surgery until after an upcoming Bass'n Gal tournament. "I couldn't even pick up a cup of coffee," she laughs of the excruciating pain. Reluctantly, the doctor set it in a cast until it was time for her to go, then placed it in a splint and taped the entire hand to cup around her rod butt. "And I went down and won that tournament," she says proudly, noting that other contenders have fished nine months pregnant or with handicaps like broken legs.

Having children also did not keep Chris and Jimmy from their beloved fishing. When Sherri, the oldest of the two, was a toddler, they would place an umbrella over the console area so she could play out of the sun, or they'd tie a rope to her life jacket so she could float behind the boat as they trolled. Later, when her children reached school age, Chris gathered up their school assignments and tutored them on the road so the family would always be together. Sherri maintained a grade-point average of 4.0 over the years, and she is duplicating the tradition with her own two children today.

Whoever invented the popular adage that a family that fishes together stays together must have been thinking about the Houstons. Over the years, Jimmy has accompanied Chris to most of her Bass'n Gal tournaments, serving as her practice partner and behind-the-scenes assistant — which means taking care of everything from changing her lines to tying on new baits the night before competition days. For his BASS tournaments, they simply switch roles. When Jimmy realized a few years ago that their hectic schedules would prevent them from spending much time with their grandchildren, he coaxed Sherri's husband, Dower Combs, into joining the BASS trail. Dower and their children also accompany Sherri to her Bass'n Gal meets. Ironically, it was Sherri who taught Dower how to fish when they were dating in high school.

Back home in Cookson, the Combs and the Houstons work the family's many businesses together. Jimmy produces and hosts his hit weekly television series, "Jimmy Houston Outdoors," on ESPN, as well as "The Bass'n Gal Tour" on various regional networks. Sherri manages their travel agency and fishing-tackle mail-order service, and she sells advertising for the shows. Dower runs their marine dealership. And Chris? "I pay the bills," she laughs.

"It's crazy, isn't it?" Chris says of her lifelong obsession with tournament fishing. And sure she asks herself, "*Why* am I doing this?" every time she's caught in another deathtrap-like storm. But as she points out, "I'm really not a competitive person until the bell rings. But when it does, that's a different story." She also doesn't get "deeply depressed if I don't do well. I go out and I do the very best that I can. I don't like to make mistakes, but if I go out and give it my best and it's not good enough to excel or do extremely well or whatever, then that's OK. There'll be another one. At the same time, of course, I've been fortunate to have won a lot of tournaments, and that didn't change anything either. I mean, the next day the sun still rose and the wind still blew."

Linda England and Fredda Lee TENNESSEE

Professional partnerships between women are almost nonexistent in the history of angling. In the early 1990s, Donna Teeny and Rhonda Sapp got together and formed Dirt Roads and Damsels in order to design and manufacture fly-fishing clothing for women. Christy Ball and Lori-Ann Murphy launched Reel Women Fly Fishing Adventures in 1994 to offer women-only fly-fishing trips to exotic locations. But it seems likely that no one has been at it longer than veteran pro bass anglers Linda England and Fredda Lee, whose collaboration under the banner of Two Star Enterprises dates back to 1982.

Though both had competed on the Bass'n Gal circuit from the beginning, they barely knew each other when Fredda got a call from a friend who had just purchased a radio station and wanted to mount a weekly fishing show. Fredda had the poise and on-air experience (as a former high-fashion model, actress, and occasional game-show guest star) to host the show, but for whatever reasons, she opted to produce and called Linda to see if she would like to host. Linda leaped at the chance. For the next several weeks, Fredda coached her, using a stuffed sock hanging down over Linda's kitchen table as a mock microphone. "Fishing with Linda England" was so successful that within a year it was airing on 163 stations nationwide. It ran with great acclaim until 1987.

Then in 1987 came their book, *Bass on the Line*, the first how-to tome on the sport authored by a woman, in this case two women. As Fredda describes it, they wrote the book literally on the road on an early-model computer "the size of a suitcase" while they fished two separate circuits and made numerous promotional appearances. Nonetheless it is undeniably one of the best sources of information available to beginning and intermediate anglers on everything from understanding the habits of bass to developing a successful fishing pattern to mastering various casting and retrieval techniques.

From 1989 to 1993, they co-hosted a fishing-tips segment for WSMV-TV's "Eyewitness Evening News" in Nashville and, in 1991, launched their current syndicated television show, "On the Line with Linda England & Fredda Lee," the first and only fishing show exclusively featuring women as the hosts. They retired from tournament fishing at the end of 1994 to devote more time to "On the Line." Although a commitment of 13 shows a season may not seem like much, Linda and Fredda are also responsible for choosing their locations, hiring their crews, handling all the on-location details, supervising the filming and editing, lining up the station groups and cable operators, and even selling the advertising. And then, of course, there are the unexpected delays when the weather isn't cooperating or the fish aren't biting.

Before Linda exited the competitive arena, she had distinguished herself as the all-time money-earner in women's competitive bass fishing, based on her combined winnings from the Bass'n Gal and Lady Bass tours. She is also a close second to Chris Houston in terms of accumulated titles: two Bass'n Gal Classic Star world championships, five Angler of the Year honors, and nine national wins. She is also the only woman to grab Angler of the Year on both circuits during the same season. And she took first place at the 1992 World Bass Society's Pro-Team Tournament in Japan, for which she and Fredda were the only women invited to participate.

Fredda currently ranks as the highest-placing woman in an open bass-fishing tournament with a second-place win at an Operation Bass Golden Blend Pro-Am Tournament in 1991, and she is the recipient of more than 10 BIG BASS Awards.

Most significant, they are the first and only women to date to compete in every BASS invitational for three seasons, from 1992 through 1994. And Linda is the only woman to place in the money in a BASS event to date.

If there is one key element that characterizes Linda's and Fredda's individual and joint careers, it is the degree of dedication that they have given to the sport. Perhaps nothing illustrates their commitment more than their decision to fish three full circuits — Bass'n Gal, BASS, and the Red Man Golden Blend — plus two Lady Bass tournaments in 1992, all while filming their weekly television show. It was a challenge that few, if any, have ever attempted, and they're to be admired for trying. In that year alone, they put over 100,000 miles on their vehicle. On many occasions, they'd finish a tournament on a Friday night and drive over a thousand miles to get to the next one by Sunday. "We barely knew where we lived anymore. It was just too much," Fredda reflects. The physical and mental toll was such that for the first time since 1978, Linda did not qualify for the Bass'n Gal Classic. "I made myself very ill and wound up in the hospital, so it was not a good year for me," she says, noting that she also underwent major surgery just three and a half weeks before she was due to compete in Japan, an event she amazingly won anyway.

For the next two years they fished BASS exclusively, then retired from competition to concentrate on their television show and promotional appearances. As a result, they were recently able to film an episode in Brazil on peacock bass and are working on a series of educational videos as well as hoping to write a sequel to their first book.

LINDA ENGLAND HAS
DISTINGUISHED HERSELF AS
THE ALL-TIME MONEY-EARNER
AND THE SECOND-HIGHEST
TITLEHOLDER IN WOMEN'S
COMPETITIVE BASS FISHING.

FREDDA LEE, IN PARTNERSHIP
WITH LINDA ENGLAND, IS
THE POPULAR CO-HOST OF A
SYNDICATED TELEVISION
SERIES ON BASS FISHING AND
CO-AUTHOR OF THE FIRST
AND ONLY BOOK WRITTEN ON
THE SPORT BY A WOMAN.

Though each has fished since childhood, no one could have guessed that Linda England, a housewife and mother who had never worked outside the home, or Fredda Lee, who had led a life of glamour since the age of 14, would end up making a living tossing a bass lure.

Born and raised in Nashville, Tennessee, where both currently reside in a outlying suburb, Linda, 49, was typical of a lot of young women who married right out of high school in the early 1960s and had two children soon after. If the family went on a car trip, say 12 hours long, her husband drove the entire way. If he felt she was not competent to take out their bass boat alone, his was the final word. It was a time, Linda laughs, when "the man drove and the woman rode, if she got to go at all." Of course, she did drive the bass boat, "but only when he wasn't around," she chuckles.

When the news reached Nashville that Sugar Ferris had formed Bass'n Gal and would be mounting its first national tournament early in 1978, Linda was 30 years old and in the midst of a depression brought on by the sudden death of her father-in-law at the age of 58, after losing her own father when she was 24. "I was really looking for some answers. I thought there must be more to life than working and dying," she says.

She turned out for that first event, the Toledo Bend tournament, "just to say I had done it." And it was a sight she will never forget. Not only were women going out in bass boats all by themselves, but many of them had their names painted boldly on their crafts, "which was really in vogue at the time," she says. "I was just totally in awe of the whole thing. I was just amazed there were so many women who were as serious about fishing as I was." Since many of the other women had fished Sugar's FEM tournaments, Linda was intimidated and didn't do that well. Or so she thought, until the final standings arrived in the mail and she realized that she was only six ounces out of the top 50 in terms of accumulated bass weight. "That really, really got to me," she remembers.

With the next tournament only five weeks away, she toyed with the idea of going again, just to see if she could do better. But she also worried about the dent it would make in the family budget and how her husband would cope for a week with their seven- and nine-year-olds. He not only insisted she go but took vacation time to join her. She finished in 21st place, just two ounces out of the money, and that's when "the bug hit! I had to do it then!"

Between her mother and homemaker duties, she read every book and magazine and watched every television show that had anything to do with catching trophy-sized bass. "I became just obsessed with proving that I could do this, because I had disappointed myself two times and knew I could have done better. So I had to take control of it and do it." It worked. Linda qualified for the Classic that first year on individual points alone.

But it would be four years before she actually won anything, leading her fellow contenders to dub her the "bridesmaid" as a result of coming in second or third on so many occasions, always within ounces of winning. Those close finishes paid off, however, when she took Angler of the Year in 1981, the most coveted title on any professional circuit, and received the keys to the first of 17 completely rigged bass boats that she would win over the course of her career. "It was the first really big accomplishment [in my life]," she exclaims of that quintessential moment. "It gave me a tremendous boost in confidence." To think that only a handful of years before, her husband wouldn't even let her drive his boat!

In 1982, Linda turned pro and began doing speaking engagements and appearances at sports shows. She also continued to devote herself to her now 13- and 15-year-old daughters.

"There'd be many times when I'd come home from a tournament completely exhausted and they'd want to go to a movie. Of course neither of them could drive, so I'd go to the movie with them and their friends and sleep through the entire show. Then they'd wake me up when it was over and we'd go home," she recalls. "But I'd still try to do these things that they needed done."

Like so many of the women who've had to balance the needs of their families with the demands of the trail, Linda was often overwhelmed with a sense of guilt. "I know you think I'm terrible for doing this," she once said to her eldest daughter about missing a school event because it conflicted with a tournament. "No, Mom, really I don't," her daughter responded unexpectedly. "All my friends' mothers are boring. You're exciting." It's a moment she's never forgotten. "I think that probably gave me more strength to continue than anything," she says. But Linda also didn't hesitate to withdraw from a Bass'n Gal Classic years later, despite all the hard work it took to qualify, so she could be at her daughter's bedside during a touch-and-go childbirth.

Born and raised in Atlanta, Georgia, Fredda's acquired passion for fishing began around the age of seven or eight, although her first encounter with a bass didn't come until she moved to Nashville at the age of 25. That she fished at all is surprising enough. By the time she was 14, Fredda was already working as a part-time runway and photography model. While still in high school, she won more than two dozen beauty pageants, including the crown at the Miss American Models Festival, for which she won a year's contract in New York.

After convincing her mother that modeling was what she wanted to do with her life, she took up residence at the Barbizon Hotel for Women in Manhattan and spent her days floating down runways in the latest designer fashions or posing for magazine shoots for top publications like *Seventeen* and *Vogue*. At night, she hostessed at New York's legendary Stork Club, which a cousin owned, putting her on a first-name basis with many of the most famous celebrities of the day. Then at 2 A.M. each morning she'd climb into her cousin's chauffeured limousine and head home to her modest apartment to catch four hours of sleep before heading back out for yet another modeling assignment. Even then, no one worked harder than Fredda Lee.

During the next four years, she also appeared on the game shows "What's My Line" in New York and "The Dating Game" three times in Los Angeles. She also tried her hand at acting with a supporting role in the Elvis Presley film, *Spinout*.

In 1970, she spent Thanksgiving in Nashville, where she "fell in love with the mountains and the countryside," and eventually relocated there. Although she had no formal training, she went on to design key displays for popular tourist sites like the Country Music Museum and to guide the overall design of the Jim Reeves Museum. Through a local Bass'n Gal affiliated club, Fredda also discovered her passion for bass fishing and bought her first boat in 1977.

Like Linda, Fredda turned out for the first Bass'n Gal tournament on Toledo Bend Lake in 1978, where she "felt so at home and so at peace and so natural," she says. Finally forsaking her design career in 1981 to fish the circuit full-time, she somehow knew she could make a living, because "I've never had that feeling about any other occupation I've ever had." Then came the fateful meeting with Linda, and the rest is, well, bassin' history.

In the event you encounter a pure-white van pulling a double-decker trailer with two identical sleek white boats, chances are you've just met up with Linda England and Fredda Lee, always a sensation wherever they go. "We have to travel in the middle of the night so people don't ask us too many questions," Linda says. "It's amazing—we stop for gas and we draw a crowd. No matter where we are, people are just in awe of the whole thing, and trying to figure out how you get the top boat off." How do you? "Very carefully! That's what we always tell them," she laughs.

Penny Berryman ARKANSAS

Penny Berryman is one of only a couple dozen women whose names can guarantee a crowd at a major fishing expo. Although she is Bass'n Gal's 1992 Classic Star world champion, the holder of three national titles (for Bass'n Gal in 1987 and 1995 and Lady Bass in 1989), and the first-place winner of Bass'n Gal's 1985 Tournament of Champions, titles are but a minor reason why Penny is so visible within the sport today. She has the spit and polish of a star, skills likely developed from her years of picking up trophies and talking to the press as a national waterskiing champion. She is also like a patient parent when it comes to answering the zillions of questions posed by enthusiastic novice anglers, a skill undoubtedly owing to her teaching certificate in elementary education from Wichita State University in 1974.

There's almost never been a time in Penny's life when she wasn't involved in one form of competition or another. At the age of 12 she took up competitive waterskiing, which led to an attic full of trophies and ultimately a ranking as third in the nation before her retirement in 1981. So when Penny stumbled upon a Bass'n Gal tournament in 1979 on Lake Dardanelle near her home in central Arkansas, in many respects she was like a honeybee waiting for another flower to bloom, though it would be another half dozen years before she felt she had the confidence and the competence necessary to fish the national tour.

Unlike most women of her generation, Penny, now 45, grew up in a family of four girls whose parents were devoted to the outdoors. They went hunting, camping, fishing, or waterskiing almost every weekend in her native Kansas, and Penny was a dyed-in-the-wool fishing nut by the tender age of four. At 17, she got her first taste of going after bass when she filled in for one of her father's regular fishing partners. "My mom and dad taught each of us girls to be very self-reliant," she says proudly.

After graduating from college, Penny shied away from teaching and headed into the business world instead, with managerial positions in sales, marketing, and advertising for an Oklahoma beverage company. In 1979, she briefly opened her own advertising agency before marrying and relocating to Dardanelle, Arkansas, to join her new husband on a 200-acre cattle ranch. And "because this itty-bitty town didn't need an advertising executive," she laughs, she was able to fish to her heart's content.

A year after Bass'n Gal paid that fortuitous visit to Lake Dardanelle, Penny heard they were coming back for an invitational but still harbored no ambition of fishing it herself. Fortunately, her husband insisted she give it a shot, to which she remembers protesting, "Who, me? You must be joking! There's no way I could compete with these great lady anglers!" "But how will you know unless you try?" he persisted.

So try she did. And she loved it, although she also recognized that there was a lot of work ahead of her if she was ever going to bring home the gold. Like an athlete in training, she spent the next five years treating fishing like a full-time occupation, venturing out on the lake alone almost every Monday through Friday. When a women's bass club formed in her area, she joined and fished their tournaments and other local events. Indisputably the greatest influence on her career, however, was

PENNY BERRYMAN, BASS'N GAL'S
1992 WORLD CHAMPION, WAS ONCE
A NATIONAL WATERSKIING STAR
BEFORE TURNING HER ATTENTION TO
COMPETITIVE BASS FISHING.

the man who would become her mentor and coach, the late Morgan Scott, who found her stranded on a sandbar one day and offered to pull her boat free. They struck up a conversation and he invited her to join him for a day on the water. Soon their expeditions became a regular thing, and before he died, Scott—a bassin' legend in those parts—shared with Penny every thread of his carefully ciphered theories about those ornery critters and how to outwit them. "When I look back on it, I think he was happy to have a little protégé to pass some of his knowledge on to, because his children didn't fish," she says of the man who grew into a surrogate father as well, since she'd lost hers years before.

In 1985, she decided she was ready to join the Bass'n Gal trail and committed to fish every event that season. She even did it the way they said you had to, showing up several weeks in advance at the first lake to pre-fish it, giving her a head start on creating a tournament strategy. And she caught fish—lots of them. She also pulled them in during the three tournament practice days, convincing her that there was no way she wouldn't be pulling home a brand-new bass boat by the tournament's end. Then came the first day of competition. She got "skunked," meaning she came in without a single keeper. Shocked, she returned the second day determined to do better but still only managed to bring in a couple of fish which were hardly worth weighing. "Welcome to the wonderful world of tournament bass fishing!" she laughs, noting that it probably helped a lot "that I had the rug pulled out from under me at such an early start in my career."

Despite the setback, Penny continued to fish the trail like a real trooper, even coming in first place at Bass'n Gal's affiliate club Tournament of Champions. But her first national win would not come for two more years, in 1987. Meanwhile, she began fishing the Lady Bass trail as well, which yielded her a national title in 1989. That same year, she also began a two-year stint as a co-host on ESPN's "Sportsman's Challenge," becoming one of the first women with a regular spot on a national fishing show.

As any veteran tournament competitor will attest, it's impossible to go out year after year on the South's massive reservoirs without at least one deadly close encounter with the elements of nature. For Penny, it was a tornado that suddenly swept over Toledo Bend Reservoir while she was fishing a protected inlet alone. Unaware that the weather had drastically changed until she got back out on the lake to head home, she suddenly noticed that trees were falling along the shore. The winds had kicked up such awesome swells that she could no longer detect the boat lane that provided the only safe passage through the barely submerged stump beds that had been left when the lake was created. All she could do was idle her way through the minefield, praying each time she crested an eight-foot swell that the boat wouldn't land hard on a stump during its precipitous descent. Penny says she has never been so frightened in her life, since at any moment a wave could easily have swamped her motor, abruptly ending any control she had over the boat. "I remember praying between every swell. Then I decided, 'I'm tougher than this. I will make it!' And I started singing between swells, mostly to keep myself calm," she says of the ordeal that lasted four hours. "It made me realize how small each of us is against Mother Nature."

There's also the time she fished and won a competition with a ruptured disk, the delayed product of too many waterskiing accidents. At first, when the pain showed up while fly fishing for tarpon in Florida, she thought nothing of it and went on to fish a tournament a month later, although her "neck hurt so bad during practice that I honestly could not turn the handle on my reel." Finally, when she got home, she visited a doctor, who recommended immediate surgery. She refused, telling him the Classic was just around the corner and there was no way she was going to miss it, excruciating pain or not. "He didn't want me to fish it, and ironically that's the Classic I won," she says, explaining how she donned a neck brace and sat on a thick layer of foam to insulate her from the shock of the boat taking the waves.

It's only glamorous on the surface, Penny says of her demanding career as a pro angler and outdoors celebrity. She flies between 175,000 and 225,000 air miles per year, mostly between the months of January and March, promoting her sponsors' products and making personal appearances wherever her agent books her. It wouldn't be so bad, she says, if she lived in a major hub city. But the nearest airport is two hours away in Little Rock and so off the beaten path that getting anywhere in the country requires changing planes en route at least once. When she was fishing both Bass'n Gal and Lady Bass, she also put on about 40,000 road miles a year, now down to 25,000 to 30,000, all of course pulling her boat. "You learn to be very thankful for the time you get off," she laughs.

To be sure, Penny is not complaining. She's not only living every weekend bass angler's dream, but when you've worked as hard as she has to get to the top, you also learn to savor the success for as long as it might possibly last.

Kathy Magers TEXAS

"I'm a 1990s woman who was born in 1945. So I'm smack dab in between what Mother raised me to be and what I really turned out to do," laughs Kathy Magers, one of the leading personalities in the bass-fishing world today.

Until 1984, when Kathy suddenly detoured into fishing the Bass'n Gal circuit full-time—eventually winning a national title in 1989—she was in most ways living the life of a modern

June Cleaver. "I've been the room mother. I've baked the cookies," says this proud mother of two grown daughters.

Kathy was typical of young women in the late 1950s and early 1960s: she served as a cheerleader, entered beauty pageants, and got her training and license as a hairdresser while still in high school. At the age of 17, she had her first child. By 20, she was divorced, but soon after married a childhood friend, Chuck Magers, a blissful union that produced a second daughter in 1972.

Fast-forward to 1995, and you would hardly know it's the same person. Now she shows up in the star billings of outdoors shows, crisscrosses the South and Midwest in the earnest pursuit of Bass'n Gal trophies, and takes celebrities like television talk-show host Regis Philbin and George W. Bush, now the governor of Texas, fishing. Besides "Live with Regis & Kathie Lee," she has also appeared on "CBS This Morning" and hosted her own television show, "Fishing Stories," for one season in 1993. And that's not counting all the articles she has written or the magazine covers she has graced or the seminars she has led.

But then, for Kathy, fishing was like a piece of buried genetic code waiting to be activated. She remembers throwing a "hissy fit" at the age of four when her grandfather, who owned a bait camp on Galveston Island in Texas, refused to take her fishing because she was a girl. "[I] wailed and cried and screamed and flailed my arms, and then I fell down in the driveway and cut my chin and big toe. But after that, Grampa took me fishing a lot," she once happily related.[1]

In 1972, that latent gene surfaced again when she and Chuck got their first taste of bass fishing with one of his co-workers who fished all the time with her husband and friends. Two years later, the Magers purchased their first boat with a tax refund. It was sort of a pitiful wooden little thing with eight

patches on the bottom, but it allowed them to join a local bass-fishing club and to participate in tournaments.

Meanwhile, Kathy had set up her own hair salon and was also busy raising two children and running a household. Chances are she'd still be doing shampoos and sets if a friend hadn't given her something to read that would change her life: an early copy of *Bass'n Gal* magazine. Filled with page after page of women's achievements on the tournament trail, it opened her eyes to the fact that there were other women out there who were just as obsessed with bass fishing as she was.

Kathy signed up for her first Bass'n Gal tournament in 1979, thinking it would be "a bunch of housewives pooling their 50 bucks to say, 'I caught more fish than you did.'" Instead, she watched in amazement as hordes of women showed up, pulling state-of-the-art metalflake boats decked out with giant outboard motors and the latest model of every accessory gadget on the market. On top of that, she got paired with one of the top women in the sport, who also happened to be married to a major BASS star. The entire experience was so intimidating that it's amazing she caught any fish. But she did, giving her enough confidence to return for other Bass'n Gal tournaments—when she could manage it—during the next five years.

By 1984, Kathy was ready to reach for the brass ring, the Classic Star, which would mean fishing every single invitational with the hope of accumulating enough points to qualify. But she was nagged by the guilt of leaving her husband and teenage daughters to fend for themselves for extended periods of time. She also had a persistent fear of towing the boat long distances by herself, since Chuck would not be able to take enough vacation time to accompany her as he had in the past. Fortunately, Chuck convinced her to go anyway.

"I felt guilty for leaving home," she reflects now. "But it's made Chuck stronger and it's made me stronger. Before, if a light bulb burned out, it was, 'Chuck, come fix this light bulb for me.' And now when things break, I do it myself. Now he goes to the grocery store. He goes to the bank. He does a whole lot more, because when I'm gone he has to."

A year later she turned pro, which is just a simple way of saying she decided to make it a career. The first thing that had to go was the beauty parlor, but that needed to happen anyway, after 23 years of standing on her feet. "My knees had gotten to hurting me real bad from standing so much doing hair. And I needed them for fishing," she laughs, joking that "somehow the deck of a boat is a lot softer than a cement floor."

Well aware that tournament earnings are never enough to sustain a career, she turned to Sugar Ferris for advice about securing sponsors. Sugar wisely told her to go after the fledgling manufacturers rather than those dominating the industry, since they've already got the top names in the sport working on their behalf. "It's like trying to go to one of the movie studios. When they've got Robert Redford, why would they want the guy who lives up the street from me?" Kathy explains of the lesson she learned early on.

So she began writing letters—lots of them—to the male CEOs who ran those upstart companies, touting the advantages of hiring her to promote their products to a virtually untapped market: women. One, now a leading producer of fishing lines, listened and featured her in an endorsement ad for which she got paid an astounding (for the time) $1,500. Suddenly, even without any titles under her belt, she had entered the sacred ground on which few women had treaded before. Of course, a decade later Kathy is but one of a half-dozen women featured regularly in product ads in the pages of leading fishing magazines, for everything from boats to motors to lines and raingear.

She has also become one of the leading ambassadors within the industry, promoting the virtues of fishing and the outdoors at fishing expos and seminars. Among her favorite speaking topics: "Survival Tactics on Fishing with Your Spouse" and "Making an Asset of Yourself," the latter filled with pointers for women on how to drive a boat, pull a trailer, and otherwise share the work load of a fishing outing.

Any doubts Kathy might have harbored about the change in direction she had taken with her life were erased in 1990 when she received the jarring news of a potentially malignant lesion on her right lung. It happened on a Friday afternoon at the start of a three-day holiday weekend, giving her plenty of time to reflect on the meaning of life. "When I thought I had cancer, all I could think was, 'Lord, I'll be dead before the Bass'n Gal Classic gets here.' I thought, 'What if I am dead in 90 days—what have I accomplished?' I got riled up. I gathered my thoughts and put 'em in a straight line. And I thought, 'I'm glad I'm doing what I'm doing, instead of having been a hairdresser all my life,'" she has said, adding, "My great-grandmother Hattie was the fiddle champion of Oklahoma. I'd like my great-grandkids to be able to say, 'Grandma Kathy was a champion pro fisherwoman.'"[2]

PART IV

Women's Legacy in Science and Industry

Gone, like the privacy of the tavern, is the all-male sanctity of fishing streams. Women undoubtedly started fishing out of curiosity, but many have learned to love it and some have actually become good at it. Mrs. C., for instance, landed one of the largest tuna ever caught off the coast of Nova Scotia. New York State now requires women to have licenses and Connecticut has a sacrosanct stream with a "Males Keep Out" sign and a lady warden. Women often trek off on their own for big game fishing in the Florida Keys, trout in Canada or salmon along the Northeast and Northwest coasts.

—*Holiday* MAGAZINE, JULY 1948[1]

Professional guides, tackle-shop owners, charter-boat captains, fishing instructors, manufacturers, writers, scientists, and conservationists—all are professions in which women are no longer a novelty.

How refreshing it is to be able to hire a woman to show you how and where to fish, to walk into a tackle shop with a woman behind the counter to answer the questions you've been too intimidated to ask, to read an angling article or book written from a woman's perspective, or to know that some of your consumer expenditures are supporting products produced by a woman. Equally comforting is the knowledge that women are at the forefront of the conservation crusade and are contributing significantly to the progress of the marine sciences. If only it were possible to spotlight each and every one of them!

CHAPTER 13

Four Pioneering Spirits

FRANCESCA LaMONTE

MOLLIE BEATTIE

MARILYN OSHMAN

JEANNE BRANSON

We commend all of the women whose conviction, dedication, and hard work is singularly and collectively changing women's status in the sport and the industry. And how proud we can be of the professional triumphs particularly represented by the four eminent women portrayed here.

Francesca LaMonte MARINE SCIENTIST • NEW YORK

"In discussing the fishing ladies of the world, the woman whose name comes at the lead, strange as it may seem, has caught very few if any fish on rod and reel and she only goes out on the deep sea occasionally. [But] she does more for fishing, fishermen, and fish than probably any other person today and she knows more about fish than probably any man or woman," wrote Chisie Farrington in her 1951 book, *Women Can Fish*.[1]

When Francesca LaMonte arrived at the American Museum of Natural History in New York in 1919 to work as a secretary in the department of ichthyology (the branch of zoology dealing with fishes), no one could have predicted that this 24-year-old woman would someday rank as one of the great pioneers in marine research or produce seven definitive books on the world's fresh and saltwater species.

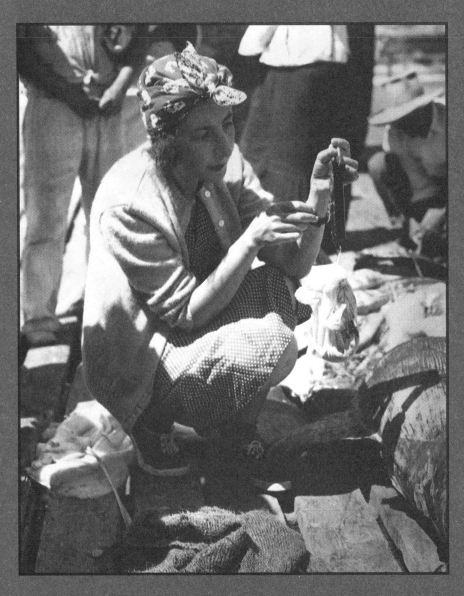

SCIENTIST FRANCESCA LaMONTE OF
THE AMERICAN MUSEUM OF NATURAL
HISTORY WAS AN EARLY PIONEER IN
MARINE RESEARCH DURING THE 1930S
AND 1940S AND THE AUTHOR OF SEVEN
LANDMARK BOOKS.

That's because Francesca had no academic credentials in the sciences; in fact, there's no evidence she even took a science class while pursuing a bachelor's degree and certificate in music at her alma mater, Wellesley College. What she did have, on the other hand, was a keen mind and a ferocious appetite for hard work that quickly made her an indispensable member of the museum's staff.

By the early 1920s, she was assisting in the creation of a complex bibliography of fishes by translating technical papers written in Italian, French, Spanish, German, Russian, and other languages into English. In 1929, she was made the assistant curator of ichthyology; in 1930, she served as a delegate to the International Congress of Zoologists in Italy; in 1934, her first book (co-authored), *The Vanishing Wilderness*, was published; and in 1935, she was appointed to the prestigious position of associate curator of the Department of Living & Extinct Fishes.

Chances are Francesca would have spent the rest of her career within the museum's hallowed halls, writing scholarly papers, planning displays, and cataloguing new specimens if her life hadn't fatefully intersected with Michael Lerner's in 1935. (See Chapter 7.) Of the seven groundbreaking scientific expeditions Lerner sponsored on behalf of the American Museum of Natural History, Francesca was a key member of the research contingent on five: Nova Scotia in 1936 and 1938; Bimini in 1937; New Zealand and Australia in 1939; and Peru and Chile in 1940 (the latter in the capacity of scientific director).

It cannot be overemphasized how critical these expeditions were to producing the first quantifiable body of knowledge on the ocean's fishes as well as how important was Francesca's role in them. During each months-long trip, the Lerners departed each morning in search of specimens, which they caught with rod and reel. In the evening, Francesca and her co-researchers met them at the dock and often worked until daybreak, measuring, dissecting, and recording every inch of the fish that came in, searching for physiological, dietary, migratory, and other clues. Francesca also became one of the chief researchers at the museum's marine laboratory and live-fish pools in Bimini, which the Lerners had constructed and donated.

It also cannot be overstated how dedicated Francesca was to her work. While it hardly seems possible that she would have the time, she produced a stream of authoritative books over the years: co-editor of *Field Book of Fresh Water Fishes of North America* in 1938; author of *North American Game Fishes* in 1945; co-editor of *Game Fishes of the World* in 1949; co-editor of *The Fisherman's Encyclopedia* in 1950; and author of *Marine Game Fishes of the World* in 1952 and *Giant Fishes of the Ocean* in 1966.

At the same time, she planned and supervised the installation of many of the museum's massive exhibits, and she kept up an amazing number of professional affiliations with organizations such as the New York Academy of Sciences, the American Association for the Advancement of Science, the American Society of Ichthyologists and Herpetologists, and the Society of Systematic Zoology, among others.

As important as her cutting-edge research was the instrumental role that Francesca played in the founding of the International Game Fish Association in 1939 and its subsequent administration. The only woman present at that historic first meeting on June 7, 1939, Francesca was designated as IGFA's secretary and was appointed to its executive committee (along with president Michael Lerner, Ernest Hemingway, and others), and she served as the editor of the organization's many publications. Most remarkable of all, perhaps, is the lack of information that exists on this mysterious spirit. She apparently wanted it that way. Her will specifically requested that no obituaries were to be released upon her death, even by the museum. All we really know, other than the fact that she was universally admired by everyone who came into contact with her, is that she was born in 1895, apparently never married, had no children, and died at the age of 87 in 1982.

One thing is certain, however: Without this great ichthyologist's bold research and literary contributions, modern efforts to salvage habitat and preserve saltwater species would have been set back untold years — perhaps years too late.

Mollie Beattie

DIRECTOR OF THE U.S. FISH AND WILDLIFE SERVICE • WASHINGTON, D.C.

"The long, drab corridor that leads to the office of the director of the U.S. Fish and Wildlife Service begins with a portrait gallery of former directors that spans six decades. On the wall are 10 black-and-white photographs of somber, middle-aged white men, stiff and self-conscious in their dark suits and pressed white shirts, each frame of uniform size. Atop them all is a new photo, this one in color. In the foreground, oblivious to the camera, stands a woman dressed in hip waders, clutching a pair of field glasses, poised at the water's edge while a Kodiak bear lingers on the opposite shore. Change has come to the Fish and Wildlife Service, and its name is Mollie Hanna Beattie," announced Ted Gup in *Audubon* magazine in 1994.[2]

On September 10, 1993, Mollie Beattie became the first woman director of the U.S. Fish and Wildlife Service, a complex federal agency with jurisdiction over nearly 500 wildlife refuges spread across about 100 million acres of public lands.

It is a formidable task involving a vast array of burning issues which routinely land Mollie and the agency on the nation's front pages. For one, there is the Endangered Species Act, which has lately been on the endangered list itself as a result of appearing to pit economically starved rural communities against targeted species such as the northern spotted owl. Another issue which has come to the fore, particularly since the great Mississippi River flood of 1993, is the agency's stance on flood control, which essentially promotes flood-plain restoration as necesssary to biodiverse habitat and is in direct conflict with classic measures like the building of dikes and other man-made river controls. The biggest issue, however, has been Mollie's advocacy of ecosystem management versus single-species protection. This stance has made her a controversial figure, particularly with hunters who fear that her policies will mean the end of the ample supply of wild waterfowl (among other game) they've historically had access to on the nation's wildlife refuges.

All in all, it's the kind of job that is guaranteed to produce ulcers and many sleepless nights. Yet this 48-year-old woman has distinguished herself for having the courage to take a leadership position rather than hiding behind her bureaucratic title, as so often happens within government. When she's not in back-to-back high-level meetings, she is crisscrossing the country, speaking before groups that often do not share her philosophy on how to manage our natural resources for the future.

From her first day on the job, Mollie barely had time to learn the location of the women's restroom before she was expected to converse fluently on such diverse subjects as Indian treaty rights and Native Alaskan mythology, the Clean Water Act, the Superfund, the Farm Bill, the Federal Power Act, the esoterica of Western and Tribal water law, the hydrogeology of aquifers in Texas and Idaho, the Convention on International Trade in Endangered Species, the wild-bird trade in Central America, GATT, NAFTA, and the biodiversity treaty—all involving her agency.

In 1993, Mollie Beattie became
the first female director of the
U.S. Fish and Wildlife Service in
the history of that critically
important federal agency.

Even with one master's degree in forestry from the University of Vermont and another in public administration from the Kennedy School of Government at Harvard University, it was a long time before Mollie discovered her calling on the front lines in the perceived battle between civilization and nature.

Seeds were certainly planted from childhood visits with her grandmother, a self-trained botanist who nursed injured wild animals on her upstate New York farm. "I got her ethic: that if it moves, feed it," Mollie told Ted Gup. But in every other way she was a typical teenage girl of the early 1960s. "I never went outside the house without being heavily made-up. I had never slept in a sleeping bag," she also related.

After receiving a bachelor's degree in philosophy from Marymount College in Tarrytown, New York, Mollie's day of reckoning with nature finally came at the age of 26 when she attended a three-week Outward Bound course in Colorado. Obviously, someone forgot to tell her she would be spending her days scaling craggy cliffs and hiking endless miles of wilderness trails, because she arrived with a suitcase packed with brand-new hiking boots which had never been broken in, electric curlers, and a hair dryer. When the grueling experience was over, she was more than ready to pack up and head to the writing job that was waiting for her at a country magazine. Instead, however, she unexpectedly accepted Outward Bound's offer to return to work as an instructor, which she did during the following three summers.

While she was getting her first master's, Mollie also taught resource management to private landowners through the University of Vermont's extension service and served as project director for an experimental game-bird habitat program. Between 1983 and 1985, she worked for the nonprofit Windham Foundation, directing a series of seminars on critical statewide issues and managing their 1,300 acres of farm and forest land with an emphasis on wildlife habitat improvement.

From 1985 to 1989, she served as the commissioner of the Vermont Department of Forests, Parks and Recreation, which administers 250,000 acres of public land, including wildlife habitat areas and 48 state parks. And she got her first taste of controversy as she moved the state towards confronting such simmering issues as clear-cutting, pesticide use, resort development, and air and water quality.

From there, she became the deputy secretary for Vermont's Agency of Natural Resources between 1989 and 1990; received her MPA from Harvard in 1991; and worked as the executive director for the Vermont-based public-policy institute, the Richard A. Snelling Center for Government, for three years.

Then came her meteoric rise to the position of director of the Fish and Wildlife Service, requiring a necessary move to Washington, D.C., from the tiny historic town of Grafton, Vermont (population 600), where she and her husband continue to maintain the rustic but solar-powered home they built there. "It's been my hardest adjustment—the lack of darkness at night, living in a place that's never quiet, the confinement of it," she has said. "On the other hand, I've been gone so long from the city, it's not been entirely unpleasant to check back in with the vibrance of humanity."

Few would argue the courage it requires to take an unpopular position and stick with it in today's volatile political climate, particularly when it comes to issues concerning the environment. Ted Williams writes in *Fly Rod & Reel* that after hearing Mollie speak at a 1994 gathering of the Outdoors Writers of America, he invited the distinguished outdoors writer Dr. Michael Frome to rate her job performance. "Mike has an abiding distrust of government at all levels; in the quarter-century I have known him, I have never heard him gush about anything, and he is downright miserly in dispensing praise for the utterances of federal bureaucrats," Williams explains. What did Frome say? "Well, I can see why you think she's so special," he told Williams. "She's too good to last."

"Maybe," Williams concludes. "But if she leaves office before President Clinton, one thing's for certain—it won't be by her choosing. Mollie Beattie is one smart, tough, stubborn Vermont Yankee. And all of us who treasure the earth ... have waited too long for her and her message."[3]

Marilyn Oshman CHAIRMAN OF OSHMAN'S SPORTING GOODS, INC. • TEXAS

Sporting-goods stores the size of Kmarts are the wave of the future, and Marilyn Oshman is determined to make sure that at least one large chain—hers—caters to women and their special needs nonetheless.

Although she didn't start Oshman's—which today reigns among the biggest independent sporting-goods chains in the country with more than 160 stores—she certainly grew up in its shadow. Founded by her late father, Jake Oshman, in 1931, the business underwent a dramatic expansion in the 1970s and 1980s under the auspices of Marilyn's ex-husband, Alvin Lubetkin. Then came the recession, and by 1989 the family empire was gushing red ink, forcing store closures as fast as they had opened only a few years before. Clearly, it was time for the company's largest stockholder to get out of the boardroom and into the showroom, and that's exactly what Marilyn Oshman did in 1991, subsequently becoming the chairman of the board in 1993.

"It's 9:45 on a Saturday morning in southwest Houston, 15 minutes before the retail day begins at one of the Oshman's

Supersports stores, and Marilyn Oshman is peptalking the 30 or so fidgeting cashiers, bike salesmen, assistant managers, and shoe-department guys. She's dressed as a lady sporting-goods commando, decked out in Oshman wear: olive city shorts and jacket, a camouflage T-shirt, and Timberland hiking boots from the shoe department. The effect is of a general rallying her troops," wrote Lisa Gray in an admiring profile in *Lear's* magazine.[4]

Forget that this finishing-school graduate (she also obtained a B.A. from Finch College in New York) spent most of her adulthood sitting on museum boards and attending art openings in addition to holding a family seat on Oshman's board. When the crisis hit, her latent instincts as a guerrilla marketer were there, like buried genetic code.

After taking a whirlwind assessment tour of Oshman's ailing retail empire, she came to the conclusion that "we were not serving women the way we should, and neither was our competition."[5] So she instigated an internal revolution that began with rearranging the merchandise displays: Swiss Army knives, which had been relegated to the hunting department, were now on view in the women's department; mace and mugger "screechers," which had been hidden away in the gun department, were now relocated to their logical place next to women's running clothes. It went on and on until Marilyn had worked her way through the inventory, relying primarily on her feminine instincts to guide her decisions on how women shop.

She also immediately created what would become an annual Oshman's tradition, the "Women & Sports" extravaganza, which is mounted simultaneously at the Oshman's SuperSports USA outlets. Now in its sixth year, this one-day event features top female athletes and outdoors personalities speaking and

As chairman of Oshman's Sporting
Goods, Inc., Marilyn Oshman has
revolutionized sports retailing
for women.

leading women through a large menu of workshops and how-to demonstrations.

Marilyn has been so effective in bringing home the point concerning how female consumers have been ignored that she was invited to appear on a four-woman panel sponsored by the Sporting Goods Manufacturers. "You would have thought we had gotten in a room and huddled, that we all had known each other for at least two years. We all said the same thing: We want to be considered, we want to be acknowledged in a sporting goods store, and beyond, that we want clothing, equipment and shoes designed for our differences and for us. That's what we want," she recounted to the trade journal, *Sporting Goods Business*.[6]

In 1994, Marilyn not only served as the chairperson of "Becoming an Outdoors Woman 1994," sponsored by the Texas Parks and Wildlife Department, she was also honored by *The Houston Post* and the Texas Executive Women organization. In addition, she serves as the only female board member of the Texas Parks & Wildlife Foundation.

Marilyn also fishes. As a child, she spent many a day on the family's pond, bass fishing with her father. One memorable day she asked him why he caught more fish than she. The sage advice that came back is as apt to business as it is to fishing: "Look at your pole. Where is your bait?" It was, of course, in the boat. "Where is my bait? It's in the water. Just remember, you can't catch a fish if your bait's not in the water."[7]

"She's a true visionary and a risk-taker," the female head of one women's athletic-shoe company told the *Houston Chronicle*, when asked to assess Marilyn's managerial performance. "Women are coming into their own in sports, and Oshman's is on the cutting edge for retailers. No one else is doing anything like what Oshman's is doing."[8]

"Jeanne Branson didn't invent the Northwest Territories
or Arctic char fishing, but she was one of the pioneers who did
much to publicize angling in the vast wilderness," praised Jim
Chapralis in a recent issue of *The PanAngler*. "I recall one day
when she had just returned from a long fly-out trip with many
happy guests and some big char. They had fished all night, in
this land of the Midnight Sun, and they couldn't wait to get back
and go to sleep. Some of the other guests, well-rested, insisted
that they wanted to do the fly-out trip for char. Jeanne got back
into the plane—totally exhausted—to lead this second group.
Clearly, she was the *Queen of the Northwest Territories*."[9]

In 1973, *The Calgary Herald Magazine* declared of this peer-
less woman: "The Jeanne Branson Show is something else again.
Whether it's a $1 million fishing lodge on Great Bear Lake, a
four-passenger float plane or a team of huskies, it is distinctly
her baby. Mrs. Branson is the boss-lady of Branson's Lodge,
located in Cameron Bay on the east side of Great Bear, a mere
50-mile cast from the Arctic Circle. One thousand miles from
nowhere. It's a tough job, a man's job really, and husband John
takes care of much of the detail. But essentially it is Jeanne who
struts on the surface, calling shots with the authority of a head
coach, and may the devil take the man—and sometimes beast—
who thinks otherwise."[10]

Calling Jeanne Branson a legend in her own time is
putting it mildly. This renowned bush pilot, crack shot, expert
angler, and highly successful entrepreneur was once the subject
of so many gushing newspaper and magazine spreads that you'd
have thought a New York press agent was hiding somewhere in
the background. But then Jeanne is the kind of tough-as-nails
character whose life will probably be made into a movie someday.

Born in Belgium but raised in northern Alberta on a wilderness ranch, Jeanne grew up under highly unusual circumstances. Her father trained circus animals for a large American circus, so, not surprisingly, she was training sled dogs by the age of 10. As the story goes, while attending a traveling show one day, Jeanne talked an attendant into letting her enter the lion's cage, which contained three large cats. The moment she stepped in, the ringmaster barked out, "Ladies and gentlemen, the youngest woman lion tamer in the world—if she lives!" And a career was born.

By the time she was 15, Jeanne was spending her summers traveling the world with the Royal American Shows as a lion and tiger trainer. Each fall, she returned home to Alberta to hunt and fish. Somewhere on the road she met John Branson, a famous dirt-track car racer who trained seals on the side and sold them to zoos and animal acts. They married in 1947, settled down, and built a large winter resort in Parker, Arizona, on the Colorado River.

With the cry of the north still in her blood, Jeanne decided to build a second resort, this one in Canada. After an exhaustive hunt for the perfect location, they opted for conceivably one of the remotest spots in the world: Great Bear Lake, in a portion of the Northwest Territories that straddles the Arctic Circle. For those unfamiliar with it, Great Bear Lake is one of the largest bodies of fresh water in the world (250 miles long and 150 miles wide), making it subject to "huge waves that can shred a small boat in minutes."[11]

Just building the lodge was a formidable task. There were no roads into the place and the nearest town was 500 miles away by air. Everything from the building materials to the work crew had to be transported in by plane. Yet Jeanne got it open in 1962.

Guests like baseball great Ted Williams arrived by turboprop jets to find a virtual oasis of civilization, with gourmet meals prepared by a mainland chef, a cocktail bar, a tackle shop, and even modern plumbing. What's more amazing, the resort remained open only two months a year, the only time the lake was not frozen. The water was so cold, even during the summer months, "that when you dipped a cup in and took a drink it would make your teeth tingle," Jeanne once joked.[12] "This is not a routine fishing hole, in case you couldn't tell. Neither is the woman who runs it," writer Harlan Bartlett of the Copley News Service announced to the country in the early 1970s.[13]

Added Jim Brezina in the *Los Angeles Herald-Examiner*: "Probably the only woman guide in the Arctic, Mrs. Branson, a statuesque brunet, outfishes most men and has a 60-pound laker to her credit. A daring woman, she thinks nothing of jumping into one of her three float planes and heading out over the huge lake or Arctic Circle to locate better fishing spots for her guests. Husband John . . . prefers to stay 'home' and maintain the lodge, boats and motors."[14]

Once a holder of two world records and an early advocate of barbless hooks, Jeanne was frequently heard preaching the philosophy, "Limit your catch, don't kill your limit."

In 1973, John's deteriorating health forced them to sell the Branson Lodge. Even so, it will always remain close to Jeanne's heart. "I've hunted and fished all over the world, but there's nothing like the fish and the serenity and quiet you get on Great Bear," she said near the end. "I used to think there must be a place where the fish hit every day and I found it. I've been there 10 years. I built it from scratch, which took intestinal fortitude, but I had fallen in love with it."

Anyone wishing to meet this incredible treasure simply has to stop by Branson's Resort in Parker, Arizona, where Jeanne still manages her motel, RV park, and marina on the Colorado River. Surely you didn't think the great Jeanne Branson would have retired, did you?

PART V

The First-Ever Women's Angling Resource Directory

Do you know of an organization or a women-owned business or service that should be included in a future edition of this directory?

If so, please mail your suggestions (with names, addresses, and phone numbers) to:

Reel Women: The World of Women Who Fish

P.O. Box 939, Welches, OR 97067

The information contained herein is provided as a courtesy. No warranties or endorsements of any business, service, product, or organization is intended.

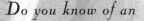

PATTY BARNES, CO-OWNER OF THE FLY FISHING SHOP IN WELCHES, OREGON, REPRESENTS THE GROWING LEGION OF WOMEN WORKING IN THE ANGLING INDUSTRY TODAY.

National and Regional Organizations

WOMEN'S

Bass'n Gal

P.O. Box 13925
Arlington, TX 76013
(817) 265-6214; fax (817) 265-6290
Founded by Sugar Ferris in 1976, Bass'n Gal boasts nearly 30,000 individual members and some 100 affiliated clubs across the country. The Bass'n Gal Tournament Trail consists of a handful of invitational tournaments, open to all interested participants, which leads to the end-of-the-season Classic Star world championship. Other events include an annual Affiliate Club Tournament of Champions. Members receive the bimonthly Bass'n Gal magazine, filled with tournament results and fishing tips. To join the national organization, call or write to the above address. To locate or start a club in your area, contact Carol Boykin at the address listed at the beginning of the next section.

"Becoming an Outdoors Woman"

Dr. Christine Thomas
College of Natural Resources
University of Wisconsin–Stevens Point
Stevens Point, WI 54481
(715) 346-4185
This increasingly-popular weekend workshop is sweeping the country as more states sign up to teach women basic outdoor skills in such areas as hunting, fishing, camping, canoeing, nature photography, and more. Thirty-two states and two Canadian provinces participated in 1995. For the dates and locations of upcoming workshops in your state, contact your state natural resources department or Dr. Christine Thomas directly.

International Women's Fishing Association (IWFA)

P.O. Box 3125
Palm Beach, FL 33480
This nonprofit organization was established in 1955 to promote angling competition among women anglers, encourage conservation, and foster and promote release tournaments. Activities include major bass and billfish tournaments for members, a members' Hall of Fame, and the IWFA Scholarship Trust to help needy students attain graduate degrees in the marine sciences.

GENERAL

The Adopt-A-Stream Foundation

P.O. Box 5558
Everett, WA 98206
(206) 388-3487
Mission: Environmental education and stream enhancement. Conducts "Streamkeeper" and "Adopt-A-Stream" workshops to train volunteers to become monitors and stewards. Present focus: Pacific Northwest.

American Bass Association

2810 Trotters Trail
Wetumpka, AL 36092
(205) 567-6035; fax (205) 567-8632
Nonprofit national association dedicated to the protection and enhancement of fisheries resources, promotion of bass fishing as a major sport, and introduction of fishing to children.

American Casting Association

Dale Lanser, executive secretary
1773 Lance End Lane
Fenton, MO 63026
(314) 225-9443
National organization with individual members, regional, state, and local groups.

American Rivers

801 Pennsylvania Ave., S.E., Suite 400
Washington, DC 20003-2167
(202) 547-6900; fax (202) 543-6142
Focus: Protection and restoration of river systems and promotion of a river stewardship ethic. Advocates strong state laws and environmental safeguards through national hydropower policy.

Anglers for Clean Water, Inc.

P.O. Box 17900
Montgomery, AL 36141
(205) 272-9530
Nonprofit organization (affiliated with Bass Anglers Sportsman Society) dedicated to the stewardship of America's aquatic resources. Plays a leadership role in conservation and clean-up efforts and the development of a number of conservation-awareness campaigns. Instrumentally involved in the passage of a significant federally funded fisheries enhancement program in 1984 and the creation of the National Lake Cleanup Campaign in 1987, among others.

Atlantic Salmon Federation

P.O. Box 429
St. Andrews, N.B., Canada E0G 2X0
(506) 529-4581; fax (506) 529-4438

International nonprofit organization comprised of groups and individual members dedicated to the preservation and wise management of the Atlantic Salmon and its habitat.

Association of Northwest Steelheaders

P.O. Box 22065
Milwaukie, OR 97269
(503) 653-4176

Regional organization dedicated to restoring and enhancing salmon, trout, and steelhead populations and their habitats for present and future generations. Contact for location of local chapters.

Bass Anglers Sportsman Society (BASS)

P.O. Box 17900
Montgomery, AL 36141
(334) 272-9530

Founded in 1967 by Ray Scott, this 600,000-strong organization sponsors the largest tournament trail in the country, a national program of affiliated chapters, and numerous educational and pro-conservation programs such as CastingKids, Anglers for Clean Water, and Living Waters Symposium. Members receive the monthly Bassmaster *magazine.*

Billfish Foundation

2419 E. Commercial Blvd., Suite 303
Fort Lauderdale, FL 33308
(305) 938-0150 or (305) 938-5311

A nonprofit organization dedicated to the conservation of billfish worldwide through scientific research and education.

Gulf Coast Conservation Association

4801 Woodway, Suite 220-W
Houston, TX 77056
(713) 626-4222

Dedicated to the protection of the marine resource on the Texas Gulf Coast through restocking programs, support of stronger conservation laws, improvement of law enforcement, and a legal defense fund.

Federation of Fly Fishers

P.O. Box 1595
502 S. 19th, Suite 1
Bozeman, MT 59771-1595
(406) 585-7592

International organization comprised of regional councils, local clubs, and individuals dedicated to education and conservation.

Future Fisherman Foundation

1033 N. Fairfax St., Suite 200
Alexandria, VA 22314
(501) 484-0055

Sponsor of the national program, "Hooked on Fishing, Not on Drugs."

Great Lakes Sport Fishing Council

P.O. Box 297
Elmhurst, IL 60126
(708) 941-1351; fax (708) 941-1196

A nonprofit confederation of organizations and individuals throughout the Great Lakes states and provinces concerned with the present and future state of sportfishing in the area, as well as the conservation and protection of its waters, wetlands, habitat, and environment.

International Game Fish Association

1301 E. Atlantic Blvd.
Pompano Beach, FL 33060
(305) 941-3474

The international arbiter of world records for saltwater, freshwater, and fly fishing. This nonprofit organization also maintains and promotes ethical angling regulations, serves as a leader in research and conservation (including game-fish tagging programs and other scientific data-collection efforts), and acts as a clearinghouse on legislative developments. Sponsors annual tournament. Maintains one of the world's largest libraries on angling literature and history. Individual memberships welcome.

International Light Tackle Tournament Association

2044 Federal Ave.
Costa Mesa, CA 92627
(714) 548-4273

Conservation organization comprised of individual clubs (all members of the IGFA) involved with billfishing on 20- to 30-pound test lines. Sponsors annual tournament and publishes post-tournament bulletin.

Lake Michigan Federation
59 E. Van Buren, Suite 2215
Chicago, IL 60605
(312) 939-2708

A coalition of citizens and organizations in Wisconsin, Illinois, Indiana, and Michigan dedicated to protecting Lake Michigan through community action and research.

Muskies, Inc.
2301 – 7th St., N.
Fargo, ND 58102
(701) 239-9540

Nonprofit organization dedicated to establishing hatcheries and introducing the Muskellunge into suitable waters, conservation, and research.

National Wildlife Federation
1400 Sixteenth St., N.W.
Washington, DC 20036-2266
(202) 797-6800

Mission: To educate and inspire, and to assist individuals and organizations of diverse cultures to conserve wildlife and other natural resources.

North American Fishing Club
12301 Whitewater Drive, Suite 260
Minnetonka, MN 55343
(612) 936-0555 or 1-800-843-6232

475,000 members in the U.S. and Canada. Promotion of members' fishing skills and enjoyment of the sport. Publishes North American Fisherman *seven times a year.*

River Network
P.O. Box 8787
Portland, OR 97207
(503) 241-3506

National nonprofit organization dedicated to helping people save rivers.

Stripers Unlimited, Inc.
P.O. Box 3045
South Attleboro, MA 02703
(508) 761-7983

Nonprofit organization formed to promote, conserve, and protect striped bass.

Trout Unlimited
1500 Wilson Blvd., Suite 310
Arlington, VA 22009-2310
(703) 522-0200

Nonprofit international organization dedicated to the protection of clean water and the enhancement of trout, salmon, and steelhead habitat. Contact for local chapter information.

MUSEUMS

The American Museum of Fly Fishing
P.O. Box 42
Manchester, VT 05254
(802) 362-3300

The Catskill Fly Fishing Center and Museum
P.O. Box 1295
5447 Old Route 17
Livingston Manor, NY 12758-1295
(914) 439-4810

The National Fresh Water Fishing Hall of Fame & Museum
Box 33
Hall of Fame Drive
Hayward, WI 54843
(715) 634-4440

State and International Clubs, Businesses, and Services Offered by or for Women

Bass'n Gal Affiliated Clubs
To locate or to start a club in your area, please contact:
Carol Boykin, director
National Affiliated Clubs
Bass'n Gal
2625 Wicker Road, Indianapolis, IN 46217
(317) 889-6549; fax (317) 353-2582

Key:

A	Adventure or travel service	HF	Handcrafted flies
C	Co-ed angling organization	I	Fishing instruction
CH	Charter fishing service	M	Marina
CR	Custom-rod builder	R	Resort or motel
F	Fly-fishing tackle store	T	General tackle store
G	Professional guide service	WC	Women-only angling organization

ALABAMA

Jean Davidson
Sandy Shore, #3
Miller's Ferry, AL 36760
(334) 682-4009
R, G

Guys & Dolls Couples Tournaments
(*See Georgia.*)

ALASKA

Cecilia "Pudge" Kleinkauf
Women's Flyfishing
P.O. Box 243-963
Anchorage, AK 99524
(907) 561-7113
G, I, HF

Capt. Leslie Anne Pemberton
Puffin Family Charters
P.O. Box 90743
Anchorage, AK 99509
(907) 278-3346
CH

Dawn Ring, buyer
Gary King Sporting Goods
202 E. Northern Lights Blvd.
Anchorage, AK 99503-4098
(907) 272-5401
T, I

Alaska FlyFishers
P.O. Box 90011
Anchorage, AK 99509
C

Alaska Women of the Wilderness
P.O. Box 773556
Eagle River, AK 99577
(907) 688-2226; fax (907) 696-3297
I

Ilene Hirsh
Flies By Ilene
2410 Eagle River Road
Eagle River, AK 99577
(907) 694-6946 (voice and fax)
HF

Claire Dubin
The Talstar Lodge
P.O. Box 870978
Wasilla, AK 99687
(907) 733-1672 (June–September)
(907) 688-1116 (October–May)
R

Pam Barnes, owner
Llama Buddies Expeditions
P.O. Box 874995
Wasilla, AK 99687
(907) 376-8472
A

ARIZONA

Jeanne Branson
Branson's Resort
R.R. No. 2, Box 710, Riverside Drive
Parker, AZ 85344
(602) 667-3346; fax (602) 667-2085
R, M

Robyn Anderson, co-owner,
c/o Carmine Isgro, manager
Canyon Creek Anglers
21 W. Camelback Road
Phoenix, AZ 85013
(602) 277-8195
F, I

ARKANSAS

Lucy Mize
P.O. Box 13
Ben Lomond, AR 71823
(501) 287-4845
G

Charlotte Downey, owner
Beaver Dam Store
Rt. 2, Box 419
Eureka Springs, AR 72632
(501) 253-6154
F, I

Bass'n Badges
c/o Kelly and Arletta Wallace
P.O. Box 1124
Gravette, AR 72736
(501) 787-9916
C

Bass'n Badges—Southern Charter
c/o John Gaddy
2712 Belmoor
Pine Bluff, AR 71601
(501) 543-5109
C

Sallyann Brown, fly-fishing instructor
8298 Adm. Nimitz Drive
Rogers, AR 72756
(501) 925-4155
I

Judy Gould, owner
Fish 'n Stuff
7430 Landers Road
Sherwood, AR 72117
(501) 834-5733
T

CALIFORNIA

Maggie Merriman Fly Fishing Schools
P.O. Box 755
West Yellowstone, MT 59758
(818) 282-3173 (November–April)
I. (See Montana for summer months.)

Marla Allison, owner
Ebbetts Pass Sporting Goods
925 Hwy. 4
P.O. Box 579
Arnold, CA 95223
(209) 795-1686
T

Josette Woolley, co-owner
Fly Fishing Outfitters
3533 Mount Diablo Blvd.
Lafayette, CA 94549
(510) 284-3474
F, G, I

Judy Warren, owner
"Horse Feathers" Fly Fishing School
20505 Hwy. 89
Markleeville, CA 96120
(916) 694-2399
G, I, HF

Debbie Elie, vice president
Outdoor Pro Shop
6315 Commerce Blvd.
Rohnert Park, CA 94928
(707) 588-8033
F

Eileen Stroud, owner
Stroud Tackle
1457 Morena Blvd.
San Diego, CA 92110
(619) 276-4822
F

Fanny Krieger, co-owner
Club Pacific
790 – 27th Ave.
San Francisco, CA 94121
(415) 752-0192
A, I

Golden West Women Flyfishers
P.O. Box 22068
San Francisco, CA 94122
(415) 752-0192
WC

Josette Woolley, co-owner
Fly Fishing Outfitters
463 Bush St.
San Francisco, CA 94108
(415) 781-FISH
F, G

Jacky Douglas, skipper
The Wacky Jacky
473 Bella Vista Way
San Francisco, CA 94127
(415) 586-9800
CH

Virginia Graves, owner
Tobacco Leaf/Delta Angler Fly Shop
123 Lincoln Center, Stockton, CA 95207
(209) 474-8216; fax (209) 477-8412
F

Pam Schuelke
Kingfish Guide Service
P.O. Box 5955
Tahoe City, CA 96145
(916) 525-5360
G

Lisa Cutter, co-owner
California School of Flyfishing
P.O. Box 8212
Truckee, CA 96162
1-800-58-TROUT
G, I

COLORADO

Naomi Keys, co-owner
Cottonwood Meadows
34591 Hwy. 17
Antonito, CO 81120
(719) 376-5660
F, G

Mountain Angler
P.O. Box 467
311 S. Main St.
Breckenridge, CO 80424
(303) 453-HOOK or 1-800-453-4669
F, I, G

Alpine Angling & Adventure Travel
48 Weant Blvd.
Carbondale, CO 81623
(303) 963-9245
F, G

Jon Marie Broz
The Flyfisher Ltd.
252 Clayton St.
Denver, CO 80206
(303) 322-5014
F, G, I

Flyfisher Ladies Angling Club
c/o The Flyfisher Ltd., Denver
WC

Western Anglers Fly Shop
2454 Hwy. 6 & 50, Suite 103
Grand Junction, CO 81505
(970) 244-8658 or 1-800-513-FISH
F

Rhonda Sapp, co-owner
The Colorado Angler
1457 Nelson St.
Lakewood, CO 80215
(303) 232-8298; fax (303) 239-9693
F, G, I

Chris Lokay, manager
Gore Creek Fly Fishermen
183 E. Gore Creek Drive
Vail, CO 81657
(303) 476-3296
F, G, I

CONNECTICUT

Fall Mountain Sports, Inc.
420 N. Main St.
Bristol, CT 06010
(203) 589-1282
T

The Better Half Bass Club
c/o Amy Perry, president
44 Parker Hill Road Ext.
Killingworth, CT 06419
(203) 663-3330
WC

Fran McDonald
Drake Rod Co.
31 Pinewoods Road
New Hartford, CT 06057
(203) 379-4371
CR

Roberta Petit, co-owner
The Riverton General Store
Route 20
Riverton, CT 06065
(203) 379-0811
T

Dawn Hubbard, co-owner
Triple T's Tackle and Variety
7 Willow St.
Torrington, CT 06790
(203) 489-8325
T

DELAWARE

Delaware Bass Chapter Federation
c/o Bill Moore
986 Bay Road
Milford, DE 19963
(302) 422-6782
C

FLORIDA

Guys & Dolls Couples Tournaments
(*See Georgia.*)

Christina Sharpe, co-owner
Sea Boots Outfitters
110 Ships Way
Big Pine Key, FL 33043
(305) 872-9005
T, F

Susan Skinner, co-owner
**Grand Slam Fishing Center and Fancy
   Rods & Reel World**
101-A Seaway Drive
Fort Pierce, FL 34950
(407) 465-6775
CR, T, I

The Pompano Beach Fishing Rodeo, Inc.
P.O. Box 5584
Lighthouse Point, FL 33074
(305) 942-4513; fax (305) 942-2974

Annual Ladies Tarpon Tournament
c/o Dave Navarro
World Class Angler
5050 Overseas Highway
Marathon, FL 33050
(305) 743-6139

Anne Denty, publisher
Florida's Fishnews
FIN Media, Inc.
1297 Venetian Way
Naples, FL 33963
(813) 597-7607; fax (813) 598-1832

South Florida Fishing Club
16345 Dixie Highway, Suite 232
North Miami Beach, FL 33160
C

Marsha Bierman
601 N.W. 110th
Plantation, FL 33324
(305) 949-1444 or (305) 423-3474
Fax (305) 949-0755

Kathy Ogle, co-owner
Bill's Tackle Shop
135 W. Marion Ave.
Punta Gorda, FL 33950
(813) 639-1305
T

**Annual Old Salt Ladies Fishing
   Tournament
(Yvonne Wisely or Jaclyn Turner)**
c/o Wiseley Marine Insurance
9300 – 5th St., N.
St. Petersburg, FL 33702
(813) 579-9579

Aledia Hunt Tush, owner
Mr. CB's Saltwater Outfitters
1249 Stickney Point Road
Siesta Key
Sarasota, FL 34242
(813) 349-4400 or (813) 346-2466
T, F, G

Capt. Merrily Pope
c/o Mr. CB's
Siesta Key, FL
(813) 371-8401 or (813) 346-2466
G

Jan Fogt, outdoors writer
P.O. Box 1847
Stuart, FL 34995
(407) 287-9272

Dorothy Gillette, owner
Sporting Classics of Tampa
1702 S. Dale Mabry
Tampa, FL 33629
(813) 254-5627; fax (813) 254-5627
F, I

GEORGIA

Laurie Lee Dovey,
    outdoors writer/photographer
160 White Pine Drive
Alpharetta, GA 30201
Fax (404) 772-9925

Joyce Parrish, co-owner
Satterfield's Sporting Goods
310 Broad St., S.W.
Gainesville, GA 30501
(404) 534-2277
T

Guys & Dolls Couples Tournaments
c/o Sandra and Terry Coursey
P.O. Box 816
Palmetto, GA 30268-0816
(404) 463-4652

Capt. Judy L. Helmey
Miss Judy Charters
P.O. Box 30771
Savannah, GA 31410
(912) 897-4921 or (912) 897-2478
CH

HAWAII

Hobbietat, Inc.
1413 – 10th Ave.
Honolulu, HI 96816
(808) 737-9582
T

J&E Fishing Supplies
(Kalihi Shopping Center, near the airport)
2295 N. King St.
Honolulu, HI 96819
T

Capt. Gary Oliver
"ELO" Sports Fishing
350 Ward Ave., Suite 106
Honolulu, HI 96814
(808) 947-5208 or (808) 373-4708
CH

Annual Tropidilla Wahine Fishing
    Tournament (women only)
c/o Capt. Jody Bright
Tropidilla Productions
P.O. Box 2158
Kailua Kona, HI 96745
(808) 322-2010; fax (808) 322-3621

Sundowner Fishing Charters
P.O. Box 5198
Kailua Kona, HI 96745
(808) 329-7253
CH

Finest Kind Sports Fishing
c/o Nancy Garnegt
P.O. Box 10481
Lahaina, HI 96761
(808) 661-0338
CH

ILLINOIS

Mary Satterfield, owner
Eagle Creek Guide Service, Inc.
R.R. 1, Box 200
Findlay, IL 62534
(217) 756-3299
G

Betty Palmer, owner
44 Street Bait & Tackle Shop
4400 – 5th Ave.
Rock Island, IL 61201
(309) 788-9479
T

INDIANA

Janet Ryan
Northwest Indiana Steelheaders
P.O. Box 701
Chesterton, IN 46304
(219) 926-7938
C

IOWA

Norma Fairbanks, owner
Fairbanks' Fishing Hole
3942 – 291st St.
Camanche, IA 52730
(319) 259-1876
R, M

KANSAS

Bass'n Badges
c/o Roy and Linda Roper
812 S. Evergreen
Chanute, KS 66720
(316) 431-3418
C

Jennifer Almond, co-owner
Old Fort Gun and Tackle
1202 E. Wall
Fort Scott, KS 66701
316-223-0001

KENTUCKY

Sunshine Bass'n Gals
c/o Marsha Phillips
P.O. Box 81
Grand Rivers, KY 42045
(502) 362-8778
WC

LOUISIANA

Capt. Mary Poe
Rt. 2, Box 281
Lake Charles, LA 70605
(318) 598-3268
G

Bayou His-n-Hers Bassmasters
c/o Donna Greer
208 Wind Ridge Drive
West Monroe, LA 71291
(318) 396-0539
C

MAINE

Women on the Water
The Ocean Institute
Maine Maritime Academy
Castine, ME 04420
(207) 326-2211
I

L. L. Bean
Casco Street
Freeport, ME 04033
(207) 865-4761 or
1-800-341-4341 (customer service)
F, I

MASSACHUSETTS

Ruth Meyer, owner
Larry's Tackle Shop
141 Main St. (Depot Corner)
P.O. Box 1290
Edgartown, MA 02539-1290
(508) 627-5088; fax (508) 627-5148
T, F, G, I, CH

Marilyn Scheerbaum, owner
Bickerton & Ripley Books
Main Street
Edgartown, MA 02539
(508) 627-8463

Capt. Leslie S. Smith
Backlash Charters
P.O. Box 879
Edgartown, MA 02539
(508) 627-5894 or (508) 627-5088
G, CH, CR

Kay and Martha Moulton
and Liz Cowie, owners
Surfland Bait & Tackle
Plum Island Turnpike
Newbury, MA 01951
(508) 462-4202
T

Janet Messineo, owner
Island Taxidermy Studio
RFD 603
Vineyard Haven, MA 02568
(508) 693-3360

MICHIGAN

Phyllis Johnson, co-owner
Johnson's Pere Marquette Lodge
Rt. 1, Box 1290
Baldwin, MI 49304
(616) 745-3972
F, I, R

Loretta Loomis, co-owner
Ed's Sport Shop
712 N. Michigan Ave.
Baldwin, MI 49304
(616) 745-4974

T

Doris Spohn, owner
Four Seasons Bait & Tackle
1210 N. Cedar
Lansing, MI 48906
(517) 487-0050

T, F

Dorothy Schramm
Rodsmith
6298 W. Longbridge Road
P.O. Box 828
Pentwater, MI 49449-0828
(616) 869-5487 (voice and fax)

CR, I

Capt. Chrisy Hills-Emory
Big John Pro-Team Charters, Inc.
2833 Neah-Ta-Wanta Drive
Traverse City, MI 49686
(616) 223-7790 or 1-800-528-5898

CH, G

MINNESOTA

Bob Mitchell's Fly Shop
3394 Lake Elmo Ave., N.
Lake Elmo, MN 55042
(612) 770-5854

F, I

**Women for Fishing, Hunting
and Wildlife**
c/o Kim Hauglie
6127 Birchwood Hills
Lakeshore, MN 56468
(218) 963-7539

WC

Women Anglers of Minnesota
P.O. Box 580653
Minneapolis, MN 55468-0653
(612) 339-1322

WC

Judith Niemi, director
Women in the Wilderness
566 Ottawa Ave.
St. Paul, MN 55107
(612) 227-2284

A

MISSOURI

Linda Redford
H.C. 1, Box 118
Blue Eye, MO 65611
(417) 779-4338

G

Patricia Rash, co-owner
Right Angle Custom Rods and Tackle
1335 W. Hwy. 76
Branson, MO 65616
(417) 335-4655

F, CR

Wanda Eager, manager
Rainbow Fly & Outfitting Co.
17201 E. 40 Hwy., Suite 106
Independence, MO 64055
(816) 373-2283

F, CR

Marilyn Evers, owner
Paul's Bait & Tackle
4421 Chippewa
St. Louis, MO 63116
(314) 773-6221

T, CR

MONTANA

Betsy French
Gallatin River Guides
Box 160212, Hwy. 191
Big Sky, MT 59716
(406) 995-2290; fax (406) 995-4588

F, G, I

Linda Madsen, co-owner
Montana River Outfitters
2427 Old Havre Hwy.
Black Eagle, MT 59414
(406) 761-1677

F, G, I

Jennifer Olsson
P.O. Box 132
Bozeman, MT 59771
(406) 587-5140 (October–May)

G, I

Lynn Corcoran, co-owner
The River's Edge
2012 N. 7th
Bozeman, MT 59715
(406) 586-5373

F, G, I

Pam McCutcheon
Big Sky Flies & Guides
P.O. Box 40
Emigrant, MT 59027
(406) 222-2004 or (406) 333-4401 (shop)
F, G, R

June Rose, co-owner/guide
Quill Gordon Fly Fishers
P.O. Box 7597
Fort Smith, MT 59035
(406) 666-2253
F, G, R, I

Patti Magnano Madsen
Wolverton's Fly Shop
P.O. Box 1963
210 – 5th St., S.
Great Falls, MT 59403-1963
(406) 761-6313
F, I

Krys Travis, co-owner
Montana's Master Angler Fly Shop
107 S. Main
P.O. Box 1320
Livingston, MT 59047
1-800-814-2270 or (406) 222-2273
F, G, I

Streamside Anglers
317 S. Orange
Missoula, MT 59801
(406) 728-1085
F, G, I

Jackie Mathews, owner
Blue Ribbon Flies
309 Canyon
West Yellowstone, MT
(406) 646-7642
F, I

Maggie Merriman Fly Fishing Schools
P.O. Box 755
West Yellowstone, MT 59758
(406) 646-7824 (April–November)
I. (See California for winter months.)

NEVADA

Karen Jones
5928 Greenery View Lane
Las Vegas, NV 89118
(702) 871-1399
G

Nevada Striper Club
c/o Peg Staten
6412 Burgundy Way
Las Vegas, NV 89107
C

NEW HAMPSHIRE

Janet Thompson, co-owner
Mountain Anglers Fly Shop
44 Main St.
P.O. Box 825
Meredith, NH 03253
(603) 279-3152
F, I

Marianne Conrad, outdoors writer
P.O. Box 743
Merrimack, NH 03054-0743
(603) 429-2018

Zyla's
Route 3
Merrimack, NH 03054
(603) 424-4373
T

NEW MEXICO

Lee Widgren, co-owner
Los Pinos Fly Shop
3214 Matthew, N.E.
Albuquerque, NM 87107
(505) 884-7501
F, CR

She Fishes!
3214 Matthew, N.E.
Albuquerque, NM 87107
(505) 884-7501
WC

Jan Crawford, co-owner
High Desert Angler
435 S. Guadalupe
Santa Fe, NM 87501
(505) 988-7688
F, G, I

NEW YORK

The Wulff School of Fly Fishing
Beaverkill Road
Lew Beach, NY 12758
(914) 439-4060
I

Georgia E. Jones, manager
Jones Outfitters, Ltd.
37 Main St.
Lake Placid, NY 12946
(518) 523-3468
F, I

Orvis New York
355 Madison Ave.
New York, NY 10017
(212) 697-3133
F, I

Renee A. Fisher, vice president
Urban Angler Ltd.
118 E. 25th St.
New York, NY 10010
(212) 979-7600; fax (212) 473-4020
F, I

Capt. Marna Rusher, co-owner
Whitaker's Sport Store and Motel
7700 Rome Road
Pulaski, NY 13142
(315) 298-6162
T, F, G, I

Sandra W. Rademacher, owner
The Royal Coachman Ltd.
9 E. Genesee St., P.O. Box 642
Skaneateles, NY 13152
(315) 685-0005
F, G, I

NORTH CAROLINA

Fran Folb, co-owner
Frank & Fran's Fishermen's Friend
Highway 12
Avon, NC 27915
(919) 995-4171
T

Wendy Eakes, co-owner
Red Drum Tackle Shop
Highway 12
Buxton, NC 27920
(919) 995-5414
T

Alice Kelly Memorial Ladies Only
   Billfish Tournament
c/o Barry Martin
P.O. Box 1879
Manteo, NC 27954
(919) 473-3700 or 1-800-537-7245

Pat Scott, co-owner
Mountain Harbor Marina
9066 N.C. 126
Nebo, NC 28761
(704) 584-0666
T

OHIO

Molly Perkins, owner
Valley Angler/Orvis
13 N. Franklin St.
Chagrin Falls, OH 44022
(216) 247-0242
F, I

Buckeye Lady Anglers
c/o Sheila Hill, president
2143 Melrose Ave.
Columbus, OH 43224
(614) 476-2876
WC

Vera Shafer, owner
Karran Shop
413 South Ridge East
Geneva, OH 44041
(216) 466-3561
T

Capt. Claudie Blaha/Capt. Michelle Blaha
Sportsman's Charter Service
2086 S. Sugar Bush
Marblehead, OH 43440
1-800-546-FISH or (419) 798-4720
CH

Jacquelyn Tibbels, owner
Jackie's Bait & Tackle at Tibbel's Marina
6965 E. Harbor Road
Marblehead, OH 43440
(419) 734-1143
T

Capt. Jane Rutschow
4566 Thompson Road
Oak Harbor, OH 43449
(419) 898-1892
CH

Capt. Robin Cover, RC Charter Service
3971 State Route 2 N.
Oak Harbor, OH 43449
(419) 898-3217
CH

Capt. Patricia Sawyer
Erie Express Charters
4568 Peachton Drive
Port Clinton, OH 43452
(419) 797-4828
CH

Walleye Mamas Fishing Club
1102 Buckingham
Sandusky, OH 44870
(419) 627-1333
WC

OKLAHOMA

Elouise Stewart
P.O. Box 520
Broken Bow, OK 74728
(405) 494-6543 or 1-800-375-2708
G

Norma and April Thomas, co-owners
Thomas Marine (boat dealer)
Highway 69 S., Route 4, Box 295
Checotah, OK 74426
(918) 473-6515

Sherri Houston-Combs, manager
Jimmy Houston Travel
P.O. Box 26
Cookson, OK 74427
1-800-775-7721 or (918) 457-5113
A

Jane Drake, co-owner
Sixshooter Resort & Marina
HC 68, Box 248
Cookson, OK 74427
(918) 457-5152
R, M

Teresa LeFlore
LeFlore's Guide Service
P.O. Box 191
Kingston, OK 73439
(405) 564-2237
G

Sue Linville, co-owner
Linville's Fishing Supply
117 W. Wilshire
Oklahoma City, OK 73116
(405) 842-8816
T

Sportsman's Calendar
2700 S.W. 27th
Oklahoma City, OK 73107
(405) 948-6635

Guys & Gals Bass Association
c/o Richard Endicott
P.O. Box 890471
Oklahoma City, OK 73189
(405) 485-9285
C

Jimmy Houston Outdoors Store
Highway 82 S.
Parkhill, OK 74451
(918) 456-1156
T

Jimmy Houston Marine (boat dealer)
Highway 82 S.
Parkhill, OK 74451
(918) 456-1157

Kay Barton, owner
Sportsman's Lodge & Motel
HC 64, Box 3520
Tuskahoma, OK 74574
(918) 569-4751
G, R

Lady Anglers Team Trail
c/o Kay Barton
Oklahoma Lady Anglers
218 E. Cherokee
Wagoner, OK 74467
(918) 485-4334 (days)
(918) 462-7391 (evenings)
WC

OREGON

Central Oregon Flyfishers
P.O. Box 1126
Bend, OR 97709
C

The Tomboy Club
c/o Brandy Church
P.O. Box 846
Dallas, OR 97338
(503) 623-8405
WC

Beverly Miller and Jim Bradbury
Totally Tubular
29455 S.E. Old Ranch Drive
Estacada, OR 97023
(503) 630-2783
I

Association of Northwest Steelheaders
P.O. Box 22065
Milwaukie, OR 97269
(503) 653-4176
C

The Lady Anglers Fishing Society,
   Portland Chapter
17084 S. Monroe
Mulino, OR 97042
(503) 829-9145
WC

Columbia River Lady Bass Masters
c/o Arlene Egan
6884 N. Hudson
Portland, OR 97203
WC

Oregon Bass and Panfish Club
P.O. Box 1021
Portland, OR 97207
(503) 282-2852
C

Deborah McQueen, co-owner
Brown's Landing (boat dealer)
50565 Brown's Landing Court
Scappoose, OR 97056
(503) 543-6526

Pat Lee, manager/guide
Steamboat Inn
42705 N. Umpqua Hwy.
Steamboat, OR 97447-9703
(503) 498-2411 or 1-800-840-8825
R, G

The Lady Anglers, High Desert Chapter
c/o Patti Burres
P.O. Box 1253
Umatilla, OR 97882
(503) 922-4046
WC

Patty Barnes, co-owner
The Fly Fishing Shop
Hoodland Shopping Center
P.O. Box 368
Welches, OR 97067
(503) 622-4607; fax 622-5490
F, G, I

PENNSYLVANIA

Kathy Heller, co-owner
Pro-Am Fishing Shop
5916 Tilghman St.
Allentown, PA 18104
(610) 395-0885
T

Evelyn B. Gulick, executive director
Forks of the Delaware Shad Fishing
   Tournament
P.O. Box 907
Easton, PA 18044-0907
(610) 250-7136

RHODE ISLAND

Anna Minicucci, outdoors writer
203 Sterling Ave.
Providence, RI 02909
(401) 943-3407 (voice and fax)

Rhode Island Ladies of the Long Rod
c/o Patsy and Heather Watson
   (401) 885-1289 **or**
   Anna Minicully, (401) 943-3407
WC

Point Judith Memorial Fly Fishing
   Tournament (annual mother/daughter
   charity event).
c/o Jo-Anne Melocarro, president
1-800-895-6491 or (401) 942-2270

TENNESSEE

Linda England and Fredda Lee
Two Star Enterprises
P.O. Box 05
Hermitage, TN 37076
(615) 847-8540; fax (615) 847-8440

Linda Hughes, owner
Tenn Guide Service
1816 E. Crabtree Road
Hixson, TN 37343
(615) 842-2249
G

Elaine Lee, owner
61 Bait and Tackle Shop
5227 Hwy. 61 S.
Memphis, TN 38109
(901) 785-9087
T

Reba Yergin
Rt. 2, Box 97C
Springville, TN 38256
(901) 593-5449
G

TEXAS

Barbara Cook-Stevenson
Rt. 2, Box 280
Alba, TX 75410
(903) 765-3120
G

Sherry D. Ruslink
Anglers Educational Seminars
6702 Forestview Drive
Arlington, TX 76016
(817) 572-3675 (voice and fax)
G, I

Cathie Coleman, co-owner
West Bank Anglers
5370 W. Lovers Lane, #320
Dallas, TX 75209
(214) 350-4665
A, F

Gail Criswell, co-owner
Amistad Marine (boat dealer)
HCR #3, Box 24E
Highway 90 W.
Del Rio, TX 78840
(210) 775-0878

Val Poe, co-owner
Val's Landing
Farm to Market Road 2946
Emory, TX 75440
(903) 473-3868
R, M

Capt. Ann Johnston
Johnston Sportfishing
314 Shark Lane
Freeport, TX 77541
1-800-460-1312
CH, G

Annual Brazosport Ladies Tournament
Bridge Harbor Marina Harbor Master
P.O. Box Drawer X
Freeport, TX 77541
(409) 233-2101

Cookie Pepper
Rt. 1, Box 185 X15
Galveston, TX 77554
(409) 737-1136
G

Doris Sorter
Lazy J Campground
Rt. 1, Box 1730
Hemphill, TX 75948
(409) 625-4689
R

Shirley Hall, owner
Frontier Park
Rt. 1, Box 1690
Hemphill, TX 75948
(409) 625-4712
R, M

Ann Thomasson-Wilson, owner
Ann's Tackle Shop
924 N. Wheeler
Jasper, Tx 75951
(409) 384-7685
T, G

Melody Edwards, co-owner
Minnow Bucket Marina
P.O. Box 833
Quitman, TX 75783
(903) 878-2500
M, G

Kathy Magers
5507 Yacht Club Drive
Rockwall, TX 75087
(214) 771-5462
I

Annual Ladies Kingfish Tournament
South Padre Island Visitors Center
600 Padre Blvd.
South Padre Island, TX 78597
1-800-343-2368

Judy Wong
7314 Emerald Glen Drive
Sugar Land, TX 77479
(713) 343-1999
G

UTAH

The Ladies Angle Fishing Society,
   Utah Chapter
992 Halycon Drive
Murray, UT 84123
(801) 268-4647
WC

Julie Hoopes Thompson, co-owner
The Flyfisher's Den
357 S. Main St.
Pleasant Grove, UT 84062
(801) 785-7461
F, CR

Anglers Inn
927 W. Riverdale Road
Ogden, UT 84405
(801) 621-6481
F, T

Anglers Inn
2292 S. Highland Drive
Salt Lake City, UT 84106
(801) 466-3921
F, T

Anglers Inn
8925 South 255 West
Sandy, UT 84070
(801) 566-3929
F, T

Lori Batty, owner
Big Foot Fly Shop
38 North 400 West
Vernal, UT 84078
(801) 789-4960
F, I

VERMONT

Orvis Manchester
Historic Route 7A
Manchester, VT 05254
(802) 362-3750 (store)
1-800-235-9763 (schools)
F, I

Mary Schirmer, co-owner
Schirmer's Fly Shop
34 Mills Ave.
South Burlington, VT 05403
(802) 863-6105
F, G, I

VIRGINIA

Eileen Davis
167 Bernard Road
Hampton, VA 23651
(804) 723-1875
I

Capt. Doreen Kopacz
Harrison's Fishing Pier
414 W. Ocean View Ave.
Norfolk, VA 23503
(804) 587-9630 (May–October)
CH, G

WASHINGTON

"Steelhead Sue"
9330-B State, Suite 257
Marysville, WA 98270
(206) 653-5924
G

Janet Schimpf
Schimpf's Nymphs Fishing Flies
111 Schafer Meadows Lane, N.
Montesano, WA 98563
(360) 249-4572
HF, I

Northwest Women Fly Fishers
c/o Avid Angler Fly Shoppe
11714 – 15th Ave., N.E.
Seattle, WA 98125
(206) 362-4030
WC

Bonnie Ward, co-owner
Angler's Choice Tackle & Marine
20222 Ballinger Way, N.E.
Seattle, WA 98155
(206) 364-9827
T

Sharon Darling, operator
Avid Angler Fly Shoppe
11714 – 15th Ave., N.E.
Seattle, WA 98125
(206) 362-4030
F, G, I

Brenda Olver & Pat Hill, co-owners
Silver Lake Motel & Resort
3201 Spirit Lake Hwy.
Silver Lake, WA 98645
(360) 274-6141
R, M, T

The Greased Line Fly Shoppe
5802 N.E. 88th St.
Vancouver, WA 98665
(360) 573-9383
F, I

WEST VIRGINIA

Upstream Flyfishing Shop
985 Harrison Ave.
Elkins, WV 26241
F, I

Upstream Flyfishing Shop
954 Maple Drive, Suite 7
Morgantown, WV 26505
(304) 599-4998
F, I

WISCONSIN

Jean Schick, owner
Wille Products (mail order)
P.O. Box 532
Brookfield, WI 53008
(414) 344-1230

Jeanne Lunde, co-owner
Lunde's Fly Fishing Chalet
2491 Highway 92
Mount Horeb, WI 53572
(608) 437-5465
T, G, I

Sara E. Johnson, executive director
River Alliance of Wisconsin
122 State St., Suite 200
Madison, WI 53703
(608) 257-2424

Wisconsin Sportswomen's Club
W237 N. 1480 Busse Road
Waukesha, WI 53188
(414) 547-8013
WC

WYOMING

Christy Ball and Lori-Ann Murphy
Reel Women Fly Fishing Adventures
P.O. Box 20202
Jackson, WY 83001
(307) 733-2210; fax (307) 733-8655
A, I

Bressler Outfitters
485 W. Broadway
Jackson, WY
Mail: P.O. Box 766
Wilson, WY 83014
(307) 733-6934 or 1-800-654-0676
G

Orvis Jackson Hole
P.O. Box 9029
485 W. Broadway
Jackson, WY 83001
(307) 733-5407
F, I

Dana Brooks
Big Horn Mountain Sports
334 N. Main St.
Sheridan, WY 82801
(307) 672-6866
F

Mary Smith
BHMS Angling Destinations
330 N. Main St.
Sheridan, WY 82801
(307) 672-6866; fax (307) 672-6016
A

INTERNATIONAL

AUSTRALIA

Sandy Murray
Interpacific World Travel Pty. Ltd.
  (tournaments)
GO FISH Australia

Shop 34A, Marina Mirage
Seaworld Drive, Main Beach
Queensland 4217
(075) 71 0000; fax (075) 71 0600

South Eastern Invitation Game Fish
  Tournament
Victorian Game Fishing Club, Inc.

186 Station St.
Aspendale, Victoria 3195

CANADA

Kathy Ruddick, co-owner
Ruddick's Fly Shop

3726 Canada Way
Burnaby, B.C. V5G 1G5
(604) 434-2420
and
Ruddick's Fly Shop

1654 Duranleau St.
Granville Island
Vancouver, B.C. V6H 3S4
(604) 681-3747
F, I

Carol Martin, co-owner
The Forks Fly Shop

74 McKenzie St.
Inglewood, Ontario L0N 1K0
(905) 838-3332
F, CR, I

Brenda Currie
Currie's Guiding

416 Connaught Drive
P.O. Box 105
Jasper, Alberta T0E 1E0
(403) 852-5650
T, G

Mallory Burton, outdoors writer

2020 Atlin Ave.
Prince Rupert, B.C. V8J 1G1
(604) 624-9694

Audrey Schrader, co-owner
The Northern Fly Fisherman

Box 9633
Saskatoon, Sask. S7K 7GI
(306) 665-0076
F, I

Annual Women's Salmon Fishing Derby
  Painter's Lodge, Campbell River
Oak Bay Marine Group

1327 Beach Drive
Victoria, B.C. V8S 2N4
1-800-663-7090
R

CAYMAN ISLANDS

The Mermaid Tournament
c/o Donna Sjostrom

P.O. Box 134 GT
Grand Cayman, British West Indies
(809) 949-7099; fax (809) 949-6819

COSTA RICA

Judy Heidt, owner
Rio Parismina Lodge

P.O. Box 460009
San Antonio, TX 78246
1-800-338-5688 (North America only)
R, G

PANAMA

Terri Kittredge Andrews
Tropic Star Lodge

Pinas Bay, Panama
635 N. Rio Grande Ave.
Orlando, FL 32805
1-800-682-3424; fax (407) 839-3637
R

Hells Anglers Billfish Tournament
c/o Dave Bishop

7404 Broadway
Merrillville, IN 46410
(219) 769-7427

PUERTO RICO

International Billfish Tournament
Club Nautico de San Juan

P.O. Box 1133
San Juan, PR 00902-1133
(809) 722-0177; fax (809) 724-8059

SWEDEN

Jennifer Olsson
Gimdalen 1426
840 60 Bräcke
Sweden
(46) 693-13056 (June–September)
G, I. (See Montana for October– May.)

UNITED KINGDOM

Davy Wotton
Heron House, Station Road
Griffithstown
Pontypool, Gwent NP4 5ES
(44) 01495 762911 (voice and fax)
F, G

Patricia Fawcett, co-owner
Stephen J. Fawcett Sporting Products
7 Great John St.
Lancaster LA1 1NQ
(44) 01524 32033
T, CR

Anne Parkinson, co-owner
Sportfish
Winforton
Nr Hereford HR3 6EB
(44) 01544 327111; fax (44) 01544 327093
F

House of Hardy Ltd.
61 Pall Mall
London SW1
(44) 71 071839 5515
Fax (44) 71 071 930 9128
F, I

Wendy Gibson
Flies by Wendy
47 Thorn Drive
Daisy Farm Estate
Newthorpe Common
Nottinghamshire NG16 2BH
(44) 0773 761645
HF

Charlotte A. Stowe, co-owner
Tom C. Saville Ltd.
Unit 7, Salisbury Square
Radford, Nottingham NG72AB
(44) 0115 9784248
F

The Orvis Co. Inc.
The Mill, Nether Wallop
Stockbridge, Hampshire SO20 8ES
(44) 0264 781212
F, I

Schools, Travel Services, Clothing, and Miscellaneous

FLY-FISHING SCHOOLS

The Maggie Merriman Fly Fishing Schools
P.O. Box 755
West Yellowstone, MT 59758
(406) 646-7824 (spring/summer)
(818) 282-3173 (winter)

Orvis Fly Fishing Schools
Historic Route 7A
P.O. Box 798
Manchester, VT 05254-0798
1-800-235-9763

L. L. Bean Fly Fishing Schools
Freeport, ME 04033
1-800-341-4341 or (207) 865-4761

The Wulff School of Fly Fishing
Beaverkill Road
Lew Beach, NY 12758
(914) 439-4060

ANGLING ADVENTURE/ TRAVEL SERVICES

Fishing the West Tours
10255 S.W. Arctic Drive
Beaverton, OR 97005
1-800-545-5729

Susie and Mike Fitzgerald, owners
Frontiers
P.O. Box 959
Wexford, PA 15090
1-800-245-1950

Sherri Houston-Combs, manager
Jimmy Houston Travel
P.O. Box 26
Cookson, OK 74427
1-800-775-7721 or (918) 457-5113

PanAngling Travel Service
180 N. Michigan Ave.
Chicago, IL 60601
1-800-533-4353 or (312) 263-0328
Fax (312) 263-5246

Cathy Beck, co-owner
Raven Creek Travel
RD-1, Box 310-2
Benton, PA 17814
(717) 925-2392; fax (717) 925-2958

Christy Ball and Lori-Ann Murphy
Reel Women Fly Fishing Adventures
P.O. Box 20202
Jackson, WY 83001
(307) 733-2210; fax (307) 733-8655

Lynn Hendrickson
Seasons International, Inc.
P.O. Box 885
Exeter, NH 03833
(603) 772-6600 or 1-800-788-4567

Women in the Wilderness
Judith Niemi, director
566 Ottawa Ave.
St. Paul, MN 55107
(612) 227-2284

WOMEN'S CLOTHING AND GEAR

Aluring Lines, Inc.
236 E. Historic Columbia River Hwy.
Troutdale, OR 97060
(503) 666-7786
Karen Riggers designs and manufactures women's hunting and fishing clothing.

Bass Pro Shops
1935 S. Campbell
Springfield, MO 65898-0123
1-800-BASS PRO
Bass Pro's mail-order catalog includes women's flyweight chest waders, fishing raingear, and outdoors clothing.

Cabela's
812 – 13th Ave.
Sidney, NE 69160
1-800-237-4444
Cabela's fly-fishing mail-order catalog includes women's neoprene waders.

Damselfly — Clothing and Equipment for Fly Fishing Women
3450 Palmer Drive, Suite 7-191
Cameron Park, CA 95682-8253
(916) 676-1529 or 1-800-966-4166
Joanne Harvey-Hills's and Chuck Hills's mail-order catalog offers a variety of cold-weather, tropical, and fly-fishing clothing, angling gear, and travel accessories, among other items.

Dirt Roads and Damsels
Rhonda D. Sapp
1457 Nelson St.
Lakewood, CO 80215
(303) 232-8298

Donna R. Teeny
P.O. Box 989
Gresham, OR 97030
(503) 667-6602
Donna Teeny and Rhonda Sapp have designed a line of women's fly-fishing clothing and gear that includes a fashionable sport/fishing vest, cotton turtleneck, fleece jacket and pants, custom waders, and rods and reels. Available through retail sporting-goods stores and by mail-order catalog.

L. L. Bean
Freeport, ME 04033
1-800-221-4221
L. L. Bean's mail-order catalog includes women's neoprene waders, flyweights, wading boots in women's sizes, and a large range of outdoors wear.

Lucky Lady, Inc.
P.O. Box 125
Mershon, GA 31551
(912) 647-1996
Manufacturer of the Dame-O-Flage brand of camo clothing and accessories for women and girls. Brochure available.

The Orvis Company
Historic Route 7A
P.O. Box 798
Manchester, VT 05254-0798
In the spring of 1995, Orvis introduced a full line of fly-fishing clothing and gear for women. Items include neoprene and lightweight waders, wading shoes, a fishing vest, wader pants, and bonefish shirts. Available through Orvis's mail-order catalog service (1-800-548-9548) or Orvis-endorsed retail outlets.

Oshman's SuperSports USA Headquarters
P.O. Box 230234
Houston, TX 77223-0234
(723) 967-8258; fax (713) 967-8254
One of the nation's largest independent sporting-goods companies with over 160 outlets nationally.

Sassy Sara's, Inc.
7400 Beaufont Springs Road, Suite 300
Richmond, VA 23225
1-800-799-1259 or (804) 763-4730
Suzanne Farrow's specialized clothing and products catalog covers freshwater, saltwater, and fly fishing, including a complete line of rods made especially for the female angler.

Suzy Smith Outdoor Sportswear
29130 W. U.S. Hwy. 160
P.O. Box 185
South Fork, CO 81154
(719) 873-5121
Suzy Smith designs and manufactures hunting and fishing clothes for women.

Zanika Outside Interests, Inc.
P.O. Box 11943
Minneapolis, MN 55411
(612) 529-1785
Vickie Morgan's breakthrough line of women's outdoors clothing features invisible zippers or unique pull-apart layers to allow women to heed nature's call without removing it all. Catalog available.

GIFTS

Angler's
4955 East 2900 North
Murtaugh, ID 83344
(208) 432-6625 (voice and fax)
Bobbi Wolverton offers a mail-order catalog of gifts with fishing motifs.

ASSISTANCE FOR THE DISABLED ANGLER

J. L. Pachner Ltd.
13 Via Di Nola
Laguna Niguel, CA 92677
(714) 363-9831
Call or write for a free catalog featuring everything from motorized rod casters, power-driven reels, and one-handed fishing vests with rod-holders for amputees to wheelchair accessories, along with businesses and services for the physically handicapped.

Project Access
P.O. Box 299
Village Station
New York, NY 10014
or
c/o Catskill Fly Fishing Center
5447 Old Route 17
P.O. Box 1295
Livingston Manor, NY 12758-1295
(914) 439-4810
Informational brochure available for volunteer groups interested in sponsoring projects to create access to prime fishing spots for physically impaired and elderly anglers.

PROFESSIONAL ANGLING SPEAKERS

Joan Whitlock
Speaker's Bureau
6730 E. 91st Place, #2
Tulsa, OK 72658
(918) 491-0826
Joan has set up the first-ever agency representing many of the top personalities (including women) in the angling world. Brochure available.

FISHING VIDEOS

"Jim & Kelly Watt's
Fly Fishing Video Magazine"
Bennett-Watt Entertainment
13101 244th Ave., S.E.
Issaquah, WA 98027
(206) 392-3935 or 1-800-327-2893
The world's largest selection of 60-minute instructional and adventure videos.

Angling Books Written by or for Women: A Selected Bibliography

GENERAL

Arms, Dorothy Noyes. *Fishing Memories.* New York: Macmillan, 1938.

Berners, Dame Juliana. "Treatyse of Fysshynge wyth an Angle," *The Boke of St. Albans.* Westminster, England, 1496. (A complete translation is available in Joan Wulff's *Joan Wulff's Fly Fishing: Expert Advice from a Woman's Perspective* and Holly Morris's *Uncommon Waters: Women Write About Fishing.*)

Borden, Courtney. *Adventures in a Man's World: The Initiation of a Sportsman's Wife.* New York: Macmillan, 1933.

Burton, Mallory. *Reading the Water: Stories & Essays of Fly Fishing and Life.* Sandpoint, Idaho: Keokee Press, 1995.

Clarkson, Joan. *Back Casts and Backchat.* London: Game and Gun, 1936.

Cohen, Sherry S. *Secrets of a Very Good Marriage: Lessons from the Sea.* Crown Publishing Group, 1993.

Cook, Beatrice. *Till Fish Us Do Part: The Confessions of a Fisherman's Wife.* New York: William Morrow, 1949.

———. *More Fish to Fry.* New York: William Morrow, 1951.

———. *Truth Is Stranger than Fishin'.* New York: William Morrow, 1955.

Dufferin, Ava. *My Canadian Journal: 1872–1878.* London: Murray, 1891.

Eastwood, Dorothea. *River Diary.* Boston: Houghton Mifflin, 1950.

Ferris, Sandra Stewart. *The King of Fish: Atlantic Salmon.* Privately published, 1989.

Foster, Muriel. *Muriel Foster's Fishing Diary.* New York: Viking Press, 1980.

———. *Days on Sea, Loch & River.* London: Michael Joseph, 1979.

Greville, Lady Violet, ed. *The Gentlewoman's Book of Sports I.* London: Henry & Co., circa 1892.

Hausherr, Rosemarie. *The City Girl Who Went to Sea.* New York: McMillan Child Group, 1990.

Helmey, Capt. Judy. *My Father, the Sea & Me.* Privately published (124 Palmetto Drive, Savannah, GA 31410), 1992.

Jenkins, Frances C. *Hey, Girls, Let's Go Fishing.* New York: Exposition Press, 1978.

Kelly, Florence. *Flowing Stream.* Gordon Press, 1972.

LaMonte, Francesca. *North American Game Fishes.* New York: Doubleday, 1945.

———. *Marine Game Fishes of the World.* New York: Doubleday, 1952.

Morris, Holly, ed. *Uncommon Waters: Women Write About Fishing.* Seattle: Seal Press, 1991.

Paterson, Wilma, and Peter Behan. *Salmon and Women: The Feminine Angle.* London: H. F. & G. Witherby Ltd., 1990. (Available through The Angler's Art and Judith Bowman Books, listed below.)

Pearse, Eleanor H. D. *Florida's Vanishing Era.* Privately published, 1947.

Popkin, Susan, and Roger Allen. *Gone Fishing! A History of Fishing in River, Bay & Sea.* Philadelphia Maritime Museum, 1984.

Prescott, Marjorie Wiggin. *Tales of Sportsmen's Wife.* Privately published, 1936.

———. *Tales of Sportsmen's Wife: Fishing.* Privately published, 1937.

Sandell, Marjorie Sandell. *A Woman's Place Is on the Water: How to Beat Men at Their Own Game.* Muskie Memories Press (P.O. Box 44400, Eden Prairie, MN 55344), 1992.

Slosson, Annie Trumbull. *Fishin' Jimmy.* New York: Scribners, 1889.

Vermes, Jean Campbell Pattison. *Enjoying Life as a Sportsman's Wife.* Harrisburg, Pa.: Stackpole Books, 1965.

Wheatley, Harriet. *Lady Angler: Fishing, Hunting and Camping in Wilderness Areas of North America.* San Antonio, Texas: The Naylor Company, 1952.

BASS FISHING

Ackermann, Joan. *"Zara Spook & Other Lures."* Samuel French, Inc. (45 W. 25th St., New York, NY 10010), 1988. (A play.)

England, Linda, and Fredda Lee. *Bass on the Line.* Atlantic Publishing (P.O. Box 67, Tabor City, NC 28463), 1987.

BIG-GAME ANGLING

Farrington, Chisie. *Women Can Fish.* New York: Coward-McCann, 1951.

Marron, Eugenie. *Albacora: The Search for the Giant Broadbill,* edited by Roger Kahn. New York: Random House, 1957.

FLY FISHING

Cooper, Gwen, and Evelyn Haas. *Wade a Little Deeper, Dear: A Woman's Guide to Fly Fishing.* New York: Lyons & Burford, 1979.

Morris, Holly, ed. *A Different Angle: Fly Fishing Stories by Women.* Seattle: Seal Press, 1995.

Page, Margot. *Little Rivers: Tales of a Woman Angler.* New York: Lyons & Burford, 1995.

Pothier, Patricia. *Float Tube Magic: A Fly Fishing Escape.* Portland, Ore.: Frank Amato Publications, 1995.

Rogers, Neal, and Linda Rogers, with Lefty Kreh and Stu Apte. *Saltwater Fly Fishing Magic.* New York: Lyons & Burford, 1993.

Stoltz, Judith, and Judith Schnell. *Trout.* Harrisburg, Pa.: Stackpole Books, 1991.

Tryon, Chuck, and Sharon Tryon. *Fly Fishing for Trout in Missouri.* Ozark Mountain Fly Fishers (1 Johnson St., Rolla, MO 65401), 1992.

Wolverton, Mike, and Barbara Wolverton. *Fly Fishing Always.* Privately published, 1984.

Wulff, Joan. *Joan Wulff's Fly Casting Techniques.* New York: Lyons & Burford, 1987.

———. *Joan Wulff's Fly Fishing: Expert Advice from a Woman's Perspective.* Harrisburg, Pa.: Stackpole Books, 1991.

FLY TYING

Dunham, Judith. *The Art of the Trout Fly.* San Francisco: Chronicle Books, 1988.

———. *The Atlantic Salmon Fly: The Tyers & Their Art.* San Francisco: Chronicle Books, 1991.

Greig, Elizabeth. *How to Tie Flies.* New York: Barnes, 1940.

Leiser, Eric. *The Dettes: A Catskill Legend.* Willowkill Press (P.O. Box 233, Fishkill, NY 12524), 1992.

Marbury, Mary Orvis. *Favorite Flies and Their Histories.* 1892. Reprint, Secaucus, N.J.: Wellfleet Press, 1988.

Shaw, Helen. *Fly-Tying: Materials, Tools, Technique.* 1963. Reprint, New York: Lyons & Burford, 1987.

———. *Flies for Fish & Fisherman.* Harrisburg, Pa.: Stackpole Books, 1989.

Tryon, Chuck, and Sharon Tryon. *Figuring Out Flies: A Practical Guide.* Ozark Mountain Fly Fishers (1 Johnson St., Rolla, MO 65401), 1990.

Wakeford, Jacqueline. *Fly Tying Techniques.* Garden City: Doubleday, 1981.

———. *Fly Tying Tools & Materials.* New York: Lyons & Burford, 1992.

HOW TO FISH

Bailey, Donna. *Fishing.* Madison, N.J.: Raintree Steck-Vaughn Publications, 1991.

Burns, Eugene. *Fishing for Women.* New York: A. S. Barnes, 1953.

Ferguson, Don, and Barbara Ferguson. *Fishing to Win.* Diamond Advertising, 1988.

Kelly, Mary. *Fishing Rod Patents and Other Tackle.* T B Reel, 1990.

Lyttle, A. Edward, and Joyce M. Lyttle. *Fishing Notes.* Ed & Joyce Lyttle (P.O. Box 935, Ketchum, ID 83340), 1987.

Pratt, Mary. *Better Angling with Simple Science.* United Kingdom: Blackwell Scientific Publications, 1991.

Robinson, Jacky. *Saltwater Adventure in the Florida Keys: An Introduction to Fishing for Kids.* White Heron Press (P.O. Box 468, Islamorada, FL 33036).

Robinson, Tara. *How to Catch Really Big Fish.* Blaine, Wash.: Hancock House, 1971.

REGIONAL GUIDES

Bareuther, Carol. *Sport Fishing in the Virgin Islands: Everything You Need to Know.* American Paradise Publishing (P.O. Box 37, Saint Johns, VI 00831), 1992.

Bark, Ann Voss, ed. *West Country Fly Fishing.* London: B. T. Batsford, 1986.

Carlander, Harriet Bell. "A History of Fish and Fishing in the Upper Mississippi River." Thesis, Iowa State College, 1951.

Bierce, Laura. *Florida Outdoor Digest.* Pisces Press, 1993.

Bradbury, Jim, and Beverly Miller. *Lake Fly Fishing Guide.* Portland, Ore.: Frank Amato Publications, 1994.

Carter, Marilyn. *Fishing Alaskan Waters.* Palmer, Alaska: Aladdin Publications, n.d.

Casali, Dan, and Madelynne Diness. *Fishing in Oregon.* Flying Pencil Publications (P.O. Box 19062, Portland, OR 97219), 1989.

Crandall, Julie V. *The Story of Pacific Salmon.* Portland, Ore.: Binfords & Mort, 1946.

Dahlstrom, Joni. *California Bass Angling Guide.* Portland, Ore.: Frank Amato Publications, 1991.

Neeley, Virginia. *Alaska Calls.* Hancock House, 1983.

Smith, Sybil. *Twin Cities Fishing Guide.* Fins Publications (P.O. Box 13005, Roseville, MN 55113), 1982.

Swenson, Margaret, and Evan Swenson. *The Angler's Guide to Alaska.* Falcon Press, 1993.

Warren, J. E. (Judy). *Angling Alpine: A Field Guide for Fly Fishing Alpine County.* Privately published (Sorensen's Resort, 14255 Hwy. 88, Markeleeville, CA 96120;1-800-423-9949).

MAIL-ORDER BOOK SERVICES AND ANGLING PUBLISHERS

The Angler's Art
P.O. Box 148C
Plainfield, PA 17081
1-800-848-1020; fax (717) 243-8603
Call or write for a catalog. Billed as "the world's largest seller of fly fishing books." Owners Barry and Gerry Serviente offer both current and out-of-print titles. (Both are devout fly fishers, and Barry is also an avid advocate for women in the sport!)

Judith Bowman Books
98 Pound Ridge Road
Bedford, NY 10506
(914) 234-7543
Call or write for a catalog. Judith Bowman, both an accomplished fly fisher and highly regarded book dealer for over 15 years, has an inventory of approximately 25,000 titles (current and out-of-print) on the subjects of fishing, hunting, and natural history.

Gary L. Estabrook Books
P.O. Box 61453
Vancouver, WA 98666
(360) 699-5454
Gary charges a fee for his catalog (which is deductible from a minimum purchase), but for the rare-book hunting/fishing purists, it will be hard to find a more comprehensive source of out-of-print literature in these categories. His vast inventory fluctuates around 30,000 volumes, many of them from prominent private collections.

Frank Amato Publications
P.O. Box 82112
Portland, OR 97282
(503) 653-8108
One of the country's leading publishers of fly-fishing titles. Order through your local bookstore or write or call for a catalog.

Lyons & Burford, Publishers
32 W. 21st St.
New York, NY 10010
(212) 620-9580
Another preeminent publisher of fly-fishing books. Order through your local bookstore or write or call for a catalog.

Books of the Black Bass
402 S. 55th St.
Tacoma, WA 98408
(206) 472-9739
Clyde E. Drury does not sell books, but he publishes one of the most comprehensive bibliographies of books, magazine articles, and newsletters written about black bass. (Clyde is another strong supporter of women in the sport.)

Bass'n Gal All-Time Earners

The Top 20 Winners Through the
Delco Voyager Class Star XVIII, September 1994

1. Chris Houston (Cookson, Oklahoma) $259,768
2. Burma Thomas (Scottsboro, Alabama) $226,658
3. Linda England (Old Hickory, Tennessee) $175,624
4. Pam Martin (Bainbridge, Georgia) $164,602
5. Betty Haire (Charlotte, North Carolina) $130,889
6. Lucy Mize (Ben Lomond, Arkansas) $124,645
7. Rhonda Wilcox (Malakoff, Texas) .... $ 97,532
8. Vojai Reed (Broken Arrow, Oklahoma) .... $ 74,744
9. Penny Berryman (Dardanelle, Arkansas) .... $ 60,973
10. Jeanette Storey (Murray, Kentucky) .... $ 56,861
11. Sherrie Brubaker (Westlake, Louisiana) .... $ 53,170
12. Mary Satterfield (Findlay, Illinois) .... $ 50,539
13. Linda Hughes (Hixson, Tennessee) .... $ 50,355
14. Joy Scott (Van Buren, Arkansas) .... $ 50,227
15. Kathy Magers (Rockwall, Texas) .... $ 49,139
16. Claudette Johnston (Pensacola, Florida) .... $ 43,492
17. Ann Thomasson-Wilson (Jasper, Texas) .... $ 37,827
18. Denise Turner (Memphis, Tennessee) .... $ 31,257
19. Mona Crawford (Welaka, Florida) .... $ 30,323
20. Dorothy Patrick (Chickasha, Oklahoma) .... $ 30,182

Other Statistics:

All-time high "Classic Star Championship" weight: **29.91 pounds**. Betty Haire, 10 bass, Hudson River, Catskill, New York, September 30–October 1, 1988.

All-time low "Classic Star Championship" weight: **7.08 pounds**. Chris Houston, 3 bass, Lake Ferguson, Mississippi, November 11–12, 1977.

Most limits caughts in a two-day event: **74**. Lake Tenkiller, Oklahoma, August 5–6, 1993.

All-time low poundage qualifying event: **6.04 pounds**. Jeanette Storey, 2 bass, Lake Clinton, Illinois, May 24–25, 1984.

All-time tournament lunker: **12.70 pounds**. Chris Houston, Lake Fork, Texas, November 14, 1991.

All-time tournament record weight: **1480.88 pounds**. 942 bass, Lake Tenkiller, Oklahoma, August 5–6, 1993.

All-time record tournament catch: **47 pounds, 2 ounces**. Betty Haire, 9 bass, Lake Talquin, Florida, February 27–28, 1981.

All-time record one-day catch: **27 pounds, 4 ounces**. Denise Turner, 5 bass, Kentucky Lake, Kentucky, August 14, 1992.

Notes

Introduction

1. John McDonald, *The Origins of Angling* (New York: Doubleday, 1963).

2. According to the National Sporting Goods Association, a total of 40.5 million anglers freshwater fished in 1994, of which 13 million (32.1%) were women; and a total of 11.5 million anglers saltwater fished, of which 3.6 million (31%) were women. In 1984, 14 million (32.6%) women freshwater fished out of a total of 41.1 million anglers; and 3.5 million (27.3%) women saltwater fished out of a total of 12.6 million.

3. A. J. McClane, in *The New Fisherman's Encyclopedia* (Harrisburg, Pa.: The Stackpole Company, 1964), estimated that there were 20 million anglers in 1963, based on annual sales of fishing licenses throughout the United States—but no estimates of the number of female anglers were available, since most states did not require them to purchase fishing licenses.

Prologue – Angling's First Great Legend: Dame Juliana Berners

1. John McDonald, *The Origins of Angling* (New York: Doubleday, 1963).

2. A modern-text translation of the "Treatyse" (as originally published in McDonald, *The Origins of Angling*) can also be read in its entirety in both Wulff, *Joan Wulff's Fly Fishing* and Holly Morris, ed., *Uncommon Waters: Women Write About Fishing* (Seattle: Seal Press, 1991).

3. McDonald, *The Origins of Angling*.

4. Silvio Calabi, *The Illustrated Encyclopedia of Fly-Fishing* (New York: Henry Holt, 1993).

5. John Bale, *Lives of the Most Eminent Writers of Great Britain* (*Scriptorum Illustria Majoris Britanniae...*) (circa 1559), quoted in John McDonald, *The Origins of Angling*.

6. Ernest Schwiebert, *Trout* (New York: E. P. Dutton, 1978).

7. Joan Salvato Wulff, *Joan Wulff's Fly Fishing: Expert Advice from a Woman's Perspective* (Harrisburg, Pa.: Stackpole Books, 1987).

Part I – Women's Legacy in Fly Fishing

1. "Letter of Margaret Penn Freame in Philadelphia, to John Penn," reprinted in *The Pennsylvania Magazine of History and Biography* (1907), quoted in Paul Schullery, *American Fly Fishing: A History* (New York: Lyons & Burford, 1987).

2. Susie Isaksen, "Carrie G. Stevens: Originator of Modern Streamer Design," *The American Fly Fisher*, Fall 1976.

3. Holly Morris, ed., *Uncommon Waters: Women Write About Fishing* (Seattle: Seal Press, 1991).

4. Austin M. Francis, *Catskill Rivers: Birthplace of American Fly Fishing* (New York: Nick Lyons Books, 1983).

5. Ibid.

6. Joan Salvato Wulff, *Joan Wulff's Fly Fishing: Expert Advice from a Woman's Perspective* (Harrisburg, Pa.: Stackpole Books, 1987).

Chapter 1 – Trailblazers in Fly-Fishing History

1. Joan Salvato Wulff, *Joan Wulff's Fly Fishing: Expert Advice from a Woman's Perspective* (Harrisburg, Pa.: Stackpole Books, 1987).

2. Victor Block, "Rangeley Lakes Region is Mecca for Fly-fishing Anglers," *Outdoors Unlimited*, February 1994.

3. Kenneth Smith, "Maine's Sportsman of the Century," *Discover Maine*, September 1994.

4. Austin S. Hogan, "Glamour Girl of the Maine Lakes: Fly Rod's Reel Was of Solid Gold," *The American Fly Fisher*, Fall 1977.

5. David Foster, "'Bonefish' Bonnie Smith," *Gray's Sporting Journal*, September 1993.

6. George X. Sand, *Saltwater Fly Fishing* (New York: Alfred A. Knopf, 1970).

7. Dick Brown, *Fly Fishing for Bonefish* (New York: Lyons & Burford, 1993).

8. Jim Chapralis, "Kay Brodney: 1920–1994," *The PanAngler*, August 29, 1994.

9. Clive Gammon, "Please Don't Fall in the Water!" *Sports Illustrated*, May 18, 1981.

10. Vic Dunaway, *Modern Saltwater Fishing* (South Hackensack, N.J.: Stoeger, 1975), quoted in the International Game Fish Association's brochure, "Webster and Helen Robinson's Fishing World."

Chapter 2 – Patterns of Excellence: Fly Tiers in History

1. Paul Schullery, *American Fly Fishing: A History* (New York: Lyons and Burford, 1987).

2. Kenneth M. Cameron. "The Girls of Summer: Part II," *The Fly Fisher*, Winter 1977.

3. Joan Salvato Wulff, *Joan Wulff's Fly Fishing: Expert Advice from a Woman's Perspective* (Harrisburg, Pa.: Stackpole Books, 1987).

4. Mary Orvis Marbury, *Favorite Flies and Their Histories* (1892; reprint, Secaucus, N.J.: Wellfleet Press, 1988).

5. Silvio Calabi, *The Illustrated Encyclopedia of Fly-Fishing* (New York: Henry Holt, 1993).

6. Kenneth M. Cameron, "The Girls of Summer: Part I," *The Fly Fisher*, Fall 1977.

7. Austin Hogan and Paul Schullery, *The Orvis Story: Commemorating the 125th Anniversary of The Orvis Company* (Manchester, Vt.: The Orvis Company, 1980).

8. Susie Isaksen, "Carrie G. Stevens: Originator of Modern Streamer Design," *American Fly Fisher*, Fall 1976.

9. Joseph D. Bates, *Streamers and Bucktails: The Big Fish Flies* (New York: Alfred A. Knopf, 1979).

10. Eric Leiser, *The Dettes: A Catskill Legend* (Fishkill, N.Y.: Willowkill Press, 1992).

11. A. River Rogue, "The First Lady's Honor Roll," *The Creel*, December 1961.

Chapter 3 – The Woman Flyfishers Club

1. Austin M. Francis, *Catskill Rivers: Birthplace of American Fly Fishing* (New York: Nick Lyons Books, 1983).

2. Susie Isaksen, "The Woman Flyfisher's Club," *The American Fly Fisher*, Fall 1981.

Chapter 4 – A Living Legend: Joan Salvato Wulff

1. Pete Woolley, "Angler of the Year," *Fly Rod & Reel: The Magazine of American Fly-Fishing*, January/February 1994.

2. Jim Chapralis, "Women in International Fishing…Then and Now," *The PanAngler*, May 29, 1993.

3. Joan Salvato Wulff, *Joan Wulff's Fly Casting Techniques* (New York: Lyons & Burford, 1987).

4. Joan Salvato Wulff, *Joan Wulff's Fly Fishing: Expert Advice from a Woman's Perspective* (Harrisburg, Pa.: Stackpole Books, 1987).

5. Silvio Calabi, *The Illustrated Encyclopedia of Fly-Fishing* (New York: Henry Holt, 1993).

6. For those unfamiliar with Lee's distinguished career, he is credited with giving birth to the conservation movement and the concept of catch-and-release ("Game fish are too valuable to be caught only once," he prophesied in 1938), the design of the first fly-fishing vest (in 1932), and the creation of a revolutionary series of dry flies (including the famous Royal Wulff) and the Triangle Taper fly lines. Besides being an angler of unsurpassed skill (from catching the first tuna on rod and reel in Newfoundland in 1938 to taking a world-record 148-pound striped marlin on a fly rod with 12-pound test leader in 1967), he was also a prolific writer, completing numerous magazine articles and eight definitive books (two of them after meeting Joan). And those are only the highlights.

Chapter 5 – Fly Fishing's Trailblazers Today

1. Silvio Calabi, foreword to reprint of *Favorite Flies and Their Histories*, by Mary Orvis Marbury (1892; reprint, Secaucus, N.J.: Wellfleet Press, 1988).

2. Pam Montgomery, "What's A Nice Girl Like You Doin' in a Business Like This?" *Fly Tackle Dealer*, January 1995.

3. Bill Barich, "Guide for Hire. 22 Years on Montana Rivers. Knows Trout. Smells Nice," *Rocky Mountain Magazine*, Fall/Winter 1994.

Chapter 6 – More Patterns of Excellence: Fly Tiers Today

1. Joseph D. Bates, *Atlantic Salmon Treasury: An Anthology of Selections from the First Quarter-Century of the Atlantic Salmon Journal, 1948–1974* (Montreal: Atlantic Salmon Association, 1975), quoted in Tena Z. Robinson, "Megan Boyd," *Fly Rod & Reel*, May 1993.

2. Tena Z. Robinson, "Megan Boyd," *Fly Rod & Reel*, May 1993.

3. Judith Dunham, *The Atlantic Salmon Fly: The Tyers and Their Art* (San Francisco: Chronicle Books, 1991).

4. Dick Talleur, "Helen Shaw: Fly Tyings' Garbo," *The American Angler & Fly Tyer*, Summer 1989.

5. Helen Shaw, *Fly-Tying* (New York: Lyons & Burford, 1987).

6. Art Smith, "Pavement's End: Fishing & Hunting," *The New York Herald Tribune*, July 7, 1963.

7. Eric Leiser, *The Dettes: A Catskill Legend* (Fishkill, N.Y.: Willowkill Press, 1992).

8. Joan Salvato Wulff, *Joan Wulff's Fly Fishing: Expert Advice from a Woman's Perspective* (Harrisburg, Pa.: Stackpole Books, 1987).

9. Runar Warhuus, "Crocheted Flies: How to Perform Torill Kolbu's Unusual Fly-tying Technique," *Fly Fisherman*, May 1995.

Part II – Women's Legacy in Big-Game Saltwater Angling

1. Chisie Farrington, *Women Can Fish* (New York: Coward-McCann, 1951).

2. According to George Reiger, *Profiles in Saltwater Angling* (Englewood Cliffs, N.J.: Prentice-Hall, 1973), "Big-game angling has an official birth date and founding father. On June 1, 1898, Charles Frederick Holder of Pasadena, California, landed a 183-pound bluefin tuna on rod and reel off Catalina Island."

3. Lady Violet Greville, ed., *The Gentlewoman's Book of Sports I* (London: Henry & Co., circa 1892). Thanks to Clyde E. Drury of Books of the Black Bass, this obscure volume was brought to the author's attention. Drury mentions that this anthology of women's writings about fishing included chapters on trout, salmon, saithe, bass, and tarpon fishing, contributed by Lady Colin Campbell, Miss Starkey, Mrs. Stewart Menzies, Diane Chasseresse, and Mrs. George T. Stagg. The existence of this book certainly indicates that women were fishing extensively during the last two decades of the 19th century.

4. Silvio Calabi, *The Illustrated Encyclopedia of Fly-Fishing* (New York: Henry Holt, 1993).

5. George Reiger, *Profiles in Saltwater Angling* (Englewood Cliffs, N.J.: Prentice-Hall, 1973).

6. Ibid.

Chapter 7 – "The Anglerettes" of the 1930s and 1940s

1. Chisie Farrington, *Women Can Fish* (New York: Coward-McCann, 1951).

2. George Reiger, *Profiles in Saltwater Angling* (Englewood Cliffs, N.J.: Prentice-Hall, 1973).

3. Ibid.

4. Ibid.

Chapter 8 – The Grande Dames of the Sea from the 1950s through the 1970s

1. Eugenie Marron, *Albacora: The Search for the Giant Broadbill*, edited by Roger Kahn (New York: Random House, 1957).

2. Dade W. Thornton, "The Princess and the Gold Cup," *Motor Boating & Sailing*, April 1992.

3. Dade W. Thornton, "Pages from the Past. Helen Grant: The Queen of Anglers," *Tournament Digest*, Summer 1990.

Chapter 10 – Women Making Big-Game History Today

1. Ken Grissom, "Dunaway Goes from Cane Poles to Record Books," *The Houston Post*, April 29, 1993.

2. Bonnie Waitzkin, "Rookie of the Year," *Motor Boating & Sailing*, January 1988.

3. Ibid.

4. Deborah Dunaway, *The International Angler*, International Game Fish Association, March–April 1994.

5. David Finkelstein and Evelyn Letfuss, "Return to Zane Grey Reef," *Yachting*, February 1986.

6. Ibid.

7. J. L. Jenkins, "Welcome Back, Panama: A Long-time Billfishing Hotspot Returns to the Fold," *Marlin*, September 1990.

8. Dan Blanton, "Sails of the Tropic Star," *Fly Fishing Saltwater*, August/September 1994.

9. Bonnie Waitzkin, "Sandy Storer: The Lady Is a Champion," *Motor Boating & Sailing*, December 1985.

10. Dade W. Thornton, "The Princess and the Gold Cup," *Motor Boating & Sailing*, April 1992.

11. Mike Leech, "IGFA Pays Tribute to...The Best of 1993!" *World Record Game Fishes*, International Game Fish Association, 1994.

Part III – Women's Legacy in Bass Fishing

1. Despite BASS's exclusion of women from its trail, Ray Scott is to be lauded for introducing the concept of catch-and-release to tournament fishing (and to the sport in general) in 1972.

2. Michael Vitez, "The Fishermen and the Females," *The Philadelphia Inquirer*, May 10, 1991.

Chapter 12 – Top Pro Bass Anglers

1. Michael Rozek, "The Big Coon," *Rozek's*, December 1992.

2. Ibid.

Part IV – Women's Legacy in Science and Industry

1. As quoted in the Zanika (Outside Interests, Inc.) catalog. The "Mrs. C." referred to by *Holiday* magazine is undoubtedly Denny Crowinshield, who landed an 882-pound tuna in 1948.

Chapter 13 – Four Pioneering Spirits

1. Chisie Farrington, *Women Can Fish* (New York: Coward-McCann, 1951).

2. Ted Gup, "Mollie Beattie, the New Director of the Fish and Wildlife Service, Has a Mission: To Reinvent American Conservation," *Audubon*, March–April 1994.

3. Ted Williams, "Management by Ecosystem: Mollie Beattie's New—and Old—Vision for the U.S. Fish & Wildlife Service," *Fly Rod & Reel*, May/June 1995.

4. Lisa Gray, "A Woman for Lear's: Marilyn Oshman of Houston, Texas," *Lear's*, April 1994.

5. Greg Hassell, "Oshman's Stores Become Female-Friendly," *Houston Chronicle*, April 27, 1993.

6. Alyssa Lustigman, "Marilyn Oshman: Chairman of the Board, Oshman's Sporting Goods," *Sporting Goods Business*, May 1994.

7. Gray, *Lear*'s.

8. Hassell, *Houston Chronicle*.

9. Jim Chapralis, "Women in International Fishing ...Then and Now," *The PanAngler*, May 29, 1993.

10. Bob Tate, "The Northern Gal Who Holds Three World's Fishing Records," *The Calgary Herald Magazine*, August 24, 1973.

11. Ibid.

12. Harlon Bartlett, *Copley News Service*, date unknown.

13. Ibid.

14. Jim Brezina, "The Best Fishing Hole in North America?" *California Living* magazine, *Los Angeles Herald-Examiner*, March 25, 1973.

Acknowledgments

It's hard to imagine any book being more blessed with generosity and unwavering support than this one. From the bottom of my heart I thank: my good friend Keppie Keplinger for her love and help when the workload was simply more than I could handle, as well as for the use of the beautiful photograph of her mother, grandmother, and aunt that graces the cover; Mark Bachmann, Mark Stensland, and Patty Barnes of The Fly Fishing Shop in Welches, Oregon, who kept me inspired through their constant words of encouragement and who provided invaluable access to their private libraries; Richard Cohn, Cindy Black, and the tireless staff of Beyond Words Publishing, Inc., for whom there are no words to adequately express my gratitude for their nurturing faith, integrity, and spirit of collaboration; my gentle, passionate, and devoted editor, Elizabeth MacDonell, whose guidance and unflagging patience were indispensable to bringing this book to fruition; Robin Rickabaugh of Principia Graphica for his brilliant creative design of this book; and Marvin Moore and Bill Brunson, who thankfully toiled around the clock to proofread and typeset, respectively, the final manuscript.

I am also grateful to every single person (many of whom were men, I'm proud to say) who sent me letters filled with suggestions or clippings as a result of reading about the book in their local newspapers or angling magazines; and to all the editors of those publications who printed my request for information or assisted in other ways, thereby crucially aiding my research efforts.

Special thanks particularly go to Margot Page and Jon Mathewson of the American Museum of Fly Fishing, Mike Leech and Gail Morchower of the International Game Fish Association, Jim Chapralis of *The PanAngler*, Bernard "Lefty" Kreh, Stu Apte, Barry Serviente of The Angler's Art, Clyde E. Drury of Books of the Black Bass, The Woman Flyfishers Club, Ben Estes, Eric Leiser, Philip Hanyok of *Fly Fisherman*, the staff of *Fly Rod & Reel*, George Reiger, Cal Cole of Oregon Trout, Chuck Tryon, Press Powell, Larry Weindruck of *The National Sporting Goods Association*, Judith Dunham, Bill Baab of *The Augusta Chronicle*, Skip Hess of *The Indianapolis News*, Jim Bertkan of the *Los Angeles Daily News*, Bill Quimby of *The Tucson Citizen*, Tom Seward, Luis Valldejuli, Juan Carlos Torruella, and Tim Lilly.

Photography Credits

The author and publisher gratefully acknowledge and thank the following organizations and individuals for permission to include the following photographs:

Dame Juliana Berners; Mary Orvis Marbury; Megan Boyd; Sara McBride's business card (end sheets); the unidentified woman fly fishing circa the 1920s (Part I opener); and the group of women trout fishing at Wagon Wheel Gap, Colorado, circa 1890, courtesy of the American Museum of Fly Fishing. Cornelia "Fly Rod" Crosby, courtesy of the American Museum of Fly Fishing and the Maine State Museum. "Bonefish" Bonnie Smith, Frankee Albright, and Beulah Cass, courtesy of Ben Estes. Kay Brodney, courtesy of Jill Ozaki. Helen Robinson, courtesy of Bernhard "Lefty" Kreh. The Woman Flyfishers Club, courtesy of The Woman Flyfishers Club. Joan Wulff (1952), courtesy of Joan Wulff. Joan Wulff (1991), photo by J. Michael Kelly, courtesy of Joan Wulff. Maggie Merriman, courtesy of Maggie Merriman. Cathy Beck, photo by B&C Beck. Rhonda Sapp and Donna Teeny, photo by Jim Teeny. Christy Ball and Lori-Ann Murphy, photo by Tom Montgomery, courtesy of The Orvis Company. Helen Shaw, courtesy of Helen Shaw Kessler. Chisie Farrington, Helen Lerner (Part II opener and p. 142), and Eugenie Marron, courtesy of the International Game Fish Association. Helen Grant, courtesy of Helen Grant. Marsha Bierman, photo by Wendy Vertz, courtesy of Harken, Inc. Deborah Maddux Dunaway, courtesy of Deborah Dunaway. Sandra Storer Donahue, courtesy of Sandra Donahue. Sugar Ferris (Part III opener and p. 206), courtesy of Sugar Ferris. Chris Houston, photo by Stan Godwin. Linda England and Fredda Lee, courtesy of Linda England and Fredda Lee. Penny Berryman, photo by Scott Liles, courtesy of Tracker Marine. Kathy Magers, courtesy of Kathy Magers. Ann Strobel (Part IV opener), courtesy of Bill Baab. Francesca LaMonte, negative #337676, courtesy of the Department of Library Services, American Museum of Natural History. Mollie H. Beattie, photo by Walter Stieglitz, courtesy of Mollie H. Beattie. Marilyn Oshman, courtesy of Marilyn Oshman, chairman of Oshman's Sporting Goods, Inc. Patty Barnes (Part V opener) and Lyla Foggia (jacket flap), photos by Mark Bachmann.

Index

The index includes women who receive significant mention in the book; passing references and mere lists of records are not indexed.

Albright, Frankee, 17–21
Andrews, Terri Kittredge, 184–86
Ball, Christy, 92–99, 103, 220
Beattie, Mollie Hanna, 247–52
Beazley, Sandra (Honey), 191
Beck, Cathy, 78–81
Benjamin, Elizabeth, 33–34
Berners, Dame Juliana, 1–6, 9
Berryman, Penny, 228–33
Bierman, Marsha, 165–78, 187
Boyd, Megan, 107–10
Branson, Jeanne, 256–59
Brodney, Kay, 21–26
Brooks, Mary, 30
Brownson, Mary, 145
Cass, Beulah, 17–19, 21
Combs, Sherri Houston, 214, 218–19
Connell, Frank (Mrs. Karl)
    Hovey-Roof, 45, 50
Crosby, Cornelia "Fly Rod," 13–17, 43
Crowinshield, Denny (Mrs. Ben),
    144–45, 240
Darbee, Elsie Bivens, 119–20
Dette, Mary, 118, 120
Dette, Winnie, 116–20
Donahue, Sandra Storer, 187–89
Dunaway, Deborah Maddux, 179–84
England, Linda, 200, 213, 220–28
Fairchild, Julia (Mrs. Tappen), 45–50
Farrington, Chisie, 128, 133–35,
    136–40, 243
Ferris, Sugar, 195–96, 199, 201,
    203–11, 213
Frost, Carrie, 43
Gardner, Mrs. Jim, 129

Grant, Helen, 158–63
Greig, Elizabeth, 43
Grinnell, Mrs. Oliver C., 145
Harrop, Bonnie, 124–25
Houston, Chris, 196, 213, 214–20
Jenkins, Conny, 200
Joy, Audrey, 44
Knapp, Margaret, 47
Kolbu, Torill, 125–26
Kunkel, Ann, 154–57, 162
LaMonte, Francesca, 140, 143, 154,
    243–47
Larkin, Gioia Gould, 48
Lawrence, Margot (Mrs. Bill), 145
Lee, Fredda, 200, 220–24, 226–28
Lehmberg, Judy, 121–23
Lerner, Helen, 140–44, 245–46
Manning, Jo (Mrs. John), 145
Marbury, Mary Orvis, 35, 36, 37–41
Marron, Eugenie, 148–54
Mason, Heidi, 191
Magers, Kathy, 233–38
McBride, Sara Jane, 35–36
McLaughlin, Pam, 191
Merriman, Maggie, 71–78
Meyer, Mrs. Maurice, 145
Miller, Louise Brewster, 31–32
Murphy, Lori-Ann, 92–93, 95,
    99–103, 220
Olsson, Jennifer, 88–92
Orford, Lady, 129
Oshman, Marilyn, 252–55
Page, Margot, 31–32
Peacock, Myrtice, 191
Powell, Earline, 43–44

Reed, Vojai, 200
Robinson, Donna, 191
Robinson, Helen, 27–30
Rogers, Page, 123–24
Sapp, Rhonda, 81–88, 220
Sears, Mrs. Henry, 145
Shaw, Helen, 111–16, 124
Smith, "Bonefish" Bonnie, 17–21
Smith, Jane, 47–48
Smith, Jennifer. *See* Olsson, Jennifer
Spalding, Mrs. Keith, 130–32
Stagg, Mrs. George T., 129

Stevens, Carrie, 34, 41–43, 124
Stolzman, Sue, 191
Teeny, Donna, 81–88, 220
Torruella, Sharon, 190
Troubetzkoy, Susan, 190
Watt, Kelly, 104–6
White, Margaret, 200–201
Wulff, Joan Salvato, 5, 51–69, 71, 73, 90, 157
Zakon, Nancy, 93
Zinck, Ruth, 125